Fearless Parenting

Handle With Love

(1 John 4:18)

Fearless Parenting

Handle With Love

(1 John 4:18)

Iverna Tompkins
&
Dr. Dianne McIntosh

Fearless Parenting
by Iverna Tompkins & Dianne McIntosh
ISBN 0-88270-691-8
Library of Congress Catalog Card Number pending
Copyright © 1996 by BRIDGE-LOGOS Publishers

Published by:
BRIDGE-LOGOS Publishers
2500 Hamilton Blvd.
South Plainfield, NJ 07080-2513

Acknowledgments

Thanks to Dianne who encouraged a re-write of an old book *How To Live With Kids and Enjoy It*, and to Shirlee who helped me upgrade it, making it applicable for today. Now watching my daughter with her daughter, I see the principles remain the same.

Iverna

This book would not be relevant to today's youth and children if it weren't for my own Michelle, David, Casey, and Daniel. Their love, faith in me and my God, and willingness to be "guinea pigs" enabled us to discover Father's heart in our home. Special appreciation goes to Wayne, my husband, who stood with me as we dicovered God's work for grace in our lives and the lives of our children.

And finally, special thanks to Shirlee Green, whose labor of love and hours of hard work enabled my heart to be clearly stated in the written format.

Dianne

TABLE OF CONTENTS

Preface

It's been many years since I raised my children, yet in reading some of my past writings, I realize that most of the principles remain strong and right, even for this generation.

Of course, there are unique situations and problems to be handled today that were not ours in the past. It's wonderful to realize that the principles of God's Word are both unfailing and unchanging.

Dr. Dianne McIntosh has worked with me over the years. I have been favorably impressed with her teachings on parenting, as well as the expression of those teachings in raising her own four children. She possesses the same spirit of counsel that rested on Jesus (Isaiah 11:12-13). It's because of this that I have asked her to share this book with me.

It is our intention to present to you both the practical and psychological aspects of parenting. My hope is that we're bringing forth a book that will be particularly beneficial to Christian parents who are struggling with today's conflicting information.

Children raised in an environment of love, and aware that all parenting is joyfully offered on their behalf, will come to appreciate their need for guidance, though they may at times feel the restraints unpleasant.

Parents who find the joy in parenting are those who recognize that it takes quality time and demands personal involvement in order to raise healthy, well-adjusted young people. Children so raised face society fearlessly, because they've sensed their own protection and likewise offer the same to others. We must not only involve our children with ourselves, but introduce them to our God and His love for them.

With all the frustrations of working outside the home, the past non-involvement of fathers with their children caused some mothers to live in a state of weariness. Many an overburdened mother has anticipated the day when her children would move away from home. This is not God's plan for us. Except in unfortunate situations where mothers are forced to raise children without the father in the home, this generation is discovering the great need for the father's involvement. A father's nurturing cannot be replaced by the mother's and vice-versa. God intended that there be a mother and a father in the home. Today, many mothers find it necessary to supplement the family income. In such cases, much effort must be made by both parents to provide daily, quality time with the children.

I trust you will read this book, not to discover something you haven't heard before, but to allow the Holy Spirit to quicken to you things that need to be remembered, or perhaps things known that have not been embraced or put into action.

I pray that the Lord will return to you the joy of parenting, indeed, the joy of living, and enable you to find true fellowship with your offspring.

Iverna Tompkins

1

Your Child and You

Iverna:

Some years ago, a young mother of my acquaintance was more than a little frustrated with raising her four children. They were growing as fast as dandelions. She told me, "Sometimes I wish I could just take them to your house and leave them. You could bring them up for me, and I could just rest."

"Betty," I said, "I want to tell you something. For your own four children, you're undoubtedly the best mother in the whole wide world."

It's almost always true that for your youngster, you're the best parent in the world. That child has an emotional attachment to you. That child has identified with you.

The *American Heritage Dictionary* defines identification as, "A person's association with the qualities, characteristics, or views of another person or group."

It's not difficult for adults to establish identification with children. I can love all kinds of children—and they know it. I could walk in, pick up a strange child, take it into my home, and in an hour, I'd feel that it was my own flesh and blood. But that doesn't mean the child would form the same kind of identification with me as it would with its mother.

After a while, he or she would cry for whoever means "Mama" to them. "Mama" might be the natural mother, a foster parent, an adoptive parent, or the maid who had taken care of him or her for as long as the child could remember. Once this "Mama" or "Daddy" identification has been made, it cannot be broken without some damage or harm to the youngster.

In wartime, fathers are taken away. Suddenly, Daddy is gone. As an adult, the mother can understand and grow to accept her husband's absence. But it's far more difficult for children to comprehend and accept.

To children, nothing is quite right anymore. They feel as if someone tore off part of their body—that it's gone and may never come back. Daddy is not a separate entity to his child—he is a physical part of that child's body, in the child's mind. The same, of course, holds true for the child's thoughts of its mother.

Psychiatrists have found a link between emotional traumas such as the absence of a parent and physical ailments like constipation. A child subconsciously might be thinking, "I got hurt when someone took something away from me, and so I'm going to hold on to everything else that's mine—forever." This directly affects the functions of the child's body.

Dianne:

What is a parent?

The normal answer is, "A parent is a mother or father of a child."

But while this is the obvious response to that question, a larger definition is needed for us to discover the goals in parenting and how to accomplish them.

By defining and establishing an understanding of the three basic types of parents—the biological parent, the bonded parent, and the biblical parent—we can discover what kind of parent we are or desire to be and find some principles for fulfilling that role.

Biological Parent

Every parent is a biological parent when the male and female genetically reproduce another human being. The destiny of a biological parent is to bring another person into this world and it is accomplished completely with the genetic reproduction. But biologically bringing a child into this world is not necessarily parenting.

Bonded Parent

The bonded parent not only realizes the child has basic needs for water, shelter, food, and clothing, but that he or she also has social needs. The bonded parent is willing to commit their time, money, energy—whatever it takes—to raise this child to become a healthy member of society. When the bonded parent meets the child's social needs, this process is called *socialization.*

> *Socialization is accomplished by training the child in the* intrapersonal skills—*those skills existing or occurring within the individual self or mind.*

Intrapersonal skills include: the ability to recognize and understand feelings; self-discipline; acceptance of responsibility; understanding their own temperament; problem-solving; the ability to evaluate and make judgment calls; loving and valuing themselves as unique individuals; and using reason, imagination, and creativity. All of these intrapersonal skills are the responsibility and focus of a bonded parent as they socialize the child, teaching him or her to recognize themselves as a human being and a social part of society.

A bonded parent socializes the child to others by training him or her in the *interpersonal* skills—those skills relating to, occurring amongst, or involving several people.

These skills include: effective communication (actively listening and giving feedback); the ability to share ideas and feelings with others; to hear and discern the feelings and needs of others; to give

3

and receive love; negotiation and conflict resolution in a healthy, productive manner; and acceptance of variations of temperament as a delightful, not difficult, part of life.

The bonded parent socializes the child to the greater community as well. This is accomplished as the parent trains the child to take what he or she has learned within himself or herself, family, and friends into the school system, the work place, and the community at large. Here the child learns how to understand differences, learns how to negotiate in varying circumstances and situations, and learns how to make evaluations. The child also learns how to offer submission and obedience beyond parental authority to other authorities.

The information source used to socialize the child is humanity and society. When the child is socialized by the bonded parent, he or she is trained in humanity's ideas regarding worship, money, school, work, sex, sleep, food, exercise, friends, acquaintances, traditions, ceremonies, and celebrations. The ultimate authority in socialization is humanity. The ultimate authorities of the humanitarian is self, society, and Satan.

However, a child is more than mere body and soul.

Biblical Parent

The biblical parent recognizes that inside the body of their child is a soul that needs to be socialized and trained in intrapersonal skills, in interpersonal skills, and at the social level to the community at large. What makes the biblical parent different is that he recognizes the child also has a spirit and that that spirit needs to find a relationship with Jesus Christ through salvation.

Once your child finds a personal relationship with Jesus Christ, his spirit can now be trained to commune with God, to worship Him, and to hear His voice. We will call this training process *spiritualization.*

In the process of spiritualization, the parent's goal is for the heart to be changed, not just behavior modification. When there is a heart change, obedience comes not because the child is in the parent's sight, but because the child wants to obey God.

If my eight-year-old son, Daniel, lies to me, I don't want him to say to me, "Okay, I'll never lie again." I want him to ask Jesus to help him. A change of heart comes when Daniel repents for lying and asks the Holy Spirit of truth to teach him how to speak the truth in love (Ephesians 4:15).

In the process of spiritualization, we teach our children that because of Jesus' blood—and not because of anything they have or haven't done—they can, and must, go into God's presence daily to seek His help and grace. As biblical parents, we model before our children the reality of that daily access into God's presence where He is cleansing, healing, and changing our hearts.

One day, we were having a prayer time as a family. Looking over at David I saw he was crying. Later I asked him what was wrong. He said, "I had been praying for Grandpa and other people when the Lord just spoke to me saying, 'Dave, I want to bless you. I want to minister to you.'" He wept as the Lord began to minister to him. This is spiritualization—presenting the reality of Christ to our children.

As a biblical parent, we need to train our children when they're young to hear God in all situations. Here is an example of teaching children to hear God in resolving conflicts.

Michelle and David just had a conflict. As the parent, I didn't know what it was about, but I sent them to their rooms to pray for the Lord to reveal what was the "log in their eye" (Luke 6:41-42)— that is, what was their own issue? For what did they need to repent? Then I went to my room and began asking the Lord for wisdom and truth—for revelation so that as the children talked with me I could hear their hearts and not just focus on their behavior.

After a while, I brought the children together, asking each one for their side of the story and for what they needed to repent. As they told me, the Spirit within me gave wisdom to bring peace between brother and sister, with understanding. Each of us had heard from God. This training is a process in learning to know what is their own voice, Satan's voice, and God's voice.

God will hear the cries of those who seek Him, whether parent or child. God is ready to answer any who turn to Him. Simply look to God and say, "Lord Jesus, I'm asking You to encounter my children. I'm asking You to encounter me. Change our hearts. I trust You to do Your work."

The responsibility of the biblical parent is to continually bring Christ into every situation their children encounter. Ultimately, our children are under God's authority, not ours or society's. This is spiritualization: training the child's spirit to commune with, hear, and worship the living God.

Prayer and Pizza

When my son, David, was in college he needed another job to make some money. As he prayed for the Lord to provide one, the only job that opened up was as a pizza delivery man. David asked me to pray with him about the situation.

As I took it to prayer, the Lord let me see that He was dealing with David's ego. David needed to be willing to do any job that God gave him. David wasn't the one to pick and choose, God would give him the job. After the Lord spoke to me, I went to David and said, "The Lord's shown me something regarding your job."

David said, "He has me, too."

"What has the Lord told you?" I asked.

"He's dealing with my pride."

My response was simply, "Yes."

The wonderful thing is that David heard the will of the Lord and embraced the dealings of God. This is the result of spiritualization.

A few weeks later, David said, "You know, this job that God gave me? I'm really being tested on it."

"What do you mean?"

David explained that the pizza company had a policy that if the pizza is not delivered within twenty minutes of the order being placed, the delivery boy was to take two dollars off the bill. One particular night David was to deliver a pizza that was already late, so the boss told him to take two dollars off the bill when he delivered it. David delivered the pizza and on his way home the Holy Spirit said to him, "You forgot to take the two dollars off the bill."

"Mom, I had already delivered four pizzas that night. I was tired. I'd only gotten a quarter tip on all the pizzas I'd delivered." The temptation was that the two dollars could be used to make up all the other tips he didn't get. But God knew. David said, "I knew God was testing me, so I went back to the house and gave the man his two dollars."

God had changed David's heart. He was learning to listen and be obedient to the voice of God. He was obedient to the Lord, not because he feared Mom or Dad's consequences, but because he knew his God and wanted to please Him.

The Final Authority

The source of information and authority for the biblical parent is the Word of God and Jesus Christ, the living Word. While the bonded parent uses self as the source of information, the biblical parent recognizes that it's the Word of God that has the final say. Anytime they read or hear a concept or idea that goes against that Word, there is no question, God's Word is the final authority.

Because of this, God becomes the frame of reference regarding friends, money, work, sex, food, sleep, etc. The Word is the revelation of God's values regarding life and it's fulfillment and goals. It is God's perspective on any situation. The ultimate authority to the biblical parent is God.

If the parent learns to love God with his or her whole heart, soul, mind, and strength—then learns to love self and then others—this godly teaching becomes life, not law.

In spiritualization, the biblical parent recognizes that once the spirit of the child is saved, the child needs the Holy Spirit to empower him or her to walk the godly walk. The Holy Spirit enables thoughts to be transformed into God's thoughts. He brings healing to the emotional life and changes man's will to align it with God's.

When the Holy Spirit comes into the will of the child and begins to teach him or her the will of God, instead of the child's own will or the will of the parents and society, the child will learn self-control for the physical body and its passions. Motives for doing everything change when the Holy Spirit is in charge of the total vessel.

When David was in high school, he said, "Mom, I'd like to go to the gym and work out and get into this health program." I asked him why. He said, " Because women love big bodies."

My response was, "That's a wrong motive; you can't go." The issue wasn't the working out; the issue was the focus on the physical body attracting others more than the body being a temple of the Holy Spirit. As a biblical parent, my responsibility was to continue to bring David back to the source, Jesus Christ, to adjust his motivation. As God changed David's heart and motivations, the working out came into right perspective in his life.

Iverna:

It is impossible to overestimate the importance of a parent in a child's life. A child is secure when he feels his parents are adequate to meet his needs. Confidence in their adequacy is vital to the child's sense of well-being.

There are two reasons why parents, alone or together, seldom communicate the vital assurance of their adequacy to their children. In the first place, they feel inadequate. So they're afraid to reassure their youngsters, because they feel there are times when they don't have the ability or strength or knowledge or myriad other requirements necessary to carry through. In the second place, there is, particularly in Christians, a false humility. They think it would constitute sinful pride to say, "I can do all things for you."

"And in This Corner . . ."

One day, my four-year-old son, Dan, brought home a playmate. His friend was about a head taller than my child. He stood, with his arms folded, looking up at me with a fierceness that had to be hereditary.

Dan said, "Mom, you can lick his dad, can't you?"

I took a deep breath, remembering as I did seeing the child's absolute giant of a father out mowing his lawn one day.

I lied my heart out. "Oh, I suppose I could."

It was not a time to let my son down. It was a time to keep him assured that I was "Superwoman."

I didn't have to worry about climbing down off my pedestal some day. When Dan got to be ten, he knew I couldn't lick anybody. He thought I was the weakest woman in the world.

"Wait, Mom, I'll do it for you," is what he said most frequently at that age. He opened all the jars for me, moved all the furniture, and replaced all the burned-out light bulbs, because he knew I was a weakling. Children just naturally outgrow their idolization of their parents; we don't have to guard against it. Enjoy it while it's there.

Just Checking!

A little boy comes home from school, sticks his head in the door and calls out, "Mom!"

"Yes, I'm right here in the kitchen," she answers. The child may go on out to play without even looking in the kitchen. He may not come in until supper time, but he knows Mom is there. That's what he needed to know. If Mom didn't answer when he called, he would probably go all through the house looking for her. His whole day would be ruined because she was out of place. Often his simple cry of "Mom!" doesn't say, "I need to talk to you now." It says, "I need to know you're here, just in case I need you. I have to have that confidence in my life. I require the stability you provide."

One mother reported that her second grader came flying in from school, grabbed an apple, gave her mother a peck on the cheek, and then went outside to play with the neighborhood children. A little later, she ran back inside again for a drink of water. She took just enough time to say, "Mom, if I didn't have you I'd be awful lonesome," and dashed back out to rejoin the games. What the child said was true—her security was in her mother, not in the gang.

Dianne:

What happens when parents do their absolute best at rearing their children according to God's standards, and yet the child still chooses to live in sin?

David must have taught his son, Solomon, about the dangers of adulterous women, as is seen from the book of Proverbs. Undoubtedly, he told Solomon the story of his mother, Bathsheba, and how they lost their first child because of their adultery and murder. Solomon was the wisest man of all, yet as an adult he turned against his own parents' training. He married heathen women who turned his heart against God.

The Basics

As parents, we must understand that our children will ultimately make choices concerning their walk that may be contrary to our instruction.

This does happen and it is best answered by looking at some basic principles regarding families and biblical parenting.

All parents are human, possessing carnal natures and are in the process of growing up—even Spirit-baptized Christians.

God knows this—and daily provides grace and wisdom so parents can be changed and effect that change in their children.

We don't have perfect kids.

If we can understand their carnality, we can help them find the areas that need changing and teach them to allow the Spirit of God to continue changing them as they mature.

Though many of our parents were believers, they were still human beings and made mistakes.

So will we. While we cannot blame our parents for our ultimate choice, neither can our children refuse to serve God due to our failures.

If parents are not obeying the principles of the Word of God, Christ can still be revealed to the children.

He is able to heal and restore them. Jesus Christ is Truth. Cain and Abel came from the same parents, but each child acted differently in his situation. Each had his own relationship with God and responded accordingly.

Jacob and Esau were in a family that showed favoritism. Dad favored Esau, because he was the athlete—the hunter. Dad didn't like Jacob because he was the cook. In this family, there was deception as one son plotted against the other. But God encountered the sons in spite of their parents.

Josiah was one of the good kings in the Old Testament, yet his father was very wicked. So what kind of parenting did Josiah get? Josiah was raised in the worship of false gods, but he chose David to be his father-example instead of Amnon. Because of that role model, Josiah became one of the greatest kings Israel ever had.

Iverna:

The kind of life we live before our children has a lot to do with how they turn out. This is true because of the nature of the identification children make with their parents. This identification develops over a period of time. But eventually, usually by the age of sixteen, most girls will develop life and relationship expectations similar to their mothers, and boys will develop the same with their fathers. For a period of time, being better, or achieving more than their mother or father creates irrational feelings of guilt.

"I shouldn't have anything better than my mother had," a girl might say to herself, and if she has an alcoholic or abusive father, she might marry an alcoholic or abusive man.

"I shouldn't have a better wife than my father has," a boy might reason, and he will marry what he saw in his mother—a terrible housekeeper, a sloppy dresser, a woman careless about her job, her home, her life. Likewise, it sometimes happens that we find a child from a dysfunctional alcoholic family who is so against liquor that you couldn't pour it down him. But that's not always the case. Many children follow in their father's—or mother's—staggering footsteps, right into the gutter.

I Wanna Be Just Like You!

To some children, the awareness that they might turn out like their parents is frightening.

The greatest fear in my daughter's young life was that someday she'd be as loudmouthed as her mother. She used to say that she just hated women preachers. Subconsciously, she was afraid that she might turn out to be one.

It is natural for your children to be proud of the good things in your life and frightened about your negatives, because they either want to be just like you, or are fearful that they will be like you! We can help them understand that while it is a natural thing for them to follow the leader, they are also individuals in their own right, not merely extensions of us.

One day my daughter seemed particularly concerned about these things. "Debbie," I said, "God won't make you just like me. He is making you, Debbie, a unique, special person."

Parents don't usually say that, because it's an ego-builder to them when their children say, "I'm going to be just like my dad." We need to encourage children to believe that they can be far more than we are if they want to be. In their struggle for independence from what we are, they may pull far away from our apron strings and do things we'd never dream of doing, just to prove to themselves, "I'm not like my dad. I'm not like my mom." This may even carry over into their Christian walk, causing them to stray from the straight and narrow path of the Lord.

We can prevent some of this. We can reassure them explicitly, "Son, in some ways, I can see you're like me; in some ways, I can see you're like your father; but in other ways, you're unique—not like either one of us, but just yourself."

If we're going to tell them they're like anyone, we can use it positively, praising them for some good quality—patience, love, generosity, athletic skill. We should never say, "You're just like so and so," in a condemning way. Chances are, we'd want to retract such a statement later, saying, "Oh, honey, I'm so sorry. I shouldn't have said that. I didn't mean it. Will you please forgive me?" This forgiveness releases the negative and makes room for the truth.

Young adults have told me that they warred for years not to be like their mother or father, but they turned out like them anyway, feeling they couldn't help themselves.

Where did they get that idea? Many grew up with it. Every time Dad was upset with them, he yelled, "You're just like your mother!"

And, likewise, Mother voiced the same exasperated prophecy. Eventually the children come to believe it. Without the skills to enable them to adjust socially, mentally, and spiritually, they fall prey to many of the undesirable actions of their parents. By understanding these things, we can guard against them.

Surrogate Parents

The relationship of parent-to-child has an overwhelming influence on the child, for good or for bad. When youngsters don't have healthy relationships with their parents, sometimes they seek to find such relationships in marriage.

A young teenage girl might feel attracted toward an older man because she needs a father. She doesn't realize the nature of the attraction; to her, it's love. They get married and live miserably ever after.

Sometimes it works the other way. A little girl, naturally having, though perhaps not understanding, maternal instincts begins to "mother" everything and everyone in her life. She may dress to look older than she is, and thereby attracts a teenage boy who doesn't have a right relationship with his mother. They get married and she assumes a mother's role, telling him where to go and what to do. The boy, being immature, accepts this until he outgrows it and comes to resent his wife's mothering of him, because the whole relationship is contrary to God's order. Likewise the girl may soon resent the lack of male leadership in her life. There's little chance for success in this instance, unless help is found and changes occur.

Strengthening the Bond

When you find a home where both maternal and paternal love are allowed to be fully expressed, you find a beautiful thing. But when either of these ingredients is missing, someone must endeavor to compensate, to make up the lack, in order to create the atmosphere of love and security.

When paternal love is insecure and a youngster appears to reject their father, Mother can step into the breach, and help the situation.

Aw Dad . . .

A father says to his teenage daughter, "Mary, would you like to go with me to the seed store? I want to plant some grass this afternoon."

It took him twenty minutes to get up the nerve to ask her, because he's so afraid she might say no. His fears are realized when she contemplates the boring business of visiting a hot, dusty, seed store. She turns her father down with a flat, "No, I don't want to go."

Mom sees that Dad is about to disintegrate, so she steps in and says (quietly so only Mary can hear), "Honey, he wants you to go with him!"

Mary calls out, "Wait for me, Dad. I've changed my mind. I'll be there in a minute."

Suddenly, everything's all right again.

Mary wasn't rejecting her father, but his ego would react as if she were. That's why it's helpful for the mother to get the child to consider the relationship reason for going—to be with her dad. Considering that, she naturally wants to go.

Many fathers don't know what to do with their teenage daughters. They don't know how to be with them in a way that is beneficial to the growing youngster. Some girls don't mow the lawn, some don't like to go fishing, they aren't interested in sports, they don't know what goes on under the hood of the car, and Dad is left not knowing what to talk about. Often, Dad ignores the teenage daughter until she gets married and furnishes him with some grandchildren to whom he can relate.

Teenage girls need a strong relationship with their father, so it behooves mothers to help in every way they can. When Dad and Mary return from the store with grass seed and weed killer, Mom can ask Mary to help her father in the yard. Doing things together can often serve the same purpose as talking things over. Maybe father and daughter will get acquainted in the process. Stranger things have happened. And when they have become acquainted, Mom won't have to be flinging the life preserver so often. Daughter will automatically respond to her father's need for her company. He, in turn, will feel sufficiently secure with her that he won't interpret reluctance to go to the feed store, or wherever, as a rejection of himself.

Daughters need their fathers during the teen years probably more than at any other time. And yet, this is the age when many girls seem to reject their fathers altogether.

This is characteristic of the teenager girl. One time she relates to Dad as the love of her life and another as the louse of her life. A teenager can be so shy and rejecting at times and so very loving at other times. It takes a few years for her to change from a little girl of thirteen to a young adult. In the meantime, she's vacillating and the father needs to go with the flow, loving his up-and-down teenager daughter through this process.

Incest

The sin of incest has been rampant in every century since the fall of man. It is not a new sin. However, because of today's media capabilities, and the outspokenness of modern victims of this sin, incest seems to be a constant headliner. It is true that more fathers than we might realize get sexually involved with their youngsters. This is especially true during the adolescent years of their son's or daughter's life. Father's may not know how to cope with being treated as the love of the young girl's life and how to cope with the passionate young girl caught up in drives she herself doesn't understand.

Trouble is a natural result. I use the word natural in the sense that the Bible uses the word "natural." Natural man, according to the Word of God, is sinful man—one who has not received the regenerating life of Jesus by confessing himself or herself a sinner and receiving Christ as Savior and Lord. So, in the "natural," this is a troublesome time for a father, facing his daughter's struggle with puberty. If an incestuous relationship develops, then the daughter points a finger of shame. Mother gets mad, the court gets mad, and

Father gets the ax. Everybody shakes their head and clucks, "Isn't that terrible? He must be sick. I can't imagine such a thing."

It is horrible, but it's natural. The possibility of improper sexual overtones can be completely overcome, however, by the Christian parent who shows frequent physical expression of the right kind with wholesome emotional warmth. We can make it a habit to maintain physical contact with our teen—a firm hug or even a back rub now and then. Father/daughter and mother/son relationships are areas where a good heterosexual transfer can be made. If daughter learns to trust Dad and his affection, then it's easier for her to reach out to other males in a right relationship, not expecting the worst from them. It is very important that fathers convey to their daughters a feeling of warmth and safety where men are concerned.

A son who doesn't have a proper relationship with his father may have identity problems; he may perhaps feeling less than male. If the mother overcompensates for that lack, as she often will, she is only reinforcing the fear in the boy that he is not really being the masculine person that he wants to be. This overcompensation on the mother's part can create a number of negative feelings and attitudes in her son—resentment, anger, embarrassment, over-dependence on his mother, desperation for attention from other males, and often an inability to develop an emotionally mature relationship with a female.

Tragic are the stories of mothers who, because of their own unmet needs and unregenerated spirits, over-related to their sons; even, at times, committing incest and thereby causing the son to be insecure about himself all his life. Fathers who encourage boys in every aspect of their lives, usually give them enough sense of well-being that they don't succumb to any wrong kinds of advances from their mother or anyone else's mother.

The ideal that we're looking for is that the father would recognize and accept his son as he is, not as the father feels maleness ought to be. Both father and mother should encourage the maleness in their boy with lots of positive reinforcement: "Son, you did a good job at this," or "I'm glad you're involved in baseball," or whatever his interests are—even if it should be a traditionally feminine pursuit, like cooking. (It might help to keep in mind that most of the world's best chefs are men.) If the father communicates to his son that the boy's interests are acceptable, even desirable, then the son will have few problems with his maleness in the light of his own life and the decisions that he makes as he grows and matures.

"Parental" Neglect

Mothers sometimes feel a real inner conflict and turmoil when husbands require attention at the same time the children do. A little advance planning can help to eliminate problems in this area. We can begin with a priority list that takes into account our own special family circumstances. If the husband is at home very little, being with him should be at the very top of our priority list when he is around.

Mothers can arrange to take care of most of the needs of the older children when their husbands are not at home. Then the children won't feel neglected at having to take a back seat for a while. Perhaps husbands can involve themselves in the activities of the older children in such a way that they satisfy one another's needs for attention.

Christian mothers have the privilege of saying, "Lord, I feel so inadequate to meet the needs of all these children and my husband. I ask You to give me the ability to show forth Your love in such a way that no one will feel slighted." The Lord will hear and He will do it.

Go Ask Your Father

When both parents are a part of the household, an additional responsibility presents itself. Each needs to do all he can to hold the other parent in an attitude of respect before the children.

At a certain age, a child might say, "Mom, Dad doesn't understand me, but you do." It's a big mistake to side with a youngster against his father. In two more years, the youngster might want to side with his father against his mother. The best thing to say is, "Well, honey, we're all different. I'm Mom, and he's Dad, and you're somebody else. But we're all in this family, and we need to work together and keep on loving each other." We can help our children to understand that there are no sides to a family, and that they have a responsibility to live in such a way as to benefit all members of it.

If children succeed in driving a wedge between mother and father, they hate what they've done. A split between parents means the child is in control. He or she has to choose sides, and that's very frightening to a youngster.

If the child's father is a very passive person who doesn't do the things a father ought to do for his children, it won't help the youngster by sitting back and waiting for something to happen, arguing, "Well, it's the father's place to do it. It's his fault that something isn't done."

We can't afford to justify our inaction that way or to waste energy on placing the blame. It really doesn't matter whose fault a particular lack is, the important thing is to do away with the lack. Sometimes that will mean that one partner has to shoulder the entire responsibility while the other just sits there. It's work, but it's worth it to provide our children with what they need.

For example, if the father refuses to set ground rules for the use of the car, or the curfew time after a date, or the age of dating, etc., chances are very good that if the mother doesn't do it, the father will vent his anger on her and she in turn will say, "I felt like it was your job to do that." The way to correct this is for the stronger parent to take control of the situation and set the rules. If it's the mother, she should represent the father in saying, "Your father and I want you in by midnight." "Your father and I want you to know that you can't use the car more often than twice a week," etc. That way each parent is protected, and, while we make the differentiation between who should do what, children do not. As long as the parents represent each other, children will accept it without difficulty.

Latch-key kids

Today, in our society, it is quite common for both mother and father to hold full-time jobs away from home, and often children

18

are left to return from school to empty houses. Where there is no opportunity for one of the parents to be home when the children return, there should be ample preparation made for it.

Heartwarming notes can be left—a reminder that, "I'll be home in a couple of hours, and I'm looking forward to talking with you about school today," or "So and so called, and I'll talk with you about it when I get home."

It's important for it to be something that allows them to be aware that we're conscious of them and lends them an awareness that our presence will be with them very soon. A phone call from work, if it is possible, will fill this need. It's surprising what a five minute phone call can do in letting a child feel loved and cared for and even protected. Tasty, yet nutritious, snacks can be made readily available.

Arranging the child's afternoon snack in a creative way— making sandwich stars, cookie faces, fruit and veggie people—can add a little fun to their homecoming. Surprise packages left on the kitchen table, a new book, the latest rage in school binders, a rental video, even a funny card will remind the child that his or her parents are thinking loving thoughts about them, even though they can't be there to greet them at the door.

Single Parents

If there is no father or mother in the home, the single parent cannot give the children the strength they need if he or she is lost in their own needs.

"Poor me, I don't have an arm to lean on."

"I don't have anyone to help me make decisions."

"I'm having to rear these youngsters all by myself now, and I'm just not capable of it."

Whether we express these things aloud or not, our youngsters will hear them if that's how we feel. And what we need to communicate to them is just the opposite:

"I am your mother/father. I am capable."

"I am your protection, your mainstay, and I can do well by you."

19

"I can support you; I can guide you; I can govern you; I can take good care of you."

"I can love you so much and so wisely that you won't miss a thing in life because you don't have a mother/father."

If you are the head of a one-parent family, you have to play a double role, so your child won't feel deprived. If you tell your child, "If you had a daddy, you could enter the soap-box derby," you're not being fair to him. If he doesn't have a daddy to do such things with him, we must find a substitute.

When other fathers and sons were going to the woods to chop down a tree at Christmas time, God always provided a Boy Scout leader or a responsible older teenage boy to take my son, Dan, out and do the same thing. He didn't stay at home because he didn't have a father, he just went tree-chopping with someone else.

One day, Dan came along as I was opening the trunk of my car to get out some filmstrips. Naturally, his curiosity was aroused.

"What's in those funny round boxes, Mom . . . Christmas cookies?"

"No," I laughed. "They're some films we're going to use at a retreat this weekend."

"Movies? Oh, boy! What are they about?"

"Well, they're about problems with children. How children are affected by different things, like death and divorce."

"Divorce? Gee! I want to see that one. I want to know how I was affected."

To me, that was heartwarming evidence that boys without fathers at home don't have to spend their lives suffering from being deprived of all the things that other boys can count on.

Trying to be both Mom and Dad to a child isn't easy, but it's possible. It helps if we understand at the beginning that at the times when we feel most ladylike, our children might need us to oil their tricycles or wrestle on the grass. And, as often happens, just when Dad is caught up in the final minutes of a football game or has his head buried under the hood of the car, his little girl will need him to braid her hair or fix her doll's broken arm. It's our responsibility to be sensitive to what they need when they need it, and to provide it for them when we can.

Détente

In one-parent family situations, the parent who lives with the children—the custodial parent—can teach them to show affection for the absent parent.

At different times in their lives, both of my children have attempted to manipulate me by saying, "Mom, why do I have to write to Dad? I don't know anything to say to him, and after all, he's not really part of our family any more."

I could have agreed, and let their rejection of him feed my ego, but they needed to keep a close relationship with their father, and I knew it. Crossing him out of their lives would not be helpful to them.

"He's your father. He loves you. He's good to you," I always told them. "You're going to write to him today." And they did it.

Children are to honor their father and their mother because God says so. The honoring is not based on what the parents do or do not do with their own lives.

Mr. Mom

In the past, mothers were almost always awarded custody of the children in a divorce situation. It's not uncommon today for fathers to find themselves in a single-parent role. And while there are some differences, the basic parenting skills are the same for father as for mother.

The difficulties arise in the father/daughter relationship as the children mature. It's a wise thing for him to unashamedly and specifically let her know that there are things about coming into womanhood that he'd like her to know. If she maintains a relationship with her mother, then the father and mother should converse about who is going to tell her the facts of life and be comfortable with it. The daughter should be comfortable in talking with either father or mother concerning all that is involved without feeling she's bringing embarrassment to them.

A father should help his daughter develop positive feelings about herself. This is done by praising her for her achievements. Most girls go through a gawky, awkward stage in early puberty and are

21

uncomfortable with their bodies overall—or with a particular part of their bodies. Dad should therefore assure his daughter that "this too will pass" and that one day she will be comfortable in her own skin. By dwelling on his daughter's achievements, whether academic, athletic, or artistic, he can help her to focus her attention on qualities and skills that can be controlled at this time in her life.

The same caring can be used with a son, though it seems a little more natural for a father and son to have conversations and a close relationship, because of their similarity of interests. However, this is not always the case, so it should not be taken for granted that your son is naturally comfortable with himself or in talking with you about his concerns.

It is really no more or less important for Dad to have a similar relationship with either son or daughter. Both need affirmation and the basic things that all children need: love, protection, and the certainty that somebody is aware of their life and involved in it.

Dianne:

Many years ago, having experienced a divorce, I prayed, "Lord, I know the statistics about children that don't have a father, and I know that a son without a father can become a wimp." The Lord told me that He would be my children's father. He promised to fill in the gap, and He has been faithful; my sons are not wimps; my daughter is not a hostile feminist. God was truly a father to my children when I was alone. Later, God used my very loving husband to step into that role.

The New Testament tells us Timothy was raised by his mother and grandmother, and that his father was a heathen. What kind of child should Timothy have been because of that circumstance? Yet, he became one of the great men of the New Testament, a man of faith. The Word of God tells us that his mother and grandmother imparted their faith to him. They were biblical parents.

Iverna:

The moment a child is born or adopted into our home, it's as if we have taken an oath before God, saying, "I assume total responsibility for preparing this child for adulthood." In one church I served, parents bringing infants for dedication were asked, "Do you, under God, in the presence of these witnesses, hereby state that you will do everything possible to live the life of Christ before them, and as early as possible lead them into an understanding of their personal acceptance of Jesus Christ as Savior?" After receiving an affirmative answer to that, we presented the child to the Lord, asking for His protection, health, and guidance throughout life.

Are you the best parent for your child? Yes. Are you the best parent you can be? Yes, when you choose to be a biblical parent and let His mind and Spirit rule your home.

2

Your Child and God

Dianne:

As biblical parents, our goal is to spiritualize our children by bringing them into relationship with the living God—teaching them how to commune with Him and how to hear His voice.

During Old Testament times, the high priest was the only one who could go into the presence of God—just once a year—through the blood of a slain animal. In the Book of Hebrews, we are told that Jesus Christ became our High Priest once and for all through His death and the shedding of His blood on the Cross, which opened the way for us to come into the Holy of Holies. As High Priest, through His death, His own blood is now on the mercy seat (instead of the blood of a slain animal) in the heavenlies, daily making atonement for us.

> *But [that appointed time came] when Christ (the Messiah) appeared as a High Priest of the better things that have come and are to come. [Then] through the greater and more perfect tabernacle not made with [human] hands, that is, not a part of this material creation,*

He went once for all into the [Holy of] Holies [of heaven], not by virtue of the blood of goats and calves [by which to make reconciliation between God and man], but His own blood, having found and secured a complete redemption (an everlasting release for us).

For if [the mere] sprinkling of unholy and defiled persons with blood of goats and bulls and with the ashes of a burnt heifer is sufficient for the purification of the body,

How much more surely shall the blood of Christ, Who by virtue of [His] eternal Spirit [His own preexistent divine personality] has offered Himself an unblemished sacrifice to God, purify our conscience from dead works and lifeless observances to serve the [ever] living God?

[Christ, the Messiah] is therefore the Negotiator and Mediator of an [entirely] new agreement (testament, covenant), . . .

Hebrews 9:11-15 (AMP)

Therefore, brethren, since we have full freedom and confidence to enter into the [Holy of] Holies [by the power and virtue] in the blood of Jesus,

By this fresh (new) and living way which He initiated and dedicated and opened for us through the separating curtain (veil of the Holy of Holies), that is, through His flesh,

And since we have [such] a great and wonderful and noble Priest [Who rules] over the house of God,

> *Let us all come forward and draw near with true*
> *(honest and sincere) hearts in unqualified assurance and*
> *absolute conviction engendered by faith, . . . having our*
> *hearts sprinkled and purified from a guilty (evil)*
> *conscience . . . .*
>
> *Hebrews 10:19-22 (AMP)*

Since it's Christ's blood that gives us access into God's presence, we know that it isn't because we're good or bad. Christ has established a new and living way. According to 1 Peter and Revelation, every believer in a household should be a priest. I'm teaching my children how to be a priest unto God, giving sacrifices of praise to Him, worshipping Him, and interceding. God desires a nation that is holy; a people who are priests unto Him (1 Peter 2:9; Exodus 19:6). He wants to start in our homes.

Iverna:

At eight years old, I would periodically hold church services in our basement. I was the preacher, and my brother, Bob, was the drunk. At every service, he'd stagger in, get saved, and sober up. Ours was not a closed congregation—all the neighbor kids were invited to attend. One of my girl friends had an alcoholic father, and a mother whose behavior was much like that of a prostitute. This friend and her brother used to come to our "play church." They took turns collecting the offering, ushering people to their chairs, and passing pretend communion. One day, after I had preached one of my sermons on John 3:16, these two friends of mine responded to the altar call. It wasn't "play church" for them, or for me, that day. They both came forward, really desiring to meet the Lord Jesus Christ, and accepted Him as their Savior. Subsequently, they began attending "real church" on Sunday. Today that boy is in the ministry.

This early experience was the first of many that persuaded me that church attendance is of vital importance for us all.

Children and Church

When parents ask me if they should make their kids go to church, I always say, "yes." When kids are in church, even under duress, they are in a good place for God to become a living part of their lives.

In many cases, kids protest so vociferously against being made to attend church that their parents back down.

"Okay, make me go to church," they threaten when they see they can't get out of it any other way. "Make me go. But after I get away from home, I'll never step inside another church as long as I live!"

Some parents are stampeded by such threats, saying, "Well, honey, if you don't want to go . . .," and they let the kids sleep in on Sunday mornings.

Kids are not able to decide wisely for themselves before they have any real basis on which to make decisions. "It is not in man to do right," the Scripture says (Jeremiah 10:23), and our own experience bears this out. Can you handle your life without God? I've tried, but, on my own, I make a total mess of things. If we know we can't run our own lives without God's help, we should know that our children can't either.

If we leave our youngsters outside the church, where are they going to be touched? How are they going to come into the presence of God? The chances of God getting hold of them are greatly increased when they are regularly in the midst of a fellowship of believers.

While our children are under our roof, we not only have the right but the responsibility to make them go to church. Later, when they have left home for good, if we don't see them serving God, we can say to Him, "Father, while these kids were in my home, I saw to it that they went to Your house. Now I'm counting on You to honor Your promise that when they are old, they will not depart from the upbringing I have given them" (Proverbs 22:6). He'll hear us. God likes to be reminded of His promises.

A family brought their youngsters to our teen choir and the kids just sat there and glared. They didn't want to attend the church, much less be an active part of the choir. How they hated it—and me! Week after week, they sat and glowered at me, especially when the Lord would move me to say something that sounded a little bit spiritual.

One day the kids' mother asked me, "Do you think we're doing right?"

In the natural, everything in me wanted to give up and say, "It isn't working. Why don't you take your kids out?" But I resisted the temptation.

"Yes, you're doing the right thing," I assured the mother. "You're doing what the Word says, and God will honor it. It's the best thing you can do."

The kids were still so hostile I was almost sorry she took my advice. But one glorious night about two weeks later, one of the boys met the Lord. Later, on an equally glorious night, the other boy opened his heart to Jesus. Those kids are serving the Lord today.

A friend of mine opened her home to unwed mothers. It was an unwritten law within that home that the girls would automatically attend church services regularly while members of that household. The rule was easy to enforce, because none of the girls wanted to stay in the house alone while the others went to church. Every young girl who lived in my friend's home went to church, met the Lord Jesus Christ, and had her life totally transformed by Him.

Church Is Not a Form of Punishment

We take our membership in the family of God so for granted that sometimes we presume our youngsters feel as we do and know they belong. This is not always true. Too often we have taught them the responsibilities of church membership without saying much about its privileges. We've hammered it into them: "In church you don't do this, and you can't do that, and you have to listen to your Sunday school teacher, and go to choir, and you have to do a million other things because God wants you to do them."

Every child needs the companionship of other people, just as adults do. I've encountered many lonely youngsters. Sometimes they're from large families, but they're still lonely. They have a desire for company, a need to belong. You can teach your youngster that he or she belongs to Dad and Mom, to brothers and sisters, and to the family of God. You can satisfy much of the need to belong in your children by teaching them that everyone in the church is part of their family.

It's time we gave our kids more positives than negatives about church attendance. We can tell them in so many words, "The people in this church love you. They pray for you. They're your brothers and sisters in Christ, and you belong in the family."

It isn't enough to see to it that your child attends church regularly. The church doesn't have a child enough hours of the week to counteract the whole impact of what the world is feeding him or her the rest of the time. Parents have to get involved in teaching the things of God to their children.

In God's Word, we are told to diligently rehearse in the ears of our children the statutes and laws of God (Deuteronomy 6:7). We are to teach our children to read the Bible and to pray. We are to lead them to become Christ-centered persons. Where this is not done, the result is often a troubled home, a home where there is no spirituality, no awareness of the presence of Christ.

Dianne:

In faith we assume the role as biblical parents and priests in our homes, just as by faith we come into God's presence because of Christ's blood.

Though church attendance is necessary, it is in the home that children come to understand the Lordship of Christ in every area of our lives.

As biblical parents, we must teach our children how to be priests unto God. Priesthood requires separation unto Him. It begins with the Cross and cleansing by Christ's blood. Then we can demonstrate that by water baptism they can separate and sanctify themselves to God to be used as His vessel. And for power to witness, we can teach them how to receive the baptism in the Holy Spirit.

Iverna:

The Age of Understanding

At what age do we introduce our children to water baptism, the baptism of the Holy Spirit, intercession, fasting, or any other "power tool" of the Lord?

This age will vary with each child.

One Sunday night, years ago, Dan said to me, "Mom, I want to be baptized in water."

I was in favor of it, of course, but instead of just saying, "That's great!" I asked him, "Why?" I thought he needed to know the answer to that with the clarity that would come from his expressing it verbally for himself.

He thought for just a minute before he answered me. Then he said, "Well, I want to be baptized in water because I'm sorry for my sins, and because I want all the people to know that I'm really going to serve the Lord—and because it's like Jesus dying and coming back alive."

At nine years old, he had grasped something of what Christian baptism is all about.

Dianne:

Does God Give the Gifts of the Spirit to Children?

The Word states that God gives believers spiritual gifts. If your child is a believer, then God includes him or her in this statement.

Do you know what gift your child most prominently demonstrates? We can ask the Holy Spirit to show us, and teach us, how to be sensitive to cultivate these gifts.

In 1 Corinthians 12:7-11, we are told that each one is given the manifestation of the Holy Spirit for good and profit. One is given a message of wisdom or a word of knowledge and understanding. Another may receive wonder-working faith or a gift of healing, miracles, prophecy, discerning of spirits, tongues, and the interpretation of tongues. The Holy Spirit is that gift, and He ministers through us in these and many varied operations.

Ministry gifts are recorded in Romans 12:6-8:

> *Having gifts ... that differ according to the grace given
> us, let us use them: [He whose gift is] prophecy, [let him
> prophesy] ...*
> *[He whose gift is] practical service, let him give himself
> to serving;* (Our children can serve, not only in the home,
> but in the local church.) *he who teaches, to his teaching;*
> *He who exhorts (encourages), to his exhortation; he
> who contributes, let him do it in simplicity and liberality;
> ... he who does acts of mercy, with genuine cheerfulness
> and joyful eagerness.*
>
> (AMP)

Our children can be encouraged in these areas of ministry.
Children can learn to show mercy. I'm teaching Daniel to forgive
any enemies he might have at school. He is learning to pray for and
bless his enemy, showing him mercy. As we discover their gifts,
we can encourage their development.

God showed me that my son, David, had the gift of counsel.
Recently, when I had a problem with rebellion in Casey, God told
me that because of David's gift, I was to allow him to counsel Casey.
It's been wonderful to see what the fruit of counsel has produced in
Casey's life because of David and the gift he's received from God.
God wants to use the gifts in our homes to bless one another, build
up one another, and to edify one another and those in the body of
Jesus Christ at large.

The Greatest Gift

Besides discovering and developing our children's gifts, we need
to heed the warning in 1 Corinthians 13—the love chapter. Though
we have all the gifts, without love, we have nothing. As biblical
parents, our first goal is to teach our children to love God with all
their hearts, souls, minds, and strength. We then need to teach them

to love themselves—and then others. With love at the center, all the other gifts and fruits grow easily, and only because of grace. Gifts and fruit, though developed by us, are seeded and watered by God.

Iverna:

Many women ask me whose responsibility it is to teach the children about God and His Word, wanting to point a finger of blame at their husbands.

Take Me to Your Leader

"It's everybody's responsibility," I tell them. "And that means if your husband won't take the responsibility, it's up to you."

Some women evade this by saying, "I feel it's my husband's place to take the lead in this, and he isn't interested in spiritual things yet, so I'm praying and waiting for him to get saved. Then he can step forth as the spiritual leader in our home. I don't want to usurp his place."

In the meantime, those mothers are letting their kids grow up without Christian training. They are letting the devil usurp God's place in their kids' lives, all the time piously insisting that they are doing the right thing.

What if the husband doesn't get saved until after the kids have left the nest? There's no way we can go back and make it up to them if they have moved out from under our sheltering wings without knowing the Lord for themselves, without any foundation in faith to enable them to stand under the pressures of life.

God doesn't see an unbelieving, unspiritual husband as the spiritual head of a household. He sees the believing wife in that position. He holds her responsible, because she's the one to whom He has revealed Himself. She's the one who has turned her life over to Him.

What if the husband tells his wife not to pray with the kids, read the Bible with them, or talk to them about God?

Such an extreme stand would be rare indeed. In such a case, the wife would have to rely on the Lord, trusting Him to give her supernatural guidance and wisdom. The usual resistance in husbands to Christian training for their children is based on unconcern or inconvenience, not on any real objection.

The Bible tells us: "For the unbelieving husband is sanctified by the wife . . . else were your children unclean; but now are they holy" (1 Corinthians 7:14, KJV). That can't mean that the believing wife is supposed to stand by and watch her children grow up without a knowledge of God. She has to bring them up to know the Lord.

Dianne:
Abigail and the Fool

In 1 Samuel 25, we find the story of Abigail and her husband, Nabal. In Hebrew, the name *Nabal* means "fool." Not only was Nabal a fool, but he was an alcoholic. This did not, however, stop Abigail's relationship with God. When Nabal did a very foolish thing, Abigail heard about it from her servant. She immediately interceded for her family by seeking out David who was coming to kill them. Encountering David, she humbled herself before him and said, "I have sinned against you." Now Abigail had not sinned. She was the righteous one in this situation. Yet, she identified herself with Nabal in his sin and interceded.

"Did too!" "Did not!"

Have you ever been in a conflict or situation with your spouse or your children where you were right and they were wrong? Or have you been in a situation where your child or spouse was doing something that you knew went against the Word of God? Most of us have. I long to be an Abigail and go before the Lord saying, "Lord, I have sinned against You. Don't lay this sin on our home. Grant us Your mercy and Your forgiveness. Christ through Calvary has already taken the punishment for this sin. Grant us Your grace and Your mercy." This kind of prayer releases us from having to fix our children or our spouse, as well as releasing God to intervene and bring them into a divine encounter.

The wonderful thing about a confrontation with God is that there is no debate. There is nothing to argue about.

When my husband, Wayne, and my children encountered God, it brought them into a closer relationship with Him personally, they became aware He is alive—He does care, He wants to speak with them, redeem them, save them, help them. Encountering God released me from having to fix them—and allowed me, with them, to find the heart of God.

Have you noticed that in all the prayers so far, we have not dealt with Satan? We've discovered a way of intercession that is effective warfare. 2 Timothy 2:24-25 says:

> *And the servant of the Lord must not be quarrelsome (fighting and contending). Instead, he must be kindly to everyone and mild tempered [preserving the bond of peace]; he must be a skilled and suitable teacher, patient and forbearing and willing to suffer wrong.*
>
> *He must correct his opponents with courtesy and gentleness, in the hope that God may grant that they will repent and come to know the Truth . . . .*
>
> *(AMP)*

This Scripture shows us effective intercession. When we bring our family before the Lord, asking the Father to forgive them, it opens the door for God to deal with them. It is God who grants the Spirit of repentance. When the Holy Spirit convicts of sin, we no longer have to play the game of manipulation; we don't have to induce guilt but allow Him to speak and convict.

In verses 25 and 26, it continues to explain that when they repent, they will come to know the truth, come to their senses, and escape the snare of the devil. This tells us that deliverance starts with God in the same way that it tells us in James 4:7—first we submit to God, then resist the enemy. In any situation we're dealing with as priests in our home, whatever we see happen—conflicts, problems, bitterness, lying, cheating—we can go to the Lord and intercede. As we submit to God, He directs the warfare. He shows us what the issue is. The focus is always on God and what He is doing about it. If He shows me the enemy is over here doing this, He also shows me how to do effective warfare against him.

If we see the enemy come in like a flood (Isaiah 59:19), we know our God is greater—He is Almighty. We look to Him, praise Him, worship Him, thank Him, and then we begin effective intercession. When we share God's heartbeat, we can teach our children to do the same. In this, they learn how to be priests that praise and pray.

Priestly Praise and Prayer

Two functions of the priesthood need to be operating in our homes. The first is praise. The priest in the Old Testament daily brought sacrifices for atonement. Hebrews 13:15, says, "By Him therefore let us offer the sacrifice of praise to God continually, that is, the fruit of *our* lips giving thanks to His name" (KJV). As priests, we should teach our children how to daily offer that sacrifice of praise.

Sacrifice means to kill or slaughter for a purpose. We need to kill our pride, our fear, our laziness, or anything that hinders us from giving and teaching the sacrifice of praise. Praise should be a daily response to God. We must, therefore, teach our children to see God in their daily lives so they can praise Him.

Once when Daniel and I were in the car going to the store, the hand of God kept us from being in a serious accident. I stopped the car and began to praise God. Turning to Daniel, I encouraged him to praise and thank Jesus for saving our lives.

That's how we model it. We set the example through what God's doing in our lives, and, from our own life of praise, teach our children to praise and thank Him, for He is a good God.

The second area we teach and train our children in is prayer. Revelation 5:8 tells us that the incense before God is the prayers of God's people. Every person in the body of Jesus Christ can be a praying priest. Daily we pray for ourselves, our families, and for the nations. It's biblical—God wants us to train our children as priests so they know how to intercede before Him.

God taught me intercession and it's power through three Bible stories. In her book *On The Ash Heap With No Answers* (Copyrighted 1992, Creation House, Lake Mary, FL), Iverna Tompkins taught about Job. She said that during his trial Job's wife said to him, "Curse God and die. Just get it over with." Iverna stated that if Job had trained his wife as he had trained the people he ministered to, she would have never wanted Job to curse God.

Hearing this, I determined, with the help, direction, and wisdom of the Holy Spirit, to teach my family what God had taught me. I wanted not only to intercede for my family, but to allow the Spirit to teach my children the things He was teaching me.

The Challenge

As priests of the most high God, our challenge is to go daily into God's presence by the blood of Jesus and pray, "Father, I'm asking You to forgive the sins of my children. Father, I'm asking You to forgive the sins of my spouse; cause him to repent. I repent of my own sins today. What do You want me to pray for regarding my spouse and my children? I know what's concerning me about them, but Lord, I lay that down and desire to pray what concerns Your heart."

This prayer not only allows the Holy Spirit to begin intercession for your children and your spouse, but also opens the intercessor up for God to reveal things we need to do to become a part of the answer.

There have been times in intercession that God has given me a word of encouragement for one of my sons, or a prophecy for my daughter, or a word of warning to watch out for a situation for my spouse. What's so exciting about this is that God knows the pitfalls and warns us. God wants us to establish His kingdom in our homes by allowing His Lordship to reign.

Iverna:

God On the Back Burner

There are instances where a child has accepted Jesus as Lord, but his or her priorities often set the things of God on the back burner. How do parents help them to see Christ as their first priority?

The responsibility for seeing to it that our youngsters walk with God is one of the most important challenges to parenthood. My boy doesn't have to grow up knowing everything other boys know; my daughter doesn't have to grow up knowing all that other girls know. With God's help, however, they will grow up to know all they can of God and His love for them.

This not only means that I should be careful to see that they receive proper Christian training, but also that I live my life before them in such a way that they can see the importance of priorities in everyday Christian living. American kids have great opportunities for outside activities—everything from tennis lessons to piano instruction—and it's all too easy for such things to push aside more necessary activities—private devotions, spiritual reading, even regular Sunday worship. It's going to be more difficult for my kids to get their own priorities in order if they see me allowing myself to be submerged by outside activities in my own life, to the detriment of the things that I say are necessary to Christian growth.

For example, if my children, knowing that I work full-time, see me at home in the evenings doing the things that must be done, getting meals, preparing for the next day's work, etc. and then spending my entire evening sitting in front of the television not involved with them and/or God; or if they see me carelessly partaking of the food at mealtime without prayer, and then I try to instill these truths in them, their minds say, "She didn't do it, why should I?"

I'm not condemning outside activities. All of them are good—if they are seen as secondary to what's lasting. But the Word has to come first. The child who knows Jesus can make it, no matter what. The child who doesn't know Jesus can't make it, no matter what.

Passing the Acid Test

Children who have been carefully brought up in the nurture of the Lord may still come to a time in their lives when they want to test their faith for themselves.

A Spirit-filled Christian woman told me that her teenage daughters were really questioning a lot of things.

"Yes, Mom, we've always believed this and this," they said, "but it's because that's what you and Dad have taught us. But what if Buddhism is right? What if reincarnation is right? What if this is right? Or that?"

"I almost died from shock," the woman said. "We had brought them up to serve the Lord, and now, all of a sudden, they wanted to check it out." But even in the midst of her distress, the woman had uncommon wisdom.

"I held in my feelings," she said. "I told them, 'Yes, you'll have to find out for yourselves that Jesus Christ is alive and that the power of the Holy Spirit is a reality. I can understand that it isn't enough for you just to take my word for it.'"

In her wisdom, she helped the girls come through the period of testing, because she wasn't afraid that her God was too little to make Himself known to them. She wasn't afraid that Christ would let them down. Intuitively, she realized that until they proved Him for themselves, they would never be satisfied, and their faith would not have the foundation that could stand against the storms of life.

Young people often ask themselves, "Is it really that great just being a Christian? It looks like people out in the world have so much fun. Do they really?" Once they have sought the answer for themselves and God Himself has satisfied them, they're on the Rock.

A teenager is at the point of life where he is testing everything he's been taught, to see whether or not it will really work. Sometimes parents interpret as rebellion what is merely a teenager's checking out the practicality of what he's been taught. What works, he keeps. What doesn't work, he's better off without, and so he throws it away.

39

If your own teenagers are going through a phase where they suddenly seem to be against all you've taught them, relax. It's temporary. Thank God that they're testing things for themselves. If you've done your job properly, training them up in the way they should go, they'll seek the truth and find it.

The likelihood that our youngsters may come to such a time of testing for themselves is one reason why we need to be careful what we teach them about God. Only what is true can stand during a time of testing. What is false will be shown for what it is.

In this, as in other areas of rearing our children, we teach through far more than our deliberately spoken words of instruction on the subject. We teach our children about God by our own example of right living, by our attitudes toward Him, and by our own relationship to Jesus as it is evidenced in our worship of Him.

Big Brother is Watching

When I was a child, I had the frightening experience of hearing the chorus, "Watching you, watching you, there's an all-seeing eye watching you." For years, all across the sky, I saw a horrible eyeball, always focused on me. I didn't like it. Nobody likes to be watched all the time. Over the years, somebody had to work extra hard at teaching me "God is love," to overcome that uneasiness.

Years ago, when I was working with the courts in probation, I went into a home where there was a picture of Jesus hanging over the table. When the youngsters complained about the food on their plates, the mother pointed to the picture and threatened to tell God on them. I became so upset, so angry, thinking that that kind of teaching could damage a child's relationship to God, that I had to withdraw from the case and send someone else to handle it.

There are so many ways that parents are tempted to "use" God in training children. Once my brother Bob couldn't find out which of his daughters had done a certain prohibited thing. The girls, who were about thirteen and fourteen at the time, conspired together, agreeing that they wouldn't tell him.

"You'll just have to lick us both," they challenged him, sure that he would back down at such a prospect. But Bob said, "That's all right. You don't have to say a word. The Lord will tell me who did it. I'm going to ask Him."

Bob went into his room to pray for a while, and when he came out, he said, "Lynette, the Lord told me it was you."

"Well," she said, "if the Lord told you I did it, then I guess you had better lick me." Years later, he learned that Judy had been the culprit, not Lynette. But Lynette had taken the licking.

The girls had no feeling that God was not omniscient in this case, but they were certain that Dad wasn't as smart as he thought. The point is that we must never "use" God in a negative manner in our relationships with our children.

Prayer in Action

One mother told me about her teenage daughter who was about to drive the whole family up the wall with her negative attitude toward helping out with household chores. She did the bare minimum that was required of her, but reluctantly. Her general approach was so complaining, so down-at-the-mouth, it was making life miserable for everyone. The mother ignored it as long as she could and then, finally, when the situation didn't improve but seemed to worsen with the passing weeks, she had to say something.

"Julie," she said, as gently as she could, "you have been acting so unhappy about doing your share of the work this summer. I don't think I've been requiring any more of you than I have of the other kids, and I'm at a complete loss to know what's wrong."

Julie was frowning when the mother began her little speech, and she was frowning even harder in the midst of it. Asked if she had an explanation, Julie offered tight-lipped, sullen silence.

"Tell you what I'd like you to do for me, Julie," her mother said. "I'd like for you to pray and seek God's will in all this."

There was no scolding, no harangue, no condemnation, just the mother's invitation for the daughter to take the matter at issue up with the highest possible Authority.

"I noticed a change in her almost immediately," the mother told me. "By the next morning, it was obvious to all of us that something wonderful had happened. Julie was doing her work cheerfully, just like in the good old days, even volunteering to do some things that were not strictly required of her. After a few days, I just had to thank her for being so helpful."

"Oh, Mama," Julie told her, "I did what you said. I prayed about my attitude, and . . ." Tears filled her eyes as she went on, "I just wish there was some way I could make up to you for how uncooperative I've been all summer."

To the mother, all the lack of cooperation was more than atoned for already.

Teaching Children to Pray

Prayer is a natural thing for a child. Sometimes parents who have turned away from God themselves learn, to their surprise, that their children have quite a regular habit of prayer. Somewhere they picked up the idea that they could talk to God, and all by themselves they began to do it.

I remember reading about the day when Helen Keller's teacher wanted to tell her about God. She began by spelling the word "God" into Helen's hand, and then she spelled more words to explain that God made the whole world and sent His son, Jesus, to die for us. Helen's face lit up, and she spelled some words back into her teacher's hand: "Oh! God has spoken to me many times. I'm so glad you told me His name."

One day Dan said, "Well, Mom, I know the Lord isn't going to come until my friend Joe is saved."

"Praise the Lord," I said, "but why isn't Joe saved already?"

"I'm not sure," he acknowledged, "but I think it's because Jesus is trying my patience to see if I'll keep on praying."

42

If our youngster reaches a point where he doesn't want to say his prayers, we don't have to crowd him about it. We can accept it matter-of-factly, and say his prayers for him: "Dear Jesus, Robert comes to You tonight, but he's too tired to say his own prayers, so I'm saying them for him. Robert loves You, Jesus . . ."

If we don't make an issue of it, the child will return to saying his own prayers before long.

One mother told me of a prayer experience with her seven-year-old. Every night after the mother had read her child a Bible story or two, the child would say, "You say my prayers for me, Mama. I'm too shy to pray out loud."

The mother didn't push her, she just said the prayers while the child snuggled under the covers. Sometimes after the mother had said, "Amen," Ruthie would remind her, "Mama, you forgot to tell Jesus about my sore toe," or whatever it was, so the mother would pray a little bit more.

There came a day when Ruthie said, "Mama, tonight I want to say my prayers myself." And she did—probably the fastest, most staccato prayer in all of Christendom. The glory of the Lord came down all over the place! As the mother was turning out the light to go downstairs, Ruthie said, "Mama, at Sunday school my teacher says that if I won't pray out loud with the rest of the kids, I have to stand outside in the hallway."

The mystery of why Ruthie hadn't been able to pray her own prayers was solved. Someone's attempt to force her to pray had pushed her away from prayer. Her mother's loving acceptance had brought her back. It's not by force but by faithfulness that parents help their children toward a closer relationship with God.

"Not one of them [sparrows] is forgotten
by God." (Luke 12:6)

It's good for our children to know that nothing is beneath God's attention. Again, they learn much by our example.

Once my daughter's dog, Babette, got sick. For two days, Babette had moped around and we didn't know what to do for her.

I knew that Debbie was worried, and I finally prayed about the situation. "This sounds dumb, Lord," I said, "but I need You to help me know what's wrong with Babette."

Almost before I could finish my prayer and say "Amen," I heard myself saying, "I'm going to take the dog to the vet to be wormed." The vet confirmed the Lord's diagnosis. Babette had worms.

"Mom, how did you know that?" Debbie asked me after we got home.

"You aren't going to believe this," I told her, "but I got on my knees before God about the dog, and He let me know what the trouble was. Honest."

Debbie did believe it, and we both had a good lesson in prayer that day—that God cares about every little thing we bring to Him.

If we can create the right kind of climate for our child to learn to take everything to God in prayer while he is still a grade-schooler, we'll have a powerful ally on our side and God's side for the child's adolescent years.

When our teenagers have been brought up to have a living prayer relationship with a God who is real, being a new creature in Christ will expand over and over again.

There will, of course, be times when our children sincerely pray and feel that their prayers were not heard or not answered. This becomes an important moment for us to keep their faith in God and in His hearing their prayers very vital and alive, because it may be setting the pattern for a lifetime of either prayer or prayerlessness.

Recently, we had a situation where some children at school committed suicide and the entire student body was extremely upset over this. Undoubtedly, there were kids who had prayed in their church circles that God would save souls and take care of the students. The enemy loves such instances, so he can come to these young minds and say, "See, you prayed and look what happened to them."

In those situations, we have to keep before them the whole counsel of God; showing them the that big picture, that only God knows who will come to know Him, and nothing can take those lives until they do know Him. We don't know who they are, so we continue to pray for the safety and salvation of all mankind.

Also, we need to make it clear to our children that sometimes God says, "Later." Sometimes He says, "No." We have to learn to hear our answers just as certainly as we know that God does hear our prayers. We affirm that He does hear prayer, because His Word promises that if we ask, He will hear. If we ask in His will and in His name, and in agreement with what's on His heart to do, He will do it.

As we explain this in clarification, we also take away the feeling that prayer is some kind of a magic wand with which our kids can get everything they want just by saying, "Dear God, in Jesus' name."

Hearing Aid

What we need to teach our children is relationship in prayer—the beauty of hearing what God is saying to them. This sometimes takes conversation: "What did you hear from God today? What's He saying to you?" If the child can't respond with any awareness, then we have our work cut out for us. We must try to create in our child a listening ear and a sensitivity to hear what the Spirit is saying.

We can use the story of Samuel who, at a young age, was able to hear from God. But he first had to run to the preacher and be told, "This is probably God. Listen to Him." We are asking our children to be sensitive, to listen, to be quiet, long enough to hear in their minds, in their spirit, the voice of God, and teaching them that if that coincides with the Bible, it is a safe hearing.

I have friends who have a six-year-old child who was in the first grade when the school decided to split the class. This really affected him, because he was one of those chosen to go to the new class and he didn't want to leave all his friends. So he came home in tears and anger and his father and mother wisely said, "Let's just pray about it and ask Father what He's saying in this." So the three of them gathered together. Instead of the father or mother leading, they just bowed their heads in quiet prayer. It was only a matter of moments until the little boy raised his head and said, "Okay."

45

His mother said, "What did Father say?"

The little boy smiled and said, "Father said, 'Move.' That's that."

Now that thrills me, because here is someone at the age of six learning that if Father says it, it's going to be all right because had instilled in him such a trust in God. When a situation arose which could have left the child angry for a long time at the school—because they changed the class—and angry with his parents because they enforced obedience to the school it was instead all resolved because a young lad was taught, like Samuel, how to hear the voice of God.

Dianne:

May we learn to pray:

> Lord, I want to be the priest in my home. I want to teach my spouse and my children by Your Word to be all that You've called them to be, with all the gifts and graces operating in their lives, so that our home will be Your altar and You will be able to come in Your fullness. Because of the blood of the Lamb, we have access daily into Your presence to praise You, to have communion with You, and to allow You to be our God, ministering to us, blessing us, and having communion with us. God, teach us how to establish Your kingdom, Your priesthood in our homes, that You may be glorified. And may our intercession be pure and effective to establish Your kingdom in our midst. In Christ's name we pray. Amen.

3

Your Child and Behavior

Iverna:

Heaving a tired sigh, I finished my work log, tucked it in my desk drawer, and rummaged in my purse for the car keys. It had been a hard day, and I was weary. Still I experienced a tingle of excitement as I put on my coat and headed for the parking lot.

My good neighbor, Barbara, took care of my children for me while I worked as a probation officer to earn a living for my family. She always had the kids ready and waiting for my return at the end of the day. I could hardly wait to swoop two-year-old Dan up in my arms and prop him on one hip while I hugged seven-year-old Debbie to me on the other side.

Stopping for a red light, I caught a glimpse of myself in the mirror on my sun visor. I was grinning a mile wide just at the thought of my children. I wondered if other parents felt the same way about greeting their children at the end of the day.

Turning the corner onto my block, I craned my neck for a glimpse of Debbie and Dan. They were nowhere in sight. They were always outside Barbara's home waiting for me unless it was raining. What could be wrong?

I hurried out of the car and into Barbara's house. The center of attraction was a large cardboard box in the middle of the floor. Debbie and Dan were on their knees peering intently inside the box at a mother cat and five wiggly, mewing, newborn kittens. Their tiny tails were poking straight up in the air.

47

For a moment, I was jealous at being upstaged by mere kittens, but then I was on my knees with the children, oohing and aaahing over the fuzzy miracles of new life.

After we went home, we talked about the new kittens while I got supper on the table. Then the three of us went to church, where I was serving as the organist for the choir.

Later that night, after I'd heard the children's prayers and tucked them into bed, I thought about the whole business of parenthood for divorcees like me and for parents in more ideal family situations.

What Makes Them Tick?

The episode with the kittens had brought into sharp focus two of the prime requisites of successful parenthood: a willingness to share with children in what is important to them and an openness to look behind their behavior to see what makes them tick.

It's years later now and I'm no longer a counselor in a probation office or a church organist, but I've not forgotten what I learned then. Today, both my children are adults and happily married. During their growing-up years, my children taught me a lot. Living with them and counseling other people's children, I learned to look behind their outward behavior to see what was really going on inside them.

Dianne:

"Mommy, Mommy! Please don't go," screamed Kyle as his mommy walked out the door, leaving him with the baby sitter. Mother entered the car where another son, Tommy, waited. Mom and Tommy took off in the car, leaving Kyle at the baby sitter's.

As an objective onlooker, what's the real problem? Is Kyle a rebellious, defiant, tantrum-throwing child who needs to be spanked? What is his behavior saying to the mother?

We must discover what is behind the behavior of our child, not merely see and correct the tantrum. What's behind the behavior that we've missed? A high percentage of the bad behavior we see is indication of a hurting child—or one who has not had his needs met appropriately and effectively.

A three-year-old was trying to put a lid on a jar, and he was turning it the wrong way. Mother came along and said, "Here, Honey, let me show you how. You should turn it this way."

The child shouted, "No!" and tried to jerk the jar from her hand. The jar crashed to the floor. Mom snatched the child up, spanked him soundly, and put him to bed. Then, still seething, she swept up the broken glass.

A five-year-old boy wanted to try fishing with an empty fishhook. When his father noticed what was happening, he pulled the hook out of the water, put a worm on it, and threw it back. A few minutes later, the child caught a whopper. He didn't seem especially pleased about it though, and when he thought his father wasn't looking, he kicked the fish off the edge of the pier back into the water. You *know* what the father did when he caught a glimpse of the action out of the corner of his eye.

Another child polished his own shoes. The shoes looked awful, but the child beamed, proud of what he had done. Then Mom came along and touched up the imperfectly polished shoes for him. Later, she wondered why she caught him deliberately scuffing his shoes along in the dirt.

In each of the three cases above, what is really happening with the child? We have what looks like rebellion but it's not that simple.

The "X" Syndrome

The "X" syndrome is established in the life of every human being as he or she learns to meet their basic needs in their environment. God has created every person with basic needs we'll call the Five A's:

*The need for **attention** (to be attended to).*

*The need for **affection** (to be loved and held).*

*The need for **affiliation** (to belong to someone or a group).*

*The need for **approval** (to be applauded and valued as special).*

> The need for **authority** *(to have boundaries and rules).*

Every child has these basic needs during his or her growing years. What happens to the child when these needs are not met? We call this the "X."

"X" Marks the Spot

Jim comes home from school. On this particular day, he has had a situation with his friend that was negative. Jim needed his friends to be a support to him, but he found out that his best girlfriend told a secret. Jim is hurting. He needs to talk to his parents about what's happened at school. Not only does he need his parents' attention, he needs their affection. He needs to be reaffirmed. Then he can learn to forgive the offenders.

Go Away Kid, You Bug Me

Jim goes into the family room where Dad's reading the paper and says, "Dad, I really need to talk to you about something that happened today."

Dad replies distractedly, "Not now, Son. I'm busy. Go talk to your mom."

Mom's fixing dinner, so Jim goes into the kitchen and says, "Mom, I need to talk to you."

If Jim was a really young child, he wouldn't state this directly, he would just come into the kitchen and stand hoping Mom would notice him. But Mom's busy too, and doesn't respond to Jim's request for attention. When she finally notices that he's in the room, she asks him to set the table and continues with her dinner preparations.

Jim now has an "X."

His legitimate needs for attention and for affection were not met. If he were to now go to God and ask Jesus to heal and meet the needs that he has, the "X" would be healed, but if he does not know how to do that, he will move into the "X" syndrome.

From the hurt, from the devaluing, from the needs not being met, Jim is going to think some wrong things about himself: "I'm no good, or no one loves me." He may also think some things about his Dad and Mom: "Dad's too busy for me; Mom's too busy; they just don't care." From this thinking, Jim will feel some things. He will feel rejected, not loved, lonely, sad, fearful, angry, and depressed. These feelings will begin to find expression in his behavior.

For example, he might say to his mom, "I'm not setting the table," and stomp out. Or, he could silently set the table thinking in his mind, I'm going to get Mom later. She doesn't like lying so I'm going to lie to her. Or "She wants me to get good grades at school, so I won't."

Please note that this is done on an unconscious level, and yet these dynamics happen often.

Iverna:

In a young child's mind, his parents are a physical part of him, just as his arms and legs are. Understanding this will help us to understand our youngsters' behavior patterns. This is why they care so deeply that we're away as much as we are, why they're concerned when we're cross, and why they pretend they don't care if we ever come home or not. They have to build up defense mechanisms in order to survive without too much pain.

When we're ignorant of these things, we unwittingly put our child in situations where elaborate defenses are necessary for his ego. What looks like misbehavior might be the child's way of trying to tell us, "I hurt."

We're not cross with our youngster when he cries in pain or when he's physically sick. Yet when he's emotionally disturbed and lashes out, we're likely to call it misbehavior, and punish it by spanking or taking away privileges. But treating the symptom doesn't get at the root of the problem. We need to see what our child's misbehavior is trying to communicate to us.

Jekyll and Hyde

Perhaps our youngster has always been very well-behaved, but all of a sudden he's fighting, being irritable, doing everything he knows is wrong. Many parents fall apart in frustration when this happens and punish the child. But the punishment doesn't help—it makes matters worse.

What we need to do is to look at our youngster's world to see if something has changed in it. We need also to look at ourselves. Have we been away from home more than usual? Has the child's father or mother been more preoccupied with work than is customary? Have we heard ourselves saying, "Leave Daddy, or Mommy, alone. He or she is busy"? If so, what the child has heard is, "Part of you is being denied," and has reacted to it.

The same kind of reaction is likely to occur when anything else claims attention the child thought was his or hers alone.

How thrilled we were the first time our child said "Mama" or "Daddy," and the first time he used a spoon successfully. Everyone in the family was called in to listen or to watch.

"Go ahead, Honey—that's right—put it in your mouth. See that! Isn't that a big boy?"

Everyone clapped. Everyone was tickled to death that the baby was learning to feed himself. He had achieved a new thing.

The first time our child brought papers home from school, we poured over them, oohing and aahing over the beautiful picture our talented child had drawn, even though we couldn't figure out which side was supposed to be up. Everything was a big deal. In the midst of it all, our youngster was basking in acceptance, security, and love.

Then came the day when Johnny brought his arithmetic home after a new baby had arrived, and Daddy and Mommy were up to their ears in diapers, bottles, and sleepless nights. That's when we inadvertently began teaching our child something other than acceptance, security, and love.

"Look, Mommy. Look, Daddy. I learned that two and three make five if they have the right base."

We took an impatient look, mumbled, "Yes, Johnny, that's nice. Run along now. Can't you see I'm busy?"

The child was baffled. Where was all the loving attention that had been taken for granted all these years? The bottom fell out of the child's world. All of a sudden he felt rejected, insecure, unloved. And we wondered why behavior problems began to erupt in him.

Dianne:
The Survival of the Fittest

Children are survivors. They look at their environment and decide how they are going to fit into the system and what role they're going to play. Each child we've used as an example has an "X." He or she doesn't know how to go to God to get healed. Perhaps they did go to their parents, and there wasn't help. Or one of the parents was the cause of the "X" instead of being the person the child could trust to fulfill his or her needs. The child has a legitimate need, and needs attention and affection, with approval. The child is going to get that need met in another way.

Role 1: The Good Child

One way a child may try to fulfill his or her needs is by being the good child. The good child will focus on getting good grades, setting the table when Mom wants it set, doing the yard work when Dad wants it done, taking responsibility for the other children in the house, etc. The child will try to fulfill his or her needs by being good and responsible. The good child will also focus on his or her appearance, clothes, material possessions, status,

53

and achievements, all to fulfill his or her needs. If recognition is won by being "good looking," that child will focus on this as the means of getting his or her needs met.

Role 2: The Caretaker

The child can seek fulfillment by becoming a caretaker. He or she will find someone that needs someone to take care of them. This may be a younger sibling, someone at school, or somebody around the neighborhood. The caretaker-child may over-relate with an alcoholic mother or father or a sickly sister who needs to be taken care of. Be assured that the caretaker-child will find someone who needs help and will meet this person's needs by being "caring," loving, sensitive, a good listener, a fixer, or a rescuer.

My daughter, Michelle, became a caretaker as a teenager. She would pick the boys to hang around with that were losers—those types who needed her to fix them and help them feel loved and valued. She didn't believe she was of worth or wanted by the normal, successful, adjusted boy. So she met her legitimate needs by meeting the needs of someone needier than herself.

Role 3: The Rebel

Instead of meeting his or her needs by being good or taking care of someone, the child can choose to have his or her need for attention met by creating problems. This child can become the black sheep of the home. The rebellious child may act up in the home or classroom, pick fights on the playground, or just misbehave in general. Our reaction to this is certainly personal attention, but it is negative attention. The rebellious child needs positive attention.

Role 4: The Invisible Child

Instead of becoming responsible, or taking on the role of a caretaker, or acting rebelliously, the child may decide to become invisible. This child won't get into trouble, or be bothersome, or feel rejected if no one sees him. This child hides in his or her room. This child envisions himself as the lost child. The invisible child's behavior may be very good. He or she doesn't talk back—becomes non-conversive in fact—and tries to become a non-person. At school, the invisible child avoids friends—friends create problems and "X"s. The invisible child will create their own little world. After school, he or she will go to their room, put on earphones, listen to music, watch TV, play video games—disappear. The invisible child will get lost in their room. The invisible child's legitimate needs will be fulfilled by himself or herself, and they will ultimately conclude that they can trust no one but themselves to fulfill their needs.

Role 5: The Dependent Child

The final option the child has in order to meet his or her legitimate needs is to become the dependent or under-responsible child. This means he or she, as a follower, will pick friends and adults to be leaders who will make all the decisions. The dependent child's thinking will be this: "If I don't make a decision, I can't get in trouble. If I don't commit myself to anything, I can't be rejected." So if Mom asks, "What would you like to do today?" the dependent child may say, "Oh, anything, Mom," which will eliminate any areas open for rejection. Eventually, the dependent child will become a non-person, incapable of making proper judgments and decisions.

The Trap

The ultimate trap of these five roles is that they work for a while, helping the child deal with his or her "X"s temporarily. But for the achieving good child, the day may come when Dad may notice the one thing the good child didn't do. Or Mom will notice that her good child got one B and not all A's on his or her report card. The very role that the child chose to meet his or her legitimate need doesn't prevent another "X."

What about the caretaker? My daughter, Michelle, found quickly that, when she chose someone needier than she was to help and heal, they ultimately got even with her. They talked about her, saying she didn't help as much as she could have, and she got "X"s from the relationship.

What happens to the rebellious one? They're always in trouble. The very thing they thought would meet their needs and avoid pain in their life creates pain.

The result for the invisible child sitting in their room thinking, "One day my parents will notice I'm not out there with them and they'll come and get me," is that the parents don't notice and they don't come to get this lost child. Sometimes the parents are too busy to notice, and if the child isn't creating problems, behaving in his or her room, why cause a fuss? So the parents leave the child alone. In that loneliness, the lost, invisible child experiences more "X"s.

And finally what about the dependent child? It takes a while for the dependent child to receive "X"s, because he or she stays safe in following everyone else's decisions. But one day the dependent child will realize what they are like and will experience self-loathing for allowing other people to strip him or her of personal identity, and so "X"s are created.

Iverna:

When a youngster misbehaves in order to get attention, we need to recognize that we might not be giving him or her enough of the right kind of attention. Giving a child plenty of the right kind of attention before it is asked for is the ounce of prevention that's worth more than tons of cure.

Attention Deficit

Infants and preschoolers are more inclined to be friendly than unfriendly, unless they've really been hurt and their natural drives stymied. But when we take our loving little dear, who's always been such an agreeable sweetheart and so easy to get along with, to nursery school, little dear meets a new thing. Everybody doesn't suddenly melt when he or she looks up at them with big blue eyes and says, "I wuv you." Instead someone says, "Shhh, sit down and be quiet." The child's behavior at home will begin to reflect this baffling rejection that has come into his or her life without warning.

Being aware of the cause allows us to know not to punish the child and thereby make the problem worse, but to show the child an increased measure of love and acceptance at home. Thus the child is able to make a satisfactory adjustment to the school situation.

We can forestall some attention-getting misbehavior by anticipating circumstances where our youngster might be deprived of attention. Making special provision to meet anticipated needs can eliminate the necessity for misbehavior on the child's part.

Look at Me!

Every parent has been in situations where a guest in the home has required their undivided attention. Perhaps this has involved extra cleaning and cooking. One or both parents may be paying exclusive attention to the guest. The child who is ignored in the midst of such circumstances is likely to become a hellion—forcing attention on himself or herself by spilling their cup of milk, jumping on the furniture, maybe even by kicking the honored guest in the shins when nobody else is looking.

The parents, embarrassed and frustrated, at a loss to know what to do, do every wrong thing in the book. First, they tell the child again and again to stop misbehaving, but neither parent enforces the instruction. Maybe their little darling is kicking the table leg. The child doesn't stop but keeps on doing it, figuring they are probably safe from punishment: "Mom and Dad won't spank me with company here." Meanwhile, the child is the center of attention and having a ball. As long as the child continues to kick the table leg, someone will be glowering at him or her. In the child's mind, unfavorable attention is better than none.

The Changeling

The next mistake the parent makes is to talk about their child's misbehavior in the child's presence, magnifying it and thereby increasing the sought-after attention that is the cause of it.

"I don't know what's gotten into Mark today," Mother apologizes to the guest, who is contemplating the run in her brand-new panty hose. Underneath the run, her leg is beginning to turn black and blue from precious little Mark's shenanigans.

"I've never seen him this naughty before," Dad adds, his eyes dangerously off Mark for an instant—just long enough for him to deliberately sling his arm against the centerpiece on the table and send it crashing and splashing. Something in Mark insists that he live up to the character that's been painted.

Suddenly, it's over.

Mom sputters something mercifully not understandable, Dad swoops the child up and, trailed by Mom, carries him as far out of earshot as possible and spanks him. He screams, Mom seethes, and then Dad, dumps him in bed, totally rejected. Gritting her teeth, Mom and Dad throw him a look of utter contempt, close the door softly, glue a fake smile on their flushed faces, and go back downstairs to entertain their guest.

But the guest is gone.

There's a note on the table beside the pieces of broken glass the thoughtful guest had picked out of the carpet. "Dear Tom and Nancy," the note reads in a rather shaky scrawl, "Thanks for the lovely lunch. Sorry I have to leave early. Love, Mary."

Mom and Dad contemplate the dirty dishes, the wrecked flower arrangement, the ruined day. Mom grits her teeth again at the loud wailing of the kid upstairs and snarls at her husband; Dad stifles a nasty comment and slams out the door—or vice-versa.

Bad scene. It's probably happened to most parents.

Preventive Measures

When we know that our child may feel threatened by our attention to somebody else, we don't have to set it up for him or her to feel neglected, making it almost certain that our child's behavior will be impossible. We can let it be a day of special attention to them from the beginning.

Hire your child's favorite baby sitter to take him or her to the park for a picnic outing. Let your child spend the night with a favorite

58

aunt. Let him or her "help" with setting the table or sweeping the front porch to get ready for the company. Go out of your way to give your child a fair share of positive attention, so he or she won't have to insist on the negative variety.

If your child feels secure in your love, he or she can be their usual sweet self. But if your child feels pushed aside and threatened, he or she will naturally fight for their life in any way they know how. None of those ways will be acceptable to us.

No Age Limitations

While our young children are this obvious in their behavior, our adolescents are less obvious. Yet they may be acting or reacting based on very similar or even the same unmet needs. Sometimes, because they act so mature, we tend to leave them to themselves far too much, and they feel we are not involved in their lives and come to have the same resentments that a three-year-old might have. Their way of expression might be to slam doors, refuse meals, sullenly respond with one word answers to questions, or be virtually non-conversive. Their grades in school may begin to drop and their social interest be completely outside the family for a period of time.

As soon as this is discovered, we must go back to the beginning and find out the cause. This is very difficult to do, because by the time it has reached this point, they are determined not to let us back into their lives. Only love can conquer.

It isn't the kind of love, however, that lets the behavior continue. It's the kind of love that realistically pursues a confrontation; "What's wrong? I know you're different than you used to be. Obviously, I have hurt you, or someone has hurt you very deeply, or someone is not understanding you." "You and I" or "You and Dad and I" or " You and Mom and I have got to come to grips with this situation so that we can make things right and remind ourselves that we are a family forever. That will never change. You are a part of us, and we are a part of you."

Whatever it takes for them to open the door, may very well not happen in one conversation, but something will happen with this one conversation. Follow it with a lot of prayer, open eyes and open ears, and soon you'll find out what's going on. Confront again and again until a breakthrough occurs. It is not just important. It is absolutely necessary to the welfare of our children that we maintain a proper rapport and relationship.

Dianne:

God has created each one of us with the ability to set up natural defenses against pain, but it's those very natural defenses that ultimately create greater pain. When we try to meet our needs through negative behavior and sick relationships, these roles and relationships eventually cause more "X"s. If as a child we don't know how to go to God and to seek healing for the "X"s and find the attention, affection, approval, affiliation, and authority we need, we will seek relief in at least three different ways.

Arousal

Let's say your teenager doesn't know how to go to God to be healed and get his or her needs met legitimately from God. He or she may seek relief by arousal. What will arouse the average teen? Anything that's risk-taking and exciting—like sex, shopping, cocaine, fast and reckless driving, bungee-jumping, gambling, stealing, any dare-devil kind of behavior, any kind of stimulating drug, any thrill worth seeking. To avoid acknowledging that the "X" is there from Mom, Dad, sister, brother, girlfriend, boyfriend, or friend, the teenager will stay busy in activities—in going, doing, and being—so he or she doesn't have to think and feel.

Satiate

Your teenager has a legitimate need, and in trying to have that need met, has an "X." He or she does not go to God for healing and ministering, but rather seeks relief through satiation or satisfying themselves to the full or even to excess. He or she will turn to food, alcohol, or any drug that's a downer. He or she may sleep for an inordinate amount of time in order to hide and escape. He or she may become a "couch potato," lethargic, not involved in activities, seeking relief from the pain and trying to bring healing.

Fantasy

Let's say your teenager is not an arousal-type person, or doesn't want to satiate—instead he or she prefers fantasy and becomes a daydreamer. He or she will read romance novels, watch soap operas, become fascinated with "fairy tales" or stories of creatures with god-like powers and immortality, and will play video games that are based in mythology and fantasy. Your teenager may create a fantasy life with a new Mom and Dad, a new girlfriend or boyfriend or best friend who will comply with his or her needs. Your teenager will seek relief and pleasure somewhere in a fantasy world.

Addictive Roles and Pleasures

As children begin to develop into adulthood, they carry with them the different roles and ways of seeking pleasures they established while growing up. Ultimately these become addictive. The responsible child becomes the workaholic adult who is performance-oriented. A caretaker becomes the controller and enabler of dependent relationships. The rebellious child becomes anti-social and a controller in relationships. The invisible, lost child becomes the adult victim. A dependent child remains a perpetual child as an adult, one who remains reliant on others.

The coping mechanisms that children choose in order to seek relief and pleasure, separating them from pain, become addictive as they grow to adulthood. For instance, if your child was an arousal-type person, he or she will become an adult sex-addict, or a gambler, or a daredevil, a shopaholic, or a drug addict. If your child was a satiator, he or she will become an adult alcoholic, a foodaholic, or a sleepaholic. If your child liked fantasy, he or she will become an adult addicted to the soaps, romance novels, or daydreaming. These addictions enable the adult to separate himself or herself from reality.

As we look at the "X" syndrome, we begin to discover that the resulting behavior is what we usually deal with instead of the "X." Most children are brought into counseling because of their addictions (their problems with drugs, relationships, sex, alcohol), not their "X."

If we, as parents, appropriately deal with the "X"s and bring healing to them, we will begin to see a change in the roles and addictions our children have embraced.

As God began to heal my daughter, Michelle, her boyfriends changed. The healthier she got, the healthier the boys she picked became. As God began to meet her needs and heal her, she didn't need to be a caretaker in a relationship. She no longer felt the need to stay dependent, or become a victim in her relationships. My task, as a biblical parent, was to discover Michelle's "X"s and bring healing, instead of attacking her behavior. As God begins to teach us how to bring ministry and healing to the "X"s, we will see the addictions vanish.

Some years ago, when Michelle was in high school, my husband and I went away to a conference, leaving a couple to oversee the home. Upon our return, the husband pulled Wayne aside saying, "I need to tell you something. My wife made a pan of brownies and when I went to get some, they were all gone. We discovered that your daughter had eaten them all."

This was very embarrassing as a parent. As a counselor, I thought, "I have failed." When the friends left, I said, "Wayne, we've got to deal with the issues with us and our ego first, before we can minister to Michelle." I knew about the "X" syndrome, I knew Michelle didn't have a food problem, but a problem with "X"s. I wanted to discover the "X"s. My natural tendency as a parent was to want to control her behavior by taking away her allowance or monitoring her food. We wanted to oversee where she went and how much money she spent on food.

Having worked with addicts before, I knew that if we played cops and robbers, Michelle would "win" for a while, but ultimately lose. By focusing on Michelle's addiction, we'd all lose. If I searched her room for food, she'd hide the food outside. If I searched outside, she'd hide the food at a friend's house. I knew I couldn't outsmart her, but I didn't want to—I wanted to heal her.

What should we do? I didn't know. I just knew she had lots of "X"s." Michelle's birth father was very abusive and didn't communicate with her. When she tried to solve a problem with him, it always ended up being her fault. Consequently, Michelle had very low self-esteem when it came to her real father. Though I didn't know what the "X"s were, I knew God did. So her step-father and I began to seek God.

A few days later, I went to her and very honestly said, "Michelle, we have a problem here, but the issue is not your food. There's lots of pain in your life. I believe Jesus Christ can heal you, and I want us to learn. The issue isn't food, but the food can be your red flag. When you begin to OD on food, after you've eaten a meal or whatever is going on, it's a red flag saying, 'Something is happening. I've got an "X." Help me'"

We watched the Spirit of God begin to teach Michelle. It took her five years for the weight to come off and stay off. Michelle learned to control her vessel in honor (1 Thessalonians 4:4). She learned that Jesus Christ can heal the "X"s. Was it painful for us? Oh, yes, because we were judged by many people by what they saw in Michelle. They saw her overweight and they wanted us to fix her. But Jesus Christ was fixing her on the inside.

We watched Jesus begin to heal her, bringing her to the place where she could start loving herself. She was no longer on a self-destructive course through eating. I watched her go to Jesus and allow Him to minister to her when she was hurt by a boyfriend or by a friend, not just turn to food to numb the pain.

The issue with Michelle wasn't getting her to stop eating; the issue was finding the "X"s and bringing healing to those areas, so she would be released from turning to food to seek relief.

If we choose to do behavior modification, we will discover a strange phenomenon. For example, if your son is addicted to alcohol, you can get him off the alcohol, but he will turn to another drug that is equally or more destructive and become addicted to that. Then you will have to get him off that drug, but he'll turn to food and gain weight. Then you will have to focus on the food, so that he loses weight. When the focus is on the addictions, no internal change happens, because you've not dealt with the real issue—the "X"s.

God needs to come in to heal the person, renew his or her mind, and bind up the broken heart. Then the child must be taught how to meet needs in a healthy fashion.

Even if your children are out of your home, it's never too late for God to intervene.

Discovering Your Child's Role

It's not enough for us to read about the different roles. We must take time to discover them in our children. Here are questions you can ask yourself that will help reveal your child's ways of dealing with "X"s.

Role 1: The Good Child

Does my child take responsibility beyond the developmental age?

Does my child want to help me in things he is unable to do?

Does my child find esteem in being responsible? In what he wears? In whom he relates to? In things such as money, cars, etc.?

Do I find my child focusing on achieving in athletics, grades, church? Does my child need to win?

Does my child feel like a failure as a person when he doesn't do really well at something?

Role 2: The Caretaker

Does my child like to take a lot of responsibility for other family members?

Does my child like to counsel or help me or my spouse with our problems?

Does my child give advice or orders to family members in an effort to get them to do what he thinks is best?

Does my child have others turn to him for help because he's a good listener or sensitive to their feelings?

Does my child seem to befriend the "losers"?

Role 3: The Rebel

Does my child often get into trouble at home?

Does my child tend to express feelings with others that seem critical or judgmental? Aggressive or hostile?

Does my child get angry often and do destructive things to self and others?

Does my child get into trouble at school and doesn't seem to care what happens?

Does my child often feel down on himself and others?

Role 4: The Invisible Child

Does my child spend a lot of time alone and seem to be more comfortable alone than with the family?

Does my child seem to keep quiet in conflicts and then disappear?

Does my child seem to feel lonely and yet wants others to seek him out?

Is my child always told how good and well-behaved he is because he doesn't bother anybody?

Does my child seem to respond passively by being quiet and compliant?

Role 5: The Dependent Child

Is my child not encouraged to grow up and be responsible?

Do we as parents do things for our child that should be done by the child?

Does my child seem to be a "follower" in a group?

Does my child seem to get away with things for which other children are disciplined?

Does my child have an uncanny ability to get others to do for him what he should do for himself?

Have you discovered the role of your child or children? In what areas do they seem to score the most? That's the role they have a tendency to walk in now. Can they walk in several, or all of them? Yes.

We understand that much of this is normal behavior for well-adjusted personalities. When they become the entire pattern of life in just one area, however, we probably are dealing with the "X" factor.

We need to begin to discover how our children are adapting and surviving in their environment, so that we can effectively intervene.

In opening communication, we may go to our children and say, "I know there are "X"s in your life, and I want you to know how sorry I am for not meeting the needs you legitimately have. I apologize for all the times you needed attention or affection or approval and I didn't know how to give it to you or I was not sensitive enough to give it to you. I'm asking you not only to forgive me, but I'm asking if you would pray with me for Jesus to heal you and that we can learn how to walk free of the roles and addictions in which we walk.

"The Holy Spirit has been given to convict us of sin and righteousness. I'm going to ask Him to teach us, show us, and alert us when it's not the role and addictions or the behavior that's the problem, but show us the real issue. What's the need? Where's the "X"? What's really going on in this situation? Will you pray this with me?"

When David was three or four years old, I told him to go upstairs and put on his tank top. He started upstairs and then stopped. He looked around at me in confusion. To me, his behavior looked like rebellion—he wasn't obeying me. I was just learning how to look beyond behavior, so I asked, "David, what's wrong?"

He said, "How do I put the toilet on?" David thought tank top meant the toilet top (we call little tee shirts tank tops). At David's level of maturity, he didn't understand what I was saying. What would have happened if I had spanked him for disobeying me? David would have had an "X," and I would have inappropriately dealt with his behavior. I would not have had a heart change or a healing in our relationship.

God will continue to give us, as biblical parents, wisdom, understanding, and revelation of the roles and addictions in which we walk, so we can repent, receive healing of the "X"s, and then reproduce that healing in our children.

We serve an eternal, all-powerful God who is present today to heal, thereby bringing release and wisdom and giving us hope for everything we need to walk the liberated, full, abundant life He has promised.

The Holy Spirit of truth will continue to set us free.

4

Your Child and Communication

Iverna:

"Mom, you don't listen to me anymore!" Dan accused me one day.

Me, not listen? I'd always prided myself on the fact that I did listen. Why, I considered myself the best listening mother in the world. But with Dan's accusation came the startling realization that what he said was true. I couldn't have been really listening, because I had just asked him if the girl he was dating was a Christian. Some corner of my memory told me that I'd asked him the same question before, about the same girl. If I had been really listening, I'd have remembered that I had asked the question before, and I'd have remembered his answer, too.

True listening involves an investment of ourselves far beyond merely making polite conversation. Real listening is in-depth identification with the child and a serious attempt to understand his or her point of view.

Dianne:

To effectively listen to our children, we should understand what affects this hearing process and some basic principles of communication.

Principle 1: Communication is a two-way street—one person delivering the message and another person hearing and receiving the message.

This may sound obvious, but have you ever tried to hold a conversation with someone who was like a monologue? They didn't really care about our response or what we said? When parents talk to their children, it becomes a monologue if the child is physically present but emotionally shut down and not listening. The child can even respond by saying, "Yeah, uh uh," but he is not really listening or responding to the situation.

Principle 2: Communication involves more than words.

Person number one attempts to impart a message, but what they need to recognize is that three things are involved in presenting this message: 1) the message itself; 2) the tone of voice; and 3) body language. All three have to be saying the same thing. If they are not, a double-level message is communicated.

For example: If I want to tell my child I love him or her, but I yell it and my body is turned around facing the other way, then my word-message says, "I love you," but my tone of voice says, "I don't like you," and my body language says, "I'm going to ignore you." What message will the child will receive?

In order to take in the message, the hearer needs to understand what affects the receiving of the message: 1) the message will first be perceived—this means the message will go through all five senses; 2) once filtered, the message is interpreted or translated, and finally; 3) evaluated.

The child who hears the parent say "I love you," but whose tone of voice says, "I'm angry," and whose body language is rejecting, is going to perceive this message through their five senses. They will hear the message and tone of voice, see an angry face and turned body, and feel the anger in the voice and rejection in the body.

Then the child will interpret what his or her senses perceive. One interpretation might be, "Mom's mad at me." Or "Mom doesn't really love me."

Thirdly, the child may make an evaluation: "I'm bad. I'm not lovable. I'd better get out of here."

The receiver of the message must now respond to the message. An appropriate response from the child would be, "Mom, I hear your words saying you love me, but when your tone of voice sounds angry and you turn your back on me, I receive another message. What are you trying to say to me?" The child is also asking for feedback regarding the double message—love/hate.

Once the child responds, the parent must now respond back.

When a child hears the message, "I love you," stated angrily, he or she will use their perceptions to interpret and evaluate that message. Being done on a conscious level, this prevents the child from effectively listening and responding. If the child evaluates this message as, "Mom hates me," the child will respond inappropriately by saying, "I hate you, too." Though perhaps not verbally spoken, he or she may defensively think it.

If spoken, the parent hearing these words may be shocked at this response to their "I love you," and will respond unsuitably: "Why are you so defensive?" or "Why do you hate me when I love you?"

Principle 3: Most problems in communication are in the area of effective or ineffective listening and responding.

Iverna:

One day, I was hollering at Dan for not scouring out his bathtub. We'd had words on the same subject in the past, but the conflict had never been resolved.

"Mom," he asked me, patiently controlling his exasperation at my tirade, "Why is it so important for me to scour my tub every day? Nobody uses it but me, and the tub doesn't look so terrible if I miss cleaning it for a whole week. Besides, I'm the only one who sees it, unless you happen to poke your head in just to check up on me. Who cares how it looks?"

Dan got through to me that day, because I was really listening, involving myself in his point of view. I had to admit it shouldn't actually matter all that much whether or not his tub was as sparkling as a cleanser commercial, but it did matter to me.

We should have been able to settle on a compromise. Dan might have promised to scour his tub once a week without being reminded, unless it got really grimy-looking, even to him. If that happened, he'd scrub it more often. In the meantime, I could have promised not to bug him about it. We could both have heaved a sigh of relief that an awful area of conflict had been ended. But it didn't happen that way, because some area of pride in me still insisted that the tub be sparkling all the time, not just once a week. I didn't change my rule, he didn't change his attitude, but we understood each other, because we had both listened. That helped.

Parents tell me the same thing happens in their parent-child relationships. The parent acknowledges the relative reasonableness of a child's attitude about something, but still insists it be done their way. There's no harm done as long as the channels of communication are kept open. We don't have to agree about everything in order to love one another. We can disagree without being disagreeable about it. But we do have to listen.

The Contender

Parents of outgoing, independent-thinking youngsters are often presented with persuasive arguments as they listen. My son could argue so logically that sometimes I reeled in my own principles for a minute.

"Look at it this way, Mom," he'd say. Then he'd present a case for his side that would sway the most able jury in the land. I almost always saw his point, but God is merciful and I saw the real point, too. Sometimes I stuck with my side and sometimes I changed my mind. The communication between us was a good thing from his point of view and mine, no matter what the outcome. When we truly listen, we can't really lose.

Dianne:

Conscious Barriers to Communication: Perceptions - Interpretation - Evaluation

A teenage girl comes home from school and announces to her mother, "I'm pregnant." Not only do the parents hear the message, but they will interpret and evaluate that message. If the parents interpret the message as, "We have failed as parents. We have failed our daughter," they will make an evaluation of themselves as being failures. And with that evaluation, the parents will give their response. They might attack the daughter by saying, "We knew you were no good. You've always been in trouble and here you are again. Will you never learn?" or, "What have we done to deserve this?"

The effective way of hearing and interpreting and evaluating this situation is by thinking, "Our daughter needs help." Now Mom and Dad's response will be appropriate. "How can we help you? We've got a serious problem here. What can we do?" Mom and Dad, through effective listening, respond appropriately to the situation at the right moment.

A teenage boy comes home in anger and states, "I'm leaving home!" What do the parents hear? Possibly, "It's bad around here. Things are really wrong in this house. We've failed. Our son is rejecting us," and if so, they will make a defensive response—not really hearing him. Listening effectively, Mom and Dad would hear beyond the words, "I'm leaving home," and realize something's going on and make themselves available to talk to the child to discover a solution to the real problem.

Visual Impairment

Another conscious barrier of perception that affects effective listening and communicating is sight. How can sight keep parents from effectively listening? Suppose your daughter brings home her boyfriend and he has spiked, dyed-purple hair. Naturally you're going to make an interpretation and an evaluation from what you see, and respond accordingly. "Are you crazy? You've picked a loser. You're better than that." When the parent attacks the boyfriend, the daughter will become hostile and respond defensively, "You don't even know him. I'll date whoever I want to. You're just old-fashioned."

Perhaps your son brings home an attractive girl who looks "together" and healthy. Again, naturally, by what you positively see, you make an interpretation, an evaluation, responding accordingly, "Oh, I'm glad you're going to go with her." You haven't effectively listened to the situation to see what the girl is actually like, because you have used sight to make an interpretation and evaluation and haven't really heard or seen her true character.

Raising a Stink

Another sense we have that affects our effective listening and responding is smell. Your son comes home from a Friday night basketball game reeking of alcohol. You're going to make an evaluation by interpreting that behavior and respond, not by listening to him, but by attacking him. "I knew that if I let you go to the game, you'd get drunk. What else have you been doing?" By imputing behavior, because of what you smell, you've shut the door to effectively listening to him and why he was drinking. (Please note this is not condoning the drinking, but looking for the "X.")

Unconscious Barriers to Communication

When a parent and a child come into a communicating relationship, not only are the conscious perceptions used to interpret and evaluate the relationship, but underneath are the unconscious barriers that affect communication, listening, and, ultimately, the relationship.

Your Value System

If your value system and your child's value system are different, it will keep you from listening effectively. For instance, if your value regarding money is that it should be saved and your daughter's value of money is that it should be spent, you'll see her spending habits as irresponsible and will make remarks that attack and put down: "You spend too much. You'll always be broke." An appropriate response is: "I've noticed you spend all your money; do you know how to save?"

Some parents think that just because they have values, their children will automatically have them, too—but that's not true. Children need to be trained and taught values. A value is anything that you spend time, effort, or money on. Watch your children. Where do they spend their time, their energy, and their money? This is where their values are. As you discover their values, you can effectively listen to why they have those values. With the help of God, you can begin to teach and train them in biblical values, rather than attack theirs.

Your Belief Systems

Your daughter comes home from school saying, "I don't believe in God any more." The parent is going to interpret and evaluate that as a negative and want to fix it by saying, "Don't be ridiculous. Everyone knows there is a God. Just look at creation!" No more discussion. Instead of listening to the heart of the child, this response shuts down communication and the child feels rejected and not worth listening to. An appropriate way to respond to the child's comment is to say, "That's interesting. What's brought you to that conclusion? I'd like to hear more." Now the door is open for heart-to-heart communication.

A teenage boy comes home from school and says, "I believe in safe sex." The child has confronted the parents' belief system and also what they value. From the parents' interpretation and evaluation, they'll probably give a negative response. "You pervert! Only heathens have sex before marriage. It's sin and God hates sin." An appropriate response will be given when the parent hears the whole message and opens the door for more communication by responding, "I'd like to hear more about that. How do we weigh this value with God's value on sex?"

A seven-year-old son comes home from school and proceeds to tell Dad that he won't cry anymore because it's bad. Now if the father's belief system corresponds with his son's declaration that crying for males is wrong, he will agree with the child. If the father's belief system is that it's healthy to cry in certain situations for healing to come, there's a conflict in belief systems. The father will have a tendency to want to change and fix it, instead of listening effectively. Listening effectively, the father will say, "What's happened today to make you come to that decision about crying?" Now the door is open for the child to begin to express his heart with the parent.

Your Expectations

Any time expectations are different, you're going to have a problem with effective listening. For example, it's time for vacation. In your teenager's mind, the expectation is, "Wow, we're going to go to the beach and I can go surfing all summer long, and I'll be able to find a new boyfriend, a new girlfriend, and that sounds like fun." Mom and Dad's expectation is, "We're going to go to the mountains and find a little cabin. It's going to be quiet and we'll be able to rest, and there will be no one in sight." The seven-year-old's expectation is, "Oh, goody, I'm going to go to a play yard and play with all the swings and the jump ropes, and I'll be able to go swimming everyday."

Before there's any discussion about the vacation, the expectations have already caused each one not to hear effectively. When parents understand that there are different expectations, then, while communicating about the vacation, they will be able to effectively listen to everyone, and to what they want to do, and plan a "family" vacation.

Because Wayne and I know about different expectations, any time we have a vacation or a period of time where we'll be able to have leisure time, we sit down with the whole family and hear everyone's expectations. We try listening effectively to each one. Then we make our decision about where to go by choosing a destination that will allow each person to do at least one of the things on his list of expectations. In this way, each is heard, each one's desires and expectations respected, and we learn about "family" vacations.

Any area where there are different expectations, there is the potential for defensiveness instead of effective listening and communication. Areas of potential problems with expectations can be school work, homework, grades, friends, snacking habits, mealtime schedules, extracurricular and evening activities, etc. Without effectively listening to each other in these areas where there are different expectations, there will be conflicts.

Your Memories

Memories may prevent you from listening effectively, because they're carried in your storehouse unconsciously and are projected into your current experiences.

If a parent has negative or positive memories from childhood regarding mealtimes, he or she will carry these into a current situation. For instance, if Dad, as a son, had negative experiences at mealtimes, because his dad and mom yelled, screamed, and fought during the meal, as an adult, (unconsciously) mealtimes will be a negative to him. Let's say that this father is at dinner with his family and Mother starts yelling at Johnny to quit picking at his food. Dad would unconsciously project his past memories of pain, rejection, fear, or anger into the current situation and respond inappropriately to Mother. He might tell Mother to shut up, she's too fussy. He might get mad and just leave. Any of these responses, because of past memories, keep Dad from listening and responding effectively.

Perhaps a parent has past memories regarding friends and phones. If, as a child, Mom was not allowed to use the phone or could only use it a short time, or when friends did call Mom and Dad would yell and scream in the background telling her to get off the phone, Mom would carry these memories into training her own children. She would either continue to regulate the phone calls or be overindulgent, allowing her children to use the phone anytime. The memories would affect her listening to her husband's counsel regarding their child and the phone and what effect Mom's regulations or indulgence has on their child. She wouldn't know how to distinguish from her child's issues, her own issues, or her spouse's issues.

Let me share an example from my own life of painful memories and how they affected me. When I was young, I was very heavy, so going shopping and buying clothes was a painful time. At the store, I either couldn't find my size, or I had gained weight and had to get a larger size. As an adult parent, I took my daughter shopping. She was in junior high school and gaining weight appropriate for her age, so it was necessary to buy some new clothes. In the store, without realizing it—unconsciously—I was in a lot of pain. I started remembering my childhood experiences, projecting them on to Michelle. I couldn't hear her saying she was having a good time—having fun. I was hearing my pain and putting it on her saying, "Oh, this must be awful having to go up another size." She said, "No, just get another size." She didn't have any problem with it. I was the one having the problem, and my past memories and former pain affected my hearing her in the present.

I was thankful to the Lord for this situation, because it made me realize I needed healing. So I asked the Lord to heal me from my past and the pain of that rejection and the trauma that I went through as a child, and He did. The next time Michelle and I went shopping, I could hear her effectively and not through the filter of my pain.

Your Emotional Words

Words that trigger responses—emotional words—affect parents' listening to their child. For instance, the word *abortion* can trigger a response causing the parent to stop listening and start reacting. Emotional words are very subjective, and parents need to identify their emotional words so that when those words are said, they will know how to respond based on what the child is really saying and not according to the emotional issue that word triggers.

Possible emotional words for a child are those that define his or her personality or appearance. Being called fat, dumb, stupid, lazy, ugly, or alcoholic. Emotional words really can become name-calling words. When these words are used in a sentence, children hear only the emotional word and stop listening to the parent. What the child will remember is the attack, the emotional words.

Your Training

Were you trained as a child to give feedback? If so, how were you trained to give feedback? If you weren't taught how to be able to convey your feelings, to express feedback, to say, "I'm confused," and then have a parent give a healthy response and continued feedback, you haven't learned the skill. If you weren't allowed to "talk back" to your parents, to ask for clarification, you will have difficulty teaching this to your child.

Iverna:

Real listening is vital because there's no way we can know another person or understand another's point of view without hearing them.

Suppose my son wants to have a dog. If I don't listen to his reasons, my answer may be a flat "No." I might even explain my quick decision: "You're involved in so much at school these days, you wouldn't have time to take the dog for his daily walk. I'd be left having to walk him, feed him, take him to the vet for shots, and all that. I just don't have time for a dog." That would be that.

But what if I listened first to his reasons for wanting a dog?

"Mom, when you're gone, I get lonesome in the apartment with nobody to play with. I don't have any friends here. But if I had a dog . . ."

Identifying with his point of view, I might make an affirmative decision after all and head for the pet shop. Since a pet would mean so much to my child, I might consider it a good investment of my time to walk the dog once in a while, and to do other things for him. By listening, I learn the real needs of my children, and I'm put in a frame of mind where I'm willing to meet those needs.

True Listening

The kind of listening required of parents is non-judgmental listening.

My child might come into the house in tears, sniffling, "Janey hit me." Times without number, my first reaction has been a negative, "What did you do to her?'

It would have been far better to say, "How did it happen?" This response does not put my child on the defensive. Such an impartial response could encourage a healing outpouring, instead of closing a damper of frustration on the cause of the trouble.

When we don't listen, we're limited to our own perspective, which may be a very one-sided thing. Besides that, our refusal to listen to our children teaches them not to listen to us. A mass of misunderstandings is the inevitable result.

Many times we don't listen simply because our mind is cluttered with other things, or we are thinking ahead about what we will say or do.

True listening is not the same thing as tolerating a period of verbiage. Neither is it merely letting the child say his or her piece so that when they're finished we can tell them what we'd already decided. Real listening has to include a willingness to change our minds and a willingness to consider a compromise.

I used to be quite annoyed over the clutter of candy wrappers, tennis shoes, stationery, pop cans, and comic books that accumulated under Dan's bed.

"But, Mom," he used to protest when I'd say something about it, "I always clean those things up in a day or two. It doesn't make sense for me to have to get out of bed to carry a pop can to the kitchen when I'm reading at night or to put my tennis shoes in the closet when I'm going to put them on again the first thing in the morning."

What he said sounded reasonable enough, but I couldn't back down all the way, and I told him so. I don't remember which of us thought of a workable compromise, but one day we got a sturdy cardboard box and cut the sides down so it could slide under his bed. He began to keep all his under-bed paraphernalia there, handy for him to reach, yet quickly slid out of the way when we wanted to sweep or dust the floor. I was satisfied because everything was in the box, and Dan was happy with the arrangement, too.

The compromise couldn't have happened if we hadn't been able to listen and really hear each other's point of view.

Many teenagers feel, with rich justification, that there's no future in saying anything to their parents, because parents never listen.

"What's the use of talking to my folks?" kids have asked me so many times. "They never listen—they never change their minds no matter what I say." Too often, that's true.

A child may say to a counselor, "I just don't have any freedom. My parents are too strict. They never let me go anywhere with the other kids."

When parents hear this, they are likely to sputter, "That isn't so at all. Johnny belongs to this and that, and he goes here and there, and every once in a while, we let him go to another place."

As long as parents are occupied with defending their own actions, they aren't listening—they aren't trying to understand their youngster. Parents need to learn to deal with the situation as their child sees it, not with the situation as they think he or she ought to see it.

Not long ago, a young girl told me, "My parents don't love me." When I conveyed that to her parents, they protested, "But that's not true! We do love our child."

Whether a parent loves their child or not, if that child thinks they don't, then that unlove is truth to him or her, at least for the moment, and something needs to be done to reassure the child.

How to Listen

"But how can I do this all-important listening to my child?" parents have asked me. "Johnny is so quiet—he hardly ever has anything to say to me."

If you have a child who is a real introvert, and you want to bring him or her out of their shell, check your memory to see if they've been an introvert all their life or if they've fallen into it recently. Introverted teenagers are generally kids who have not learned to give of themselves. The only way some people can learn to give of themselves is to have it demanded of them.

With your teenager, you can begin by letting him or her know that they are needed. You can ask their opinions about things without using questions they can turn off with yes or no answers. You can involve him or her in discussions, asking, "What do you think about the national political situation?" If they say, "I don't know," you can acknowledge that, "Of course, no one knows," but "we'd just like to hear what you think about it." You may be amazed at the depth of his or her response when they think their parents are really interested.

There's an art to keeping conversation coming from your children instead of always telling them what's what. When they become comfortable talking with you, they will begin to respond to others as well. It will be a progressive thing if you'll get it started and give them some practice.

The Purpose

In the midst of doing this, keep in mind the purpose of the conversation. It's not that your children might impart accurate, scientifically verifiable information, but that they might be open in sharing with you. For that reason, it would be wrong to correct them if they misquote a statistic, mispronounce a word, or draw some illogical conclusion, embellishing it with knowledge they don't have. Keep in mind that you're not working on their intellectual content, you're working on their ability to converse in a meaningful way. There will be other opportunities to correct any misinformation, without squelching the flow of communication.

Dianne:

God wants to teach us how to train our children effectively to respond according to the heart and not according to the message—not according to the words that are being said, but to what the heart is saying behind the words.

As for the components of communication, giving and receiving, most of us have had one or two of the parts missing in our training. For instance, as a sender, I was able to send the message but was unaware that I was giving a double message. As a receiver of the message, I didn't know I had the responsibility to receive the message and to evaluate it, to understand my perceptions in it, and also to ask for clarification regarding an unclear message. Finally, as initial sender of the message, my responsibility was to receive the feedback without feeling defensive, threatened, attacked, but by responding according to what I wanted to say, giving a healthy response to the feedback. As parents, we need to understand that our perceptions, values, expectations, memories, and training all affect our ability to adequately talk with our children.

Defensive Responses

We've discussed that in not listening effectively, parents often react inappropriately to the message and the messenger. Here, in more detail, are some ways parents hinder or stop good communication and hearing the heart of their loved ones.

Defensiveness - When parents find walls going up inside themselves, they're becoming defensive and attacking *(fight)* or becoming silent *(flee)*.

Becoming angry - When parents find themselves or their child responding angrily, they've stopped listening and something else is being affected in the situation. (We'll discuss in detail what's behind anger in a later chapter.)

Having a need to correct or fix - When there's the need to fix or correct, the parent has stopped listening and is now seeking to control the message or messenger.

Feelings mixed up with responses - Anytime a parent feels proud, resentful, fearful, or embarrassed, they're responding defensively and not listening effectively.

The silent treatment - When a child is pouting, quiet, and not wanting to talk, that's a defensive response.

Interrupting - Anybody who interrupts has not listened to the whole message and is reacting to only some part of the message.

Moralizing - When parents feel the need to give a moral evaluation of the situation, they have stopped listening effectively and now want to preach and to talk the child into their position.

Criticizing - When criticism enters the communication, someone is defensive and not listening effectively.

Rationalizing - When either party begins to explain away actions, behavior, or what was said, he or she has stopped listening and is reacting defensively.

Name-calling - Any time name-calling is used, it's a weapon and a defensive response, which is not effective listening. Examples of name-calling are dumb, old, lazy, unloving, whore, drunk.

Teasing - When someone says something and then says, "Just kidding," it's a defensive response to communication and keeps effective listening from happening.

Ignoring or changing the subject - When someone brings up a subject that's too painful to talk about, the defensive response is to ignore or change the subject. This defensive response stops effective listening.

Daydreaming - When a child that is being spoken to is sitting there looking at the speaker straight in the eyes, yet the speaker knows the child is in a daze, the child is responding defensively to the speaker and is no longer listening to what is being said.

Blaming and accusing - Anytime there's blaming and accusations being leveled, effective listening has stopped. Examples: "How many times do I have to tell you?" or "You always . . ."

Threatening - When, in the course of conversation, anyone starts issuing threats, it is a defensive posture and effective listening has stopped. Examples: "If you do that one more time . . ." or "You'll be sorry," or "Do you want to live here?"

Commanding - When a parent has to command behavior, especially with teenagers, they've moved into a defensive position and have stopped listening effectively. Example: "Stop . . ." "Don't . . ."

Comparing - When comparisons are made between children: "Why can't you be like your brother?" parents have stopped listening effectively to behavior and are now trying to manipulate and move defensively.

Improper feedback - When the questions for feedback are given as a challenge and not to obtain honest and useful feedback, this will cause a defensive response and effective listening has stopped. Children have a right to give feedback and to ask for clarification, but not to irreverently talk back. There is a difference.

Iverna:

Every listening parent knows that nothing is off-limits for discussion as far as a child is concerned. Things adults might discuss in veiled terms, if at all, a youngster feels free to blurt right out at the least opportune moment.

"Mom, I can't stand to talk to Mrs. So-and-So. Her breath stinks."

It's easy for us to react to such embarrassing outbursts with a careful, "Shhh! It's not nice to talk about such things." But it's better for us to seize every opportunity to teach our child something he

85

needs to know. Instead of just shushing the child, we can tell him, "That's why we use mouthwash, so our breath won't offend anybody."

A surprising number of teenagers have never been taught by their parents to use an underarm deodorant, and somehow the TV commercials haven't sunk in either. They might get some instruction in such things at school, but may not realize the importance without follow up at home.

A teenage girl spoke to me one day about a very fine Christian young man.

"He's just perfect in every other way," she said, "But I can't stand to be around him because he has such strong body odor. What can I do about it?"

There wasn't much she could do, without dying of embarrassment. Fortunately, a church counselor took it upon himself to go to the boy and tell him why he should use an underarm deodorant. The boy received the advice graciously, in spite of his embarrassment. The last I heard, romance had flourished, wedding bells had rung, the union had been blessed with beautiful children, and the whole family used deodorant.

Admittedly, we all have other things to do than just to listen to our youngsters and respond to what they're telling us. But we can try to give them our undivided attention for a few minutes—however long they need—before they leave home in the morning and the first time we're together after that.

Talk to Me, Baby

We need to know the frustrations of the night and the problems of yesterday, even though they're past. Sometimes kids need to make a confession, express a change of attitude, or confess their fear of going back to school. They need to unload all this to somebody, and it's better for them to talk to us than to some kid at the bus stop. The hearer needs to be the one who can give guidance.

When you've been out and come back home, don't glance at the headlines first, shuffle through the mail, or rush off to change your clothes. First, give yourself to your kids, let them get off their chests whatever they need to. Learn to read them. When you're paying real attention, you'll pick up the import of what they don't say, as well as what they do say.

Working parents can't consider themselves off-duty when they leave the office at five o'clock. They remain on-duty, but in a different role.

The kids have probably been living for the moment when Mom and Dad come in from work. They want to tell them everything that has happened to them.

If Mom and Dad come home with an attitude that says, "I've got to get dinner on the table so I can get that over with; I've got to get the grass cut; I've got to pay the bills . . . and then I can relax," they defeat the whole evening with their kids. But if they go in and invite their kids to pour out to them whatever they need to, they will avoid a lot of unnecessary frustration for their children and for themselves.

After dinner is over, the dishes are done, and kids' immediate needs have been met, Mom and Dad can have some time for themselves. It's good for children to recognize that mothers and fathers are persons, too, with needs of their own.

Mom and Dad don't say to the kids, "Okay, your time is up. Shove off. Now it's my time for me." They get it across in more subtle ways, saying, perhaps, "I'm going to take my shower now, Honey" or "When you're done watching you're favorite show, or reading your chapter in your history book, you and I will sit down and talk about it."

If Mom and Dad have been really available to them up to that time, they'll be happy and accepting, not clamoring for more because they've been shortchanged to begin with.

When parents try to avoid the extra two hours of "duty," they will find themselves feeling so guilty they don't enjoy any of the time they've kept for themselves. And the kids don't leave them alone either.

If parents have a good rapport with their youngster, occasionally they can afford to say, "Honey, I'm busy right now.

I can stop what I'm doing so we can talk, or we can talk in about an hour when I'll be finished with all this. Which would you like?"

When the rapport is there, and they have treated their child in a trustworthy manner in the past, not letting him or her down when they have promised something, the child will know they can count on Mom and Dad, and the child's decision will be an honest one.

But if that rapport hasn't been firmly established, and the child comes out with something like, "Oh, it really doesn't matter, Mom. I don't have to talk to you about it," then Mom would be well advised to stop whatever she's doing and let her son or daughter know that he or she is more important to her than anything else. Meeting your children's need to be heard, giving them the assurance and security of your attention and love, should always have the highest priority in your schedule.

Places to Go—People to See

This is a busy world. We're all busy people. Even mothers or fathers who are not working outside the home, or who work from a home office, have so much to do that they make schedules for themselves. By nine o'clock in the morning, they have an idea of what their day is going to include. We all live a scheduled life—or we get run over. But schedules are made to be broken when your youngsters need you. Parents need to listen to them—even if they have to leave the rug half vacuumed, or re-schedule an appointment, or if dinner will be an hour late—because it's an eternal life we're dealing with.

A simple, "What are you doing?" should often be translated, "I need attention from you." If you can't involve your child in what you're doing, you can quit it. If two minutes of your undivided attention is all your child requires, wonderful—if it's twenty minutes, that's wonderful, too. But let your child judge the time according to his or her needs. Don't try to hurry them off. You only defeat your own purpose that way.

If you don't always have lots of time with your youngster, it's doubly important that the time you do spend with them is unsparingly theirs. Remember, quality time wins over quantity time, every time!

Quality, not Quantity

The quantity of spoken conversation is never the criterion of real listening. Father and son can sit side-by-side for hours, not talking, and know they've been together. On the other hand, they can talk a mile a minute without really meeting minds if either of them is preoccupied with something else. Real listening is paying attention to the other person—whether or not any words are spoken. Real listening is the stuff of which family togetherness is made.

Real listening is hearing the heart of your child, not reacting to his or her behavior or negative words. This all sounds easy, but what does keep parents from being able to hear effectively?

Your preconceived judgment of the behavior or the content of the conversation, your own guilt from things you have done or believed, is often upsetting when you hear it coming through your children, and you react to that, rather than hearing their heart when they speak. Your great goals for your children to excel beyond you in every aspect of life are sometimes injured by hearing that they're not interested in those areas at all and have, in fact, interests in areas that seem very unimportant, unnecessary, and even undesirable to you. But listening is hearing with the third ear, not the two that are so obvious.

Dianne:

Solomon prayed that God would give him a hearing heart to judge His people, and be to able to discern between the good and evil (I Kings 3:9). As parents, we need to ask God for the same, so we may hear the hearts of our children and hear our own hearts. We need the Holy Spirit to show us the times we move into defensive positions, so that we can repent, ask forgiveness, and let the Lord teach and train us how to be effective listeners and communicators.

5

Your Child and Love

Iverna:

One of the duties of mothers mentioned in the Word of God is the duty to love their children. Titus 2:4 says that the older women are to teach the younger women "to be sober, to love their husbands, and to love their children."

When babies are little and helpless, mother-love instinctively flows out like a river to meet their every need. As the mother meets the needs of her offspring, her own needs are met, and she's happy. In the same way, the father's needs to be in charge and to take care of others are often met in the care of his infant. But in that kind of dependent relationship the story couldn't end with everyone "living happily ever after."

The child is weaned from total dependence on the parents as he or she grows old enough to handle some things for himself or herself. The parents have to let the child learn self-feeding, self-dressing, and how to drink from a cup instead of a bottle. This is not done so that the parents can call long-distance and tell Grandma, but because children are meant to grow up and to develop a responsible maturity of their own.

As children grow, they naturally begin to rebel against what Mommy or Daddy requires of them. If the parents don't learn to love their youngsters in this new kind of relationship, life is going to be full of negatives—constant spankings, nagging, scolding—a disappointment for all concerned.

Learned Love

We've all made the mistake of saying, "When you're a good girl, Mommy/Daddy loves you." What needs to be communicated is, "No matter what, Mommy/Daddy loves you." That's learned love—love that keeps on loving whether the object of the love behaves in acceptable or unacceptable ways. When a child has misbehaved, he or she probably needs a parent's love even more than when he or she is in a right relationship with the rest of the world.

If parents take the wrong approach with their children, they begin to think, "When I am pleasing, then I am loved." Little girls who grow up with that notion believe that anytime they displease their husbands, their husbands no longer love them. Little boys with this attitude become men who believe the same things about their wives. It leads to an attitude that says, "I'm going to be late getting home, or I didn't get that promotion we were counting on, or I forgot our anniversary—so she'll be furious and won't love me because I've displeased her." So he doesn't go home at all. Instead, he stops by a bar and finds someone who acts as if she'll love him no matter what.

Divorce courts are full of people who were brought up to believe that unacceptable behavior automatically results in a withdrawal of love. For the non-Christian world, it's pretty hopeless. But children of God know that "while we were yet sinners, Christ died for us" (Romans 5:8). Even though we have behaved unacceptably, the Lord Jesus Christ loved us enough, in spite of our behavior, to die for us. And we are called to follow His example and love others as He loved us (John 13:34).

Having the model of God's love—which never leaves us or forsakes us (Hebrews 13:5), regardless of our behavior—Christian parents can pray that He will enable them to learn that kind of love for their children—and to communicate it to them.

Tell Me, Tell Me, Tell Me

Adults often say to me, "You know, when I look back on it now, I realize that my mother and father loved me, but I honestly didn't believe that when I was growing up."

That you love your children does not automatically mean that they know you love them. They need to know it. Oh, how they need to know it!

One way that you can help yourself express love to your children is to look back in your life and recount what you wish would have happened to you: "I wish my dad had said, 'I love you;' I wish my mother had said, 'I love you;' I wish I had heard it at times when I wasn't particularly pleasing them," and learn from that. Make a concerted effort to pick times to express your love when your children least expect to hear it: "Do you know how much I love you? Do you know how much you mean to me?"

While it is true that there are many expressions of love other than verbal, it is equally true that without the verbal expression something is lacking. From time to time, do the unexpected— whether it be taking the kids out of school just to play because it's a good day for you, saying, "I just love you and you love me, and we want to have a day," or leaving a shirt on his or her bed that you found at the store and that you know your child would love or buying a ticket to a game, or making them something special that they didn't expect you to make. Whatever it is, when you do it, don't do it without the expression, "I did this because I love you."

When everything is going fine, and everyone is happy with life—not having any real battles—you probably show a measure of joy that your kids might interpret as love. But when everything is just like dynamite about to explode, it's a different story. If parents and children are in the midst of a disagreement, they probably won't know that you still love them unless you verbalize it and follow up with loving action.

Dianne:

"Mom," Michelle cried as she ran into the house. "I got it. I got the house." We were all rejoicing with her, for it had been only two years prior that she had been in rebellion against God, but through repentance and restoration, God had done a miracle in her life.

As I watched my son rejoice with my daughter, I thought, "Lord, You've brought healing in their relationship, because here the prodigal has come home and You've blessed and restored—and her brother is able to rejoice in it."

The next day, I was praying about it and I thought, "You know, I really need to see if David is doing okay with this."

So I went to him, saying, "Dave, are you doing okay with all that's happening for Michelle?"

His response was, "Mom, at first I thought she doesn't deserve it and, well, you know, she's been a bad kid. But then I began to rejoice because I serve the same God, and He's a good God."

It takes a heart change to have that kind of response! That's not behavior modification.

"David, do you know you can have the same thing?"

He looked at me, "No, Mom, I didn't know that. I knew from God that He loved me enough, but I didn't know you loved me enough to sacrifice for me."

"That's the good news. The elder brother didn't know, and he never asked (Luke 15:11-32). Dave, all you have to do is ask for it."

Embracing Calvary

One day, when I had done something wrong and God was dealing with me, I really felt bad about it. As I was repenting, I sensed that I wanted to punish myself for what I had done. I heard the Lord say to me, "I took punishment at Calvary. Dianne, all the punishment you deserve because of what you've done, I've already taken."

I thought to myself, "God, I don't know how to embrace Calvary. I've learned to earn that grace."

I watched with my daughter—she didn't earn anything back. She just came back in repentance to God, and God began to breathe on her and began to bless her. I kept saying, "Michelle, it isn't anything you've done. It's Jesus Christ. It's Calvary. It's Christ's blood that's cleansed you."

What's the point? Jesus Christ wants to teach us how to reproduce His kingdom of love on this earth. In Ephesians 6:4, we are told as parents to train our children in the nurture and admonition of the Lord. In other words, we're to train them by acts and counsel or words.

The most powerful form of training is modeling, found in Deuteronomy 6:4-7:

> Hear O Israel: the Lord our God is one Lord . . .
>
> And you shall love the Lord your God with all your [mind and] heart and with your entire being and with all your might.
>
> And these words which I am commanding you this day shall be [first] in your own minds and hearts; [then]
>
> You shall whet and sharpen them so as to make them penetrate, and teach and impress them diligently upon the [minds and] hearts of your children, and shall talk of them when you sit in your house and when you walk by the way, and when you lie down and when you rise up.
>
> (AMP)

This passage is commanding parents to first love the Lord their God. When it's in their own hearts, then they can reproduce it in their children. It isn't something parents just tell them with words or by discipline—it's something they model before them.

Iverna:

In my home, we were very verbal about our feelings for one another. It was not at all unusual for Dan to be outside playing basketball, come in for a drink of water, yell, "I love you, Mom," and then slam out the door and be half a block away before I'd finish yelling my love back at him.

There are many non-verbal ways to communicate love, too. I've been in homes where I never heard anybody say, "I love you," and yet I could sense the love just thick in the air.

Love You Can Count On

Parents can't ever afford to withhold love—or expressions of love—on account of bad behavior.

Many times, a little child will scream out in frustration, "You don't love me!" and the result is punishment, either physical or verbal:

"Shame on you! You know I love you! Don't you?"

"Yeah."

"Then don't ever, as long as you live, say such a terrible thing again!"

What comes through is a far cry from love, and the big scene sets up a defense mechanism in the child's mind that says, "Okay, I won't say it, but I'll sure think it."

A lot of behavioral problems stem from the fact that children are still thinking things their parents have taught them not to say. True, they need to be guided as to appropriate times and places when these things need to be said, but when your youngster bursts out, "You don't love me!" it's time to take inventory.

That would be an excellent time to say, "What have I done to make you believe I don't love you?" Rather than, "What don't I do? What have I done to somehow show you I don't love you?" If it is some form of correction, "You won't let me do this," then you know that you must explain to them your measure of decision-making. "The reason I didn't let you go there is . . ." or "The reason I had to restrict this was . . . and that is love whether you see it as such, love isn't just permissive," and make it clear to them.

Admittedly, there are kids who will try to manipulate their parents with this. Maybe you've had to correct them about something, and they've come up with, "You don't love me." If you catch them watching out of the corner of their eye to see how you'll take it, that's not a case of feeling unloved, it's a case of testing you to see if you're sucker enough to fall for their little scheme.

If you dissolve into something like, "Oh, Honey, Mommy/ Daddy doesn't . . ." apologizing all over the place and maybe backing down on the restricted privileges you were going to enforce, the child will think, "Chalk one up. I just won again." Everyone will have lost a lot. You can't fall for manipulation, but you can make sure your kids know you love them.

Debbie knew she was secure in my love, but sometimes, when I wouldn't permit her to have her way about something, she'd whimper, "You don't love me."

It was a little joke we had. I'd say, "That's how I prove I love you, by not letting you do what's not right." She knew it was true.

The Silver-tongued Warbler

Children are tremendous manipulators, and they seem to know their parents much better than the parents know their children. They know your soft spots, and they know just how and when to nestle up and say, "Oh, Dad, you're so great. Mom, you're the best cook in the whole wide world."

We probably ask, "What do you want, Son?"

"Oh, nothing. You're just great, that's all."

If there's a pause of any length, it's just so he can get up his nerve to ask, "Can I go swimming this afternoon?"

After a build-up like that, how can a parent refuse? But rather than viewing that as manipulation, you can see it as a fun game. You probably let him go swimming. But if there is a good

97

reason not to let him go, don't change your mind for all the sweet-talk in the world.

To Err is Human

Sometimes when a parent is nervous and upset about something—husband, wife, home, health, finances, job, neighbors, politics—their youngster will come running in the front door yelling, "Hey, Mom/Dad!"

Instead of listening to what the "Hey, Mom!" is about, the frenzied parent will yell, "Shut the door, and get out of here!"

The child doesn't know what they've done wrong. They don't know that you're bearing other burdens. The child feels simply that he or she has just got blamed for them all. It makes the child look at himself or herself negatively, as no-good or unloved, or at Mom or Dad as an unreasonable parent.

All parents do stupid things like that sometimes, but the mistake can be remedied. The moment you become aware of what you've done, you can tell your child, "Honey, I'm sorry I was so awful toward you. I was upset over something else, and I just took it out on you. But I shouldn't have done it. Please forgive me."

You may get a dirty look, but you'll have corrected an error.

Let's face it. You'll be wrong lots of times. You're human—you can't help it. But your kids won't respect you any less when you admit to them that you fall short of perfection. It can even make the bond of love stronger.

One day, Dan and I had reached what seemed an absolute impasse in our relationship. I didn't know what was wrong, exactly, but I sensed that something was really bothering him about me. He hadn't had a kind word for me, or even a friendly look as far as I could recall, all day. It was too uncomfortable a situation to be ignored.

"Dan," I said, "do you know what a stroke is?"

He kind of glared at me, and his tone when he spoke was on the brink of real impatience.

"Yeah, Mom, of course I know what a stroke is. It's something that happens to people and leaves their mouth kind of hanging open on one side."

"No, Son," I interrupted, "I'm talking about another kind of stroke, the kind psychologists talk about. To them, it's called a stroke when you pay a compliment or do a kindness for someone. When you do something that makes someone think you like them. When what you do or say meets their ego needs.

"I haven't had any strokes from you for a long time, Dan," I went on. "Why, I get more strokes from my son-in-law than I get from you!"

I could have bitten my tongue off as soon as the words were out of my mouth, but it wouldn't have done any good. They were said; I couldn't unsay them.

Dan just looked at me, I looked back at him, and we went our separate ways. The hurt was a solid wall between us.

Later, when I was getting ready to go to a meeting, Dan hung around as if he wanted to say something to me.

"Where are you going, Mom?" He knew the answer to his question before he even asked it, but still, it was a start.

"To church, of course." I was still unbending.

"Well, would you like for me to drive you?"

It was a perfect opportunity for me to acknowledge his efforts to do something nice for me, but I was bristling inside, so I blew it.

"I'm quite capable of driving myself, thank you."

When I saw the stricken look on his face, I woke up to the obvious—that he was ready to be reconciled to me. And suddenly, I was ready, too.

"Thanks for offering, Dan," I told him. "That was nice of you, and I really appreciate it." My voice had gotten kind of quivery by then, but when his six-foot-one frame bent to give me a good-bye hug, the lump in my throat melted.

The problem he had with me was obviously my independence from him, my lack of need of him. The way he expressed that was withdrawal from me. When I became vulnerable enough to let him

99

know my tremendous need for him—and he reached out to meet that, then I had to see my own defenses that would have kept me from the solution.

Though I had to leave him at that time, the door was open for us to reinstate the relationship that we had known so consistently for so long. Dan came to realize that my need of him was as great as his need of me.

Dianne:

In the New Testament, Jesus summed up the law by telling us to love the Lord our God with all our mind, soul, strength—everything within us—and then to love our neighbor as we love ourselves (Luke 10:27).

What are you modeling for your children as far as loving God?

Does your child see you seek God's kingdom first before money, before status, before friends?

When God blesses you financially, does your child see you use the money to be greedy and covetous?

Does your child hear you talk about the Lord when you're in your home as well as wherever you go outside your home?

Do your children hear about the Lord from you? If things have happened, do they hear how God has brought His life into the situation, not in super-spiritual terms, but in what has actually happened?

Does your child see you include the Lord in your plans and thoughts?

Does your child see you turn to the Lord and depend on Him when you're scared, when you're successful, when you're lonely, when you're anxious, when you're needing something?

Does your child see your love for God displayed in love for His Word?

Does your child understand that you tithe because you love God, not because you're going to get something for tithing?

Does your child understand that you attend church because you love God and not because it's your duty?

Does your child know that your love for God is displayed by your obedience to Him and His will? I've heard Wayne say to the children many times, "You need to know that I've done this because God said to do it, and I love Him."

Does your child see that you're a recipient of God's love?

Do your children see that you're a recipient of His mercy and His grace?

Do your children see that you're able to repent? When the Holy Spirit convicts you of sin against your children, do you go to them and ask for their forgiveness? That's the love of the Lord displayed in relationship.

Does your child see that you love God more than being popular, successful, having pleasures, or always getting your own way?

Does your child see that your life's goal is to actually learn how to love God more, to walk in the reality of who He is?

In summary, in modeling the love of the Lord, can your children see that love in your walk, in your life, and in your spouse's life? Are you teaching your children that it's a blessing to love the Lord; it's not a pain; it's not work? What are you modeling about your love for the Lord?

The second aspect of the commandment is that we are to love ourselves as we love our neighbor.

What are you teaching your child about loving yourself?

Is your child learning to esteem himself or herself valuable and lovable because he or she sees you loving yourself when you're good and bad, or does your child only see it when you've been successful.

When you're down in the pits and when you've failed, does your child see you touch God and find a love that is not based on how you feel and what you're experiencing?

Does your child see that God's love is redeeming? That you're being changed? That Christ loves you so much He has come to set you free? Or are you playing a game with your children and pretending you're something you're not? Or do you love yourself enough to say, "Jesus, here I am. I don't want to stay in this condition; teach me how to grow up; teach me how to love myself?"

Does your child see you able to receive God's love so that you can forgive yourself? There's nothing you've done that hasn't already been handled at Calvary. Jesus is ready to take it, cleanse you of your sin, and heal you.

Does your child see you turn to Christ when you need nurturing, comfort—when you need correction? Or does your child see you turn to food, sleep, alcohol, church activities, or worldly pleasures?

Does your child see you glory in your weaknesses so that Christ may be greater and stronger than you are? Or does your child see you play a game and pretend you don't have anything wrong with you?

Does your child see you learning the differences between a healthy self image and false pride or false humility? The more you believe Jesus loves you and sets you free, the more you'll be able to love yourself, and that love will not elevate or demote; it is just accepting who you are and where you're at.

Does your child see that loving yourself means a healthy self image and a healthy value of who you are and who others are?

Does your child understand that your home will be a place where all can encounter God's unconditional love?

Our parents came to visit. Sitting in our living room, they stated, "It's so peaceful in here." The Lord said to me, "It's because I'm here." Afterwards, I went to the children and made sure that they understood the comment from Grandma and Grandpa—that it was because of Jesus Christ. When Jesus is Lord of a home, His presence is there. Does that change our problems and our issues and the things we're dealing with? No, but He rules over us because He's Lord of our home and He is teaching us to walk in His Lordship.

Is your life of God's love one of "salt" to your children?

There was a period of time with my children when I was not healthy salt. I was causing them to rebel against God, so I went to the manual for biblical parents, the Word of God. In 1 Timothy 4:1-2, it says that there are those who are going to turn away from the faith because of the hypocrites.

God challenged me and said, "Dianne, whenever you've been a hypocrite, you're going to turn your children away from Me." And I said, "Okay God, make my life right. Make me say and walk the same thing. I can't do that. I don't know how to, but You can."

That's the kind of salt Jesus wants us to be. We don't have to be perfect, but we're saying, "Here I am; change me."

You must ask yourself what are you modeling about loving self and others? Are you refraining from comparing self to another—and finding the unique place each one has in the home. Are you allowing the individual qualities, gifts, and temperaments to be expressed and valued as each grows in the grace and knowledge of Jesus Christ?

Iverna:

Many children are burdened with low self-esteem. They believe their parents don't like them, because of all the negatives, negatives, negatives consistently hurled at them. "Don't do this. Don't do that." Parents need to make their children know that their actions are designed to ensure their happiness, not to deprive them of it. When they come to understand that, they'll be secure in the knowledge that because their parents love them they are doing the best they can for them.

Dianne:

How are you responding to the command to love your neighbor?

Are you training your children to love others as they love themselves?

Do your children see you able to show grace and mercy to your enemy?

Do your children see you able to pray and do good for your enemy?

Do your children see you resolve conflicts biblically, not passively or aggressively?

Do your children see you get the log out of your eye first (Matthew 7:3)—deal with your issues first before you deal with your brother?

Are your children learning to esteem others above themselves (Philippians 2:3), but not to the exclusion of self?

Are your children hearing your family speak the truth in love (Ephesians 4:15)?

103

Do your children see that you treat enemies and friends and neighbors the same way when it comes to forgiveness, grace, and mercy?

What do your children see about your love for your neighbor when you talk about him? Are they hearing your conversation as a valuing of the person with a desire for their restoration or is your conversation gossip?

Do your children see that anybody, Christian or non-Christian, is to be treated with respect and valued and prized exactly the way they are? If they do, they will well represent Jesus.

I watched our son, Daniel, at age seven, as his soccer team was playing the best team in the league. Both teams were undefeated. Daniel was positioned as the goalie, a position which he had played fairly regularly during the season. During the game, I watched as he began to keep the pucks from scoring, but one got by him and the opposing team scored. The parents celebrated. I watched Daniel shake it off and get back in his position for the next try. When the game was over (and, by the way, Daniel's team won), Daniel said, "You know, that other goalie played a really good game."

I said, "Yes, you did, too. Daniel, what were you thinking when that puck went by you and they scored?"

He said, "I did the best I could." That's being loved for who we are, not by what we do. It didn't go to Daniel's ego. He kept it in perspective. That's what Jesus does. It's the kind of love He's giving us, and that's what He's teaching us—love that's valued and that values others.

What are your children learning of the love of the Lord—that *agape* love—that unconditional love that's not based on performance? It can't be earned or lost. It flows from the presence of God, brought by the Holy Spirit (Romans 5:5).

As parents, your responsibility is to daily experience God's love so that you can reproduce it in your children. It isn't by success or failure that you're parents. God has blessed you with children, and He requires you to teach them how to love Him as He births it in your hearts. As you love God with your whole mind, soul, strength, and might, you will be able to teach this unconditional love to your children as they sit, walk, and stand.

Iverna:

We all blow it—time after time—in the business of bringing up our children. But if we keep our relationship to God up-to-date, He can—and will—mend all our mistakes.

Have you worried that you might spoil your youngsters by showing them too much love? Don't. Life is so short. Shower your kids with love. They'll get unspoiled soon enough—slapped around at a university, knocked around in the service, kicked around in their first job. While they're still with us, we can give them tenderness, kindness, concern. We can let them know that no matter what they do, there's someone who loves them. I've seen adults get unspoiled rapidly, but I've never seen adults come into love suddenly who were deprived of love during their growing-up years.

6

Your Child and Emotions

Dianne:

When the basic needs of children are not met—attention, approval, affection, affiliation, and authority—they feel devalued as a person. Depending on their temperament, the situation, and whether they know how to go to God to satisfy those needs, "X"s can develop. These "X"s will ultimately turn into responses and behavior that are maladaptive in expression as the child seeks to meet the need.

Fight or Flee

Each child is born with the capacity to respond to situations with *fight* and *flee* reflexes. The emotions that go with these reflexes are anger and fear. It's not enough just to deal with the behavior that's in response to fear—the parents must deal with the why of the fear, so that the child can be set free.

For instance, let's say my seven-year-old son, Daniel, has had a bad day at school. His friends were mean to him, so he had some "X"s. Not feeling too good about himself, he just needs to be held. But he is insecure about asking for that need to be met, and because of experience (there were times when I disregarded him), he's afraid I will ignore him or say, "Not now."

So he has learned to meet this need by waiting until he sees Wayne hug me, and then he puts his arms around both of us, saying, "Group hug, group hug." We've learned to separate ourselves from each other and hug Daniel, realizing he has a need.

If Daniel calls for a group hug and we respond by saying, "Go away. We don't have time. Don't bother us now," Daniel now has an "X." He is going to think, "Mom and Dad don't care. They don't have time for me. They only have time for my brothers." This thinking results in feelings of lack of love, rejection, self-pity, fear, or anger.

If Daniel responds out of fear, he'll retreat—deciding not to do that again so he won't be rejected—or in anger—trying to strike back and get even. He may go to his room and throw his toys around—or hit the neighbor boy.

Fear

When the emotion of fear occurs, certain responses and behaviors result. The body will respond to this emotion physically. There may be a churning in the child's stomach, resulting in a nervous stomach. The child's heart may start pounding a little faster, and his or her palms may get sweaty. The child will start feeling anxious and fidgety. From these fidgety, anxious feelings, he or she will try to find behaviors that will temporarily calm and alleviate the physical symptoms, such as riding their bike, eating a snack, nail biting, or bedwetting.

When a child has an "X" and doesn't turn to the Lord for help, fear will manifest itself non-verbally four ways: overtly, covertly, psychosomatically, and obsessively/compulsively.

Fear Expressed Overtly - Infancy to 18 Months

An infant may exhibit a fear response by bodily jerking and screaming. The baby cannot verbally say, "Excuse me, Mom, I would like to tell you that a loud noise just scared me because I don't know what it is." The baby doesn't know how to express what's going on so they'll express it through crying-and through their body.

108

But that crying may also mean, "I'm wet; I'm hungry; I'm thirsty; I'm tired; I want to be left alone; or I'm scared." So when an infant cries, the parent must discover the reason.

Fear Expressed Overtly - Ages 2 to 7

The growing child gains an awareness that there is more to life than just their toes, fingers, and other body parts. There are other people around him or her who are sometimes friendly and sometimes frightening.

Although not a complete list, here are some ways two-year-olds might express fear:

Shyness.

Self-violence—The child will hit himself or herself.

Escape into fantasy—They wander or drift off into their own thoughts.

Compulsive behavior—Biting nails and pulling hair may be examples of this.

A friend of mine had a little girl who, in fearful situations, would pull out her eyelashes, and then start pulling out her eyebrows. Other compulsive behavior is twirling or twisting their hair, tapping fingernails on the table, bouncing their leg. These are all ways the body tries to calm itself, but it's saying to you as a parent, something's going on. There's anxiety in the situation. The child may develop a tic, where the body will respond in little jerks. It can be in the face, in the shoulders, or in the back. The child is no longer able to repress the physical symptoms, so it comes out in compulsive behaviors.

Some kids will establish rituals trying to control their fears. They may wash many times or repeatedly perform any other act or gesture. One little girl would pass a particular table in her house and touch it three or four times as she walked by it. This was a ritual she established to deal with fear.

A young person came in for counseling because he was compulsive. In describing the child's behavior, his mother told of the three to four-hour baths he took every day and how he put pieces of paper on the floor to walk on so he wouldn't get his feet dirty.

109

I asked her to tell me about him when he was two or three.

She remembered an incident when she had bought him a comforter with ducks on it for his bed. She put him in bed, laid the comforter over him, then sat down on the bed to talk with him before he went to sleep.

He sat up in bed and started crying, "Mommy, Mommy, get up. Get up." She thought it was ridiculous. She was just sitting on his bed. So she tried to talk him out of his fear, but she couldn't.

I explained that at age two or three, children think anything that moves is alive, so when she sat on the comforter, the ducks moved, and the child thought the ducks were alive and that his mother was killing them. The child was trying to tell Mom, "Get up. I'm afraid you're killing the ducks." But he didn't know how to say that to her, so all he could do was scream, "Get up!" When she tried to talk the child out of his fears, they went underground into ritualistic behavior. The rituals were one way of alleviating the guilt he felt about the ducks.

Stuttering.

Bed-wetting.

Thumb-sucking. It's normal for children to suck their thumb at this age, but if they're anxious, you will find thumb-sucking will become more prevalent.

Nightmares.

Changes in the child's behavior. For instance, if the child has a very good appetite and suddenly doesn't want to eat or picks at their food, take note. If the child was a finicky eater and now can't stop eating, take note. This change in behavior is an indication that he or she is turning to food as an outlet, and the issue isn't food. The issue is the anxiety.

Fears. At this age, children begin to encounter the world in front of them with a limited understanding of why things operate the way they do, so they begin to be fearful. For instance, when a car moves, the child may think the car is alive. If they are told to get in the car, they're afraid because they think the car will eat them. When the parents see the child not getting into the car, they want to threaten and discipline. They don't understand that the child is afraid of being

110

eaten, not afraid of getting into the car. The biblical parents can simply ask, "Why don't you want to get in the car?" and the child will tell them. If they say, "The car will eat me," the response is not to talk them out of the fear—the response is: "How can I help you? What will make the car not eat you?" Then the child will give a response. Sometimes it won't make any sense, but to the child it begins to alleviate the fear. Remember, emotions don't have to make sense to be felt or alleviated.

Fear Expressed Overtly - Ages 7 to 13

Some typical behaviors that might indicate the child is responding fearfully to a situation are:

Pulling out hair, eyelashes.

Chronically escaping to their room.

Lying.

Night terrors.

Compulsive cleaning, washing, touching.

Worry. They'll start worrying about homework, worrying about being liked, worrying about friends. Remember, the issue is the "X," some need which wasn't met.

Over or under-eating.

Nervous habits. Nail-biting, twisting their hair. At this age, you will not see the child biting their nails, but you'll see the effect of it—jagged, broken nails never needing to be clipped.

Tics that manifest in facial grimaces, eye blinking.

Fears. Fear of school, peers, rejection, or of failing. The fear will start to manifest itself in their peer group and in school. A friend who teaches elementary school said she knows immediately when a child is in a home where divorce is happening, because the child will go from straight A's to F's. The child is so obsessed with what's going on at home that the fears absolutely paralyze intellectual ability. The emotional problems are affecting performance at school. My friend says that once the child receives help, the grades return to normal.

The grades weren't the issue—it was the fear of rejection and abandonment that had affected the performance in school.

Fear Expressed Overtly - Adolescence

Some behaviors that we might see manifested in the lives of adolescents indicating much anxiety and fear are:

Driving fast. This is evidenced by the number of tickets they get or by accidents.

Cursing.

Failing at school.

Alcohol or drug abuse. This is when the abuse of alcohol and drugs can be seen. Often, alcoholism and drug addiction will start earlier, but their effects are hidden. At this age the resulting effects are shown in their lifestyle, i.e., drunkenness, apathy, excessive sleep, etc.

Promiscuity.

Truancy.

Compulsive behaviors firmly entrenched.

Changes in self-esteem.—For example—inferiority or a child who has been basically introverted before may become very brash and arrogant.

Clumsiness.

Laziness.

Embarrassment.

Inability to make decisions.

Negativism.

How Fear is Expressed Covertly

When a child has an "X" and is feeling emotional pain, they will covertly deal with that pain by choosing what has been called defense mechanisms. Here's a list of some typical defenses that a child will use to defend against the pain. It doesn't heal it—but shields them against recognizing the pain.

Denial. The child will say to him or herself, "This is not really happening to me."

Repression. The child is saying to himself or herself, "It never happened. The situation never happened."

Disassociation. The child will begin to separate himself or herself from the situation by saying, "I don't remember what happened." A classic example is the adult who had been raped by her father as a child. She handled the traumatic situation by focusing on the candy that was in her hand while her dad abused her. By focusing on the candy and away from what was happening, she did not remember the abuse. This is a form of disassociation.

Projection. A child says to himself or herself, "It's not happening to me, it's happening to you." This defense forces children to become gossips and backbiters. In families, this is pretty common between siblings. A sibling will say, "My brother just lied," when in essence that child had just lied, projecting the issue on to someone else.

Minimization. The child begins to say, "Oh, it's not a big deal. It's really not that important." They minimize the situation. "Mom and Dad really didn't mean to do that."

Displacement. The child will deal with a safe object instead of the one causing the pain. For instance, when Johnny is rejected by Dad and fears him, he's not going to deal with him but with the brother of whom he's not afraid. He will yell at his brother or steal from his brother to get even with Dad.

The classic example of displacement: the boss yells at the employee, the employee goes home and yells at the spouse, the spouse yells at the children, the children kick the dog. Each one displaced to a safer object.

Rationalization. The child will explain to himself or herself—and re-explain—so that they don't have to take responsibility for their actions. Example: "If Mom hadn't rejected me, I wouldn't have hit Tommy." He explains away his behavior of hitting Tommy. He's not lying—he's just explaining his behavior as not "bad."

Regression. The child will go back to behavior that was safe. Example: Michelle, my oldest, was two years old when her brother was born. Believing David got more attention, she tried to act like David, regressing to baby behavior, climbing into the crib, pretending to be David's age. She was trying to take the place back as the littlest child that she had lost to her younger brother, regressing in behavior to get the attention she feared she was losing. This is not a behavior problem of climbing into the crib; this is a child who feels an "X" and needs some attention and love.

Another example of regressive behavior is a child that's been potty-trained and out of diapers for a long time who starts bedwetting again.

Psychosomatic Illnesses

Another way a child tells you that he or she is fearful is through physical somatic (bodily) symptoms. For instance, in the age range of two-to-seven, the child manifests headaches and a nervous stomach to the where the child thinks they need to throw up. An older child will start having more symptoms, such as diarrhea, more vomiting, more migraines. With an adolescent, there will be ulcers, colitis, heart murmurs, hair loss, or itchy skin. They'll have nail problems and infections because of biting their nails.

The point with psychosomatic illness is that it does not start out with a physical problem—a germ, a disease—it starts out with an emotional problem.

For instance, your child comes to you in the morning with a stomach ache. Ask questions such as: Are you having a test today? What's going on at school? If your child is having problems with a certain kid or a bully, that nervousness and fear will cause a somatic effect. The issue isn't the physical, which does need to be taken care of—the issue is that your child has a problem at school, or on the bus, or with friends, or in the home. When the problem and fear is resolved and alleviated, the physical can stay healed.

Obsessive/Compulsive Behavior

In chapter three, we discovered that when children have "X"s they turn to behaviors and roles to deal with their environment. Those roles may ultimately become obsessive/compulsive roles. The good, responsible child becomes performance-oriented and a workaholic. The caretaker becomes relationship-dependent and a chronic fixer or rescuer. The child who went to his room to be invisible becomes the lost child and victim. The rebellious child becomes anti-social. The dependent child remains a helpless child. Your child will begin to take particular roles to live out in the hope of alleviating the anxiety.

Recognizing this behavior, parents can deal with it because God, by His Holy Spirit, has given His children, through the Word of God, antidotes to fear.

Antidotes to Fear

Love. 1 John 4:18 tells us that in *agape* love there is no fear. When parents observe a certain behavior in their child's life, they need to ask themselves, and the Lord, "Is it because my child lacks love? Do they need to know that God's love will cast this fear out, that nothing will separate them from God's love?"

Natural love is conditional, but it is God's love that sets captives free. When I was dealing with my fear responses as an adult, God brought this back to me many times, saying, "Dianne, you don't feel loved."

"Well then, Lord Jesus, I need You to love me." I can't tell you what He did—I just know I encountered Him and I was different after that divine encounter. Paul tells us in 1 Corinthians 3:18 that when we behold the Lord we are changed from glory to glory. We don't know how, but it happens, and when we've encountered the living God, we're loved.

Power. This word, "power", is like dynamite, *dunamis*. It's the inherent ability to do greatness. Power is greatly needed today. The church is impotent in many areas—not moving in the resurrection power of Christ. Children need to know that they can be strong in the Lord, not strong in themselves. The world will make your children strong in themselves by self-defense classes, but God will empower your children to the point that nothing will cause them fear and they will know first-hand the power of their God.

Children should be taught that there is nothing of which to be afraid. When the enemy is around them, God encamps about them and protects them (Psalm 34:7).

God showed His power to His people in the wilderness. God did not desire that His people be without water; He wanted to show them He was the source of water. He didn't want them to go without food; He wanted to show them that He was their Provider. Is the power of God still in the midst of His children? Yes! Parents need to begin to show that to their children. He is all powerful—*dunamis*—and we're strong in Him.

In 2 Timothy 1:7, three antidotes to fear are given: "God hath not given us the spirit of fear; but of power and of love and of a sound mind" (KJV). Does your child need power? Is there a situation at school with bullies in which he or she needs to know that, "greater is he that is in you, than he that is in the world" (I John 4:4)? Help your children release the Holy Spirit to minister power to their fear.

Soundness of mind. Is your child fearful of failing a test? Then he or she needs to know that God has not only the power—the *dunamis*—but He wants to give your child a sound mind. He wants to renew his or her mind. All you and your child need do is pray and believe that God will do what He wants!

If the child is thinking, "I'm no good; I'm a failure; Mom doesn't like me," the parents need to ask the Holy Spirit of truth (John 14:17; 15:16; 16:13) to come with the truth and minister it to their child. The Holy Spirit renews the child's mind by bringing truth into his or her thinking, so every thought can be taken captive to Jesus   (2 Corinthians 10:5). Philippians 4:6 says to think on those things that are true, worthy of worship, and praise, those things that are pure and noble. Instead of your child thinking: "Mom hates me, Mom doesn't love me; Mom rejects me; or Dad hates me and doesn't love me," what's the truth? "Lord Jesus, the truth is that my mom and dad are too busy, but I know they still love me. They don't know how to show the love to me just now. So God, please begin to minister that love to me. I want my thoughts to be Your thoughts. You allow me to see as You see." That's how God gives a sound, healthy mind.

If your mind and your children's minds are fixed on Jesus Christ and on what He is saying about each situation, not on what we think, then He'll cause a soundness of mind, a self-controlled mind, to release you from fear.

116

Faith. Jesus said to His disciples when the storm was raging on the sea, "Why are ye fearful, O ye of little faith?" (Matthew 8:26, KJV). When your child is fearful, he or she doesn't have enough faith. Your child's faith needs to be increased. Because "faith cometh by hearing, and hearing by the Word of God" (Romans 10:17, KJV), you need to open your Bible and ask God to speak to you through His Word. Ask for a sovereign word that speaks to your child's situation. Pray, "Increase my child's faith to believe what You're going to do so she won't need to walk in fear of what man or the situation (the storm) can do to her."

When my son is afraid of the bully, that means that he has faith in the bully, not in Jesus Christ. So I need to pray, "God, I'm asking You to give faith to my child. Stir it within so he has faith in You, faith to believe Your Word more than his experience." God is waiting to be proven. He is waiting for us to bring the revelation of Himself to our children in the midst of their day-in and day-out situations. He wants us fearing Him and no one else. The fear of God is an awe—worshipful reverence—because He is Almighty God.

God's presence. Isaiah 12:2 says, "Behold, God is my salvation; I will trust, and not be afraid" (KJV). Beholding God is what released the fear. The key to this verse is that the Lord is the salvation. That is the hope for parents, because they are human beings—and as such are going to fail their children. At one time or another, all parents will fall short. They won't be sensitive all the time, but God is their salvation. When your children behold Him, they are released and saved from fear.

Children learning to trust God will discover that He will never fail. He will be there. A parent's role is to bring them to Jesus Christ, to show them His reality in the present situation. I want Daniel to know that he can turn to Jesus anywhere: at school, when he stays overnight with a friend, or wherever and whatever the circumstance. Anyplace he has an "X," he can trust Jesus to minister to him.

Children must learn the presence of the Lord. He goes with them to school, to their after-school jobs, on dates. He wants to reveal Himself—His presence—to them in each of those situations and

117

circumstances. "The Lord is my light and my salvation; whom shall I fear?" (Psalm 27:1, KJV). When my child is afraid, he doesn't have the revelation of God's salvation. So I pray, "Jesus, my child needs You to save her from her fear."

When children are afraid, they need a revelation. That's the light. They need the truth—the illumination that Jesus is the salvation. He can come and save them. He can deliver them. He's Almighty God. Point your children back to Calvary where Jesus Christ came to set them free, to minister to them, and to break the power of that fear. Feed them Scriptures, such as Psalm 23, and John 20:12, that talk about God's presence.

Peace. Jesus said in John 14:27, "Peace I leave with you, my peace I give unto you. Let not your heart be troubled, neither let it be afraid" (KJV). In situations where your children are anxious, upset, or troubled, and the psychosomatic effects of tension appear, pray that God's peace would be ministered to your child's body as well as to their soul and spirit.

God is teaching parents how to teach their children. Instead of turning to roles and addictions to deal with the "X," turn to Him, and through prayer and supplication allow Him to release the anxiety, minister to you, and release you from the fear (Philippians 4:6).

When you are fearful, ask, "Lord Jesus, which of these antidotes do I need? Obviously, I need Your presence. Do I need Your love, Your salvation, Your peace? Do I need a revelation of You? Do I need my faith increased?" As you pray that reality in your own life, begin to reproduce it in your children's lives. It's fine to use techniques to deal with fears. Don't discount them. But as spiritual parents, you're required to bring God into the situation so there is an eternal change.

Ask for the healing blood of Jesus Christ to break the power of fear so that your children will learn to walk in wholeness and soundness of mind. Your children will learn that when they have an "X," instead of going into the fearful behaviors and psychosomatic reactions, they can turn to Jesus Christ and He will fill their needs.

118

Anger

Every human being has the capacity for anger. Ephesians 4:26 tells us that when we're angry we should not sin. The emotion of anger is not the problem, but rather what we do with anger that can open the door to sin. In the same way fear became a response to an "X"—an unmet need—so can the emotion of anger. Certain aggressive behaviors may result from this emotion, but neither the aggressive behavior nor the anger is the issue. The issue is the "X."

We can see in each age group the kinds of aggressive behavior that would indicate an "X."

Overt Behavior - Aggression - Ages 2 to 7

Because two to seven-year-olds have limited vocabulary and communication skills, they use their body to express their pain. They'll hit, shove, push, bite, or scratch, become stubborn, throw a tantrum, or become verbally aggressive by saying, "No. Don't."

Watch how a young child plays house. Many children will express their aggression and their anger by the way they treat their dolls—they will push, shove, or aggressively squeeze the dolls.

From two to four years old, my son Daniel's temperament had a tendency to become more aggressive in response to pain rather than fearful. When I would pick him up at school or from the babysitter's, I would usually hear that he had hit someone. I knew that I wasn't dealing with an aggressive person, but I was dealing with a person who had somehow been hurt that day. Sure enough, when I would sit down and talk with Daniel, there was always something that had happened that he interpreted as an evaluation of himself as a loser—less than, not smart enough, or good enough. At the time, the only way he knew how to deal with his pain was by hitting back. "Because I feel pain, I want you to feel pain."

Saturdays were special days for Jack, because that was the day Mom would play with him, giving him her undivided attention. One Saturday, Grandma came over to play with him and Jack didn't notice until later that Mom was gone. When he went through the house looking for her and wasn't able to find her, Jack angrily said to Grandma, "Get out of my house." This is a child with an angry

119

response. But what's the real issue? He didn't know how to say, "I'm angry; Mom's not here. I'm hurt; Mom's gone. I'm lonely." He only knew how to express his anger in an aggressive response.

Taking this example at face value, we would see the child as being very disrespectful to his grandmother. But was he really? That wasn't the issue. Training against disrespectful behavior would have only solved part of the problem. Jack needed to work through the issue of Mom not being there.

Overt Behavior - Aggression - Ages 7 to 13

During early childhood through the pre-adolescent ages, there are rapid changes happening within and around the child. He or she is starting school and is suddenly exposed to other children and to the discipline of the classroom. This means more avenues for rejection and pain, more opportunity for his or her needs to go unmet, and more instances of not knowing how to respond appropriately to each situation.

As the verbally aggressive child encounters the teacher, he or she will learn that aggressive behavior is inappropriate. Then they will learn how to deal with their anger by becoming passively aggressive. The child will wait, hold in the anger, and then expose and express it later. For example, a child may look as if they have handled the correction from the teacher but the anger will surface on the playground by aggressive behavior towards other children. The cause of the anger was never dealt with, the heart never changed—only the behavior was modified by discipline and correction. Certainly behavior needs to be corrected, monitored, and disciplined, but not in place of an internal heart change.

What kind of behaviors will parents observe in a child that is passive/aggressive?

School tardiness. The child wants to get even, and this is one way he can do it.

Procrastination. If you want the trash taken out now, the child will wait and wait and wait.

Dawdling.

Forgetfulness. Ask the child to do something; the child says, "Yes, I'll do it," fails to do it, and says, "Oh, I forgot," in a helpless manner. If this forgetfulness is coming from anger and the "X," it's a way of getting even.

Misunderstanding. You explain the rules to your child the way behaviors are to be, and the way things are to be done. When the child fails to comply, he or she will say, "Oh, you meant that? I didn't understand."

Aggression *in play*. In their play, there will be aggressive behavior evidenced by spanking of their dolls, in how they play with their cars, or in war games.

The child becomes inert. They're immovable, able to sit for a long period of time. Ultimately, it's stubbornness and defiance.

Laziness. Lethargy—the anger is going inward and, instead of dealing with the "X" and what they're feeling, they become lazy and don't want to do anything. The areas that are important to the parents are no longer important to the child.

Stealing. In this age group, a child may deal with his anger and get even by stealing. A boy who recently moved to our town was caught shoplifting. He had moved here from a place where he was very popular, liked the high school, liked what was going on. He had not wanted to leave his old neighborhood and classmates. Dad and Mom made him move with them, and he was angry, thinking they didn't care what he felt. He wanted to get even. Stealing in this family was considered an "unpardonable sin," therefore it was his way of getting even. The issue wasn't the shoplifting. He was trying to scream out to Mom and Dad, "You don't care about me." The issue wasn't the moving, rather, the child felt as if they didn't hear him and care about him and know how to meet his needs.

Arguing. Arguing is a definite way of showing hostility. It's another way of punching someone in the nose, but it's done verbally. If parents find themselves arguing with their child, the question to ask is, "Does this child need to win? Have I in some way put this child down, made him feel "less than" and now he's got to find his ego in winning?" The issue is the "X," not the arguing.

121

Being critical or name-calling. A very overt way of dealing with pain is calling someone fat, lazy, or stupid. If a child feels put down by Dad, he or she might not say it to Dad's face but will to his or her own friends. The child will call Dad names and be critical and judgmental of Dad. This is a form of aggression.

Teasing. The tease is a person who makes a comment about you that's negative and then says, "Just joking. Can't you take a joke?" while the comment was really made in hostility. It's a cover for the anger. The issue here is that the person is not dealing with you correctly—or honestly—but hiding behind the "Can't you take a joke?" attitude.

Impatience. Impatience is another form of intolerance. It can be a sign of anger. They may be impatient and intolerant of others, lack mercy in a situation, or become very legalistic and judgmental in dealing with people. The bottom line are the "X"s. What's going on? The hurt the child feels should be the focus of attention, not the criticalness or the attack. They've cloaked the "X" in their impatient and intolerant attitude.

Overt Behavior - Aggression - Adolescence

The adolescent learns that they can't be overtly angry in speech or behavior because of the negative consequences, so they become more passive or more aggressive. The following are indicative of this behavior:

Bad grades.

Speeding in the car.

Not cleaning his or her room.

Sleeping late or sleeping in past the time he or she is supposed to get up.

Missing classes or truancy.

Listening to rock music or any kind of music the parents don't like.

Playing the stereo loudly.

Staying out late or sneaking out.

Promiscuity.

Stealing. Stealing things from home, not necessarily big or major things, but doing so chronically.

Taking risks.

Cursing.

Covertly competitive.

When an adolescent is pushed to the wall, he will become overtly aggressive through some of the following:

Yelling, screaming.

Fighting.

Running away.

Throwing things.

Becoming hostile in attitude and tone.

Being disobedient.

Becoming violent.

Becoming resentful.

Acting cruel.

Dominating.

Acting self-righteous.

Becoming egotistical.

Exhibiting inflated pride.

Becoming selfish.

Acting irritable.

In one instance, there was a girl who was being sexually abused by her dad. She didn't want to report him because it was his word against hers, and he had threatened to beat her if she told. She skipped school most of the time. Often she ran away from home. She was sexually active. These were aggressive behaviors coming from her life.

The sad thing was that she was being labeled as a bad person even though she was the victim. She had the bad reputation, not her dad. She used destructive behavior as she was trying to scream out and say, "Please notice; help me." She ran away for a reason, but the intervention had been ineffective and inappropriate. The parents put more restrictions on her behavior so she wouldn't run away again, but that was not the issue. The real issue was the abuse that no one knew about.

The abused daughter was reacting in the only way she could according to her limited, frenzied rationale. She needed help to break the cycle of destruction she was trapped in—abuse in the home resulting in her own aggressive behavior that labeled her wrongly as a "bad girl." She had "X"s and was hurting from the abuse in her life, and she needed help for it.

Parents must lay down their concepts and ideas about what rebellion means and what they think they see in their children's behavior. Is it a parent's pride or their belief that they can't be wrong that hinders parents from seeing the real issue in a child's misbehavior? It can be very humiliating to be a biblical parent. As God begins to deal with the children, those things that are in their nature that need correction have to come to the forefront in order for God to deal with them. Jesus Christ always has a way out, and He wants to minister to everyone involved.

When you see your children acting out aggressive behavior, that's the time to say, "Lord Jesus, give me wisdom. Where's the "X"?—so that there can be a heart change and not just behavior modification."

Intervention

Biblical parents can deal with anger and fear through their ministry to their children. Here are some steps that can help:

Discover why the child is fearful or angry. What's the event? Where's the pain? Why the reaction?

For what does the child need to repent? In other words, when they were angry and sinned, the action brought on by their feelings of anger is what they need to be sorry for. "I need to repent for hitting." Hitting was the sin. "I need to repent for talking back." That is disrespectful.

Forgive the child.

As a parent, did you have a part in the situation that requires repentance? Then repent.

Ask for and receive the child's forgiveness.

Establish appropriate discipline or consequences. For instance, if the child is caught stealing, he or she needs to return what was stolen and perhaps make restitution. They need to realize there are consequences for their behavior. Discipline will allow and provide consequences.

Uncover the child's hidden need. What's the "X"? What did the child need? Attention? Affection? Affiliation? Approval?

Pray effectively. Ask the Holy Spirit for wisdom in how to pray. What's the antidote for the fear that's needed at this time? What are the boundaries around the anger that God wants to establish? What patterns need to be broken? Where does the Blood of Jesus Christ need to come in and cleanse and heal? Where does the Word need to come and speak encouragement and the truth? Allow the Holy Spirit to minister His life, His peace, His health, His holiness.

Conclude with a commitment to the Holy Spirit, asking Him to continue to allow growth to come in this area, that both parent and child may walk in this holiness, free of the anger and free of the inability to go to Him for healing. Ask the Holy Spirit to convict of sin and establish righteousness, that the parent's and children's ears would be circumcised to hear Him, their hearts sensitive to Him.

When Daniel gets "X"s, he's very aggressive. He has more of a hostile, dominant temperament. He was in his room throwing some toys around in one of those attitudes, so I knew something was up. Something must have happened at school.

Going to his room, I began to talk with him. As much as Daniel and I have talked, and as much as Wayne and Daniel have talked, it's still not easy for him to tell us what he feels. It took a little while, but finally he told me the story.

He has two boys he plays with. The one that's usually the leader was going "eeny meeny," deciding which one of the two he would play with that day. Daniel was not chosen. Not only was he not chosen (which was an "X"), but the other boy who was chosen turned to Daniel with a smirk on his face and a gesture that Daniel didn't know the meaning of but he knew it was not a positive one. The kid was, in essence, going, "Ha, ha, ha, ha."

And I said to Daniel, "Well, that would have said to me, 'Ha, ha, ha, ha. You're not picked and I am.'" He just hung his head. I knew that's what the issue was. I prayed, "Lord, I want to teach Daniel how to come to You for healing. I don't want him to have to learn aggressive behaviors."

I asked the Lord, "Jesus, You were present in that situation. Show me what You were doing. What would You have done if Daniel had turned to You right there in that incident?"

Jesus so sweetly said to me, "I would have chosen him."

I turned to Daniel and said, "You need to know in the incident today, what Jesus was doing."

Daniel doesn't yet know how to ask Jesus, but he's learning. I touched him on his shoulder and said, "Jesus was saying, 'But I choose you, Daniel. I choose you.'"

His face brightened up. The issue was over.

Iverna:

In dealing with adults, I have found that their problems often stem from a childhood of suppressed emotions. They have wanted to say, "I'm mad. I hate. I want to kill." But if they had given verbal expression to such feelings as these, they'd have been killed themselves.

Don't tell me that you've never hated. I won't believe you. Don't tell me that you've never had an urge to kill. I know you have. I've been there. If you haven't had those feelings toward someone else, you've had them toward yourself, wishing you could drop dead to get out of something that was unbearable to you.

Kids have the same feelings. And more times than not, when they voice them, they are punished for them. By doing that, children learn to suppress their feelings, to deny even vocal expression of their natural instincts. The result of all this suppression produces psychopaths, liars, killers, and people who crack up because they've been denied the natural expression of normal feelings.

Why do we do it? Pride. We've been taught to control ourselves—not to let our feelings show. And we try to teach our children to do the same thing.

Parents want to be proud of their children's behavior, and, because they know that the average person might not understand if their child yelled or stomped his or her foot, they try to keep their children from expressing themselves in this manner. The parents don't want anyone to think they've lost control over their kids, so they make them inhibit the natural expression of their emotions. Too often, children learn to suppress their emotions, not control them.

Express Yourself

Wise parents will encourage their child to express his or her feelings verbally instead of requiring their child to stifle them.

A friend of mine spoke with her son a short time after he'd been involved in a fight with a playmate. She was anxious for him not to feel guilty about the feelings he had.

"I'll bet it really made you mad when Johnny tipped over your tricycle," she said.

"Yeah, it sure did," her son replied. "I wanted to slug him."

"I can understand how you feel," she said. "I've felt that way myself when someone has bothered something of mine."

"You have?"

"Oh, yes. Lots of times."

Her son was surprised to learn that his mother had feelings of anger, too. This knowledge made his own feelings more acceptable to him, and he was open to learning from her how to deal with anger and other feelings.

If parents are careful not to seize every available opening for preaching at their youngsters, the children will come to maturity more quickly. By not giving them any advice to resist, parents will sometimes clear the way for them to move forward at a surprisingly rapid rate.

If my friend had told her son that his anger was wrong instead of encouraging him to understand it and work through it, the situation would undoubtedly have become worse as her son added his bottled-up frustration to his initial, natural response of anger and guilt.

A Chemical Surge

Kids from age six on need to understand what happens in their systems when they become angry. They don't have to know the word adrenaline, but they can understand that some chemical is released inside their bodies when they become angry. When that happens, they automatically want to fight. And they're stronger when they're angry—because of all that adrenaline.

Simply telling a child that anger and fighting are wrong won't change how he or she feels. The next time the adrenaline pours through their system, that child is going to want to hit somebody, just as they did before the physical process was explained. But parents can help their child act acceptably if they say, "Yes, the chemical that comes into your bloodstream when you are angry has to be gotten rid of somehow, but you don't have to hit anybody. Instead, you can let it help you run fast as lightning around the block."

Your youngster will probably find this an intriguing thing, and the next time he or she gets mad, they might leave their tormentor standing mystified in their dust while they race around the block just to see how much faster they can go with the extra chemical helping them out.

It is important to help a child understand what goes on inside their body, to give him or her tangible reasons for their feelings so they won't develop the notion in their mind, "I'm just no good."

In actuality, parents think it's worse for their child to hit a person than to speak evil of them. And yet, in the idealism of parenthood, Mom and Dad make the mistake of teaching their children that one is as bad as the other because they were taught that the Bible said that thinking the wrong thing is the same as doing it (Matthew 5:28; 1 John 3:15).

Mom and Dad are going to have trouble if they teach that to their children. If they say to their youngster, "Johnny, it's just as wrong for you to say it as to do it," he may go out and clobber the first kid who crosses him. Society places a greater penalty on the actual striking than on the threatening words, and children have to learn this so they can govern themselves accordingly. When they're old enough to understand—and the age of understanding varies greatly from one child to another—parents can deal with the attitudes behind wrong actions. But behavior patterns have to come into line before then.

Pocket Protector

Dan's fast fists had resulted in bloodied noses and irate mothers a number of times before it occurred to me to train him to do something to prevent such undesirable results of anger.

"The first thing to do when you feel yourself getting mad is to put your hands in your pockets," I told him. "And keep them there."

The idea sounded so kooky, he was willing to try it. I'd look out the window and see a very red-faced little boy, his hands shoved ferociously down in his pockets, and breathe a sigh of relief that he was learning to control his temper.

Parents can actually use their child's emotional outbursts to strengthen family relationships. There's nothing more binding in love than to join another person in an emotion. When your youngster is full of hate, you can tell him or her you understand it. If your child hates flies, hate flies with them. If your child hates birds, don't preach to them about how beautiful birds are, and how God made them for

129

us to enjoy. Agree with him or her that your windshield is really ugly when it's all splattered with droppings from the sparrows in the trees. Confess that you didn't like it when the crows plucked up the corn in your garden as soon as it sprouted.

When your child says he or she hates people, if you say, "Oh, Honey, you mustn't hate people," you haven't taken their hate away. You may have intensified it by making him or her think it's not okay to express feelings verbally. As a result, he or she resolves to bury such feelings from now on, and later you have to pay a psychiatrist a hundred dollars an hour to dig them up again.

Instead of trying to stifle your child's animosities when someone has done something he or she doesn't like, you can try to get them to put himself or herself in the other person's place—to examine their motivation. "Why do you think he did it?" Thinking things through, your child may learn a lot.

If your child's immediate answer is, "I don't know why he did this," then you have to try to think through the other person.

Let's say your son's best friend suddenly turned against him and made up with another group of boys who were not his friends, and he came home very hurt. You could say, "What do you think he was thinking when he turned away from you and pretended not to know you? What do you think the other kids were saying about you when he went to them? Was there anything that took place in your conversation today that was different than in the past?"

What should not be said is, "What did you do to him?" because that sets your son up for a great defensive reaction—and usually ends in silence, or a claim of "I didn't do anything." But if you can stimulate an interest in the offended one about the person who offended them enough to say, "Was he hurting today; was he insecure—did you have on your new team jacket? Maybe he was jealous of that?" you can help the child find out if perhaps it was this situation or that situation. This does two things. First, it helps the child to know how to reconcile with the person who hurt him or her, and, secondly, it gives understanding and takes away the extreme feeling of anger that would result in such a hurt.

When a child is frustrated because he or she has lost something vital, the best thing I can recommend to the parent is to join their child in his or her frustration. It's not the time to lecture the child, saying, "Well, I've told you that if you continued to be so careless about your things, keeping your room in such a mess, that someday you'd lose something very important to you."

When your youngster is already upset, you don't want to add guilt to his or her burden with an "I told you so." That's not what your child needs. If you give them moral support, your child will learn to be their own judge. That will result in changed behavior patterns eventually, whereas your preaching will result only in resistance to change.

Make It a Family Affair

Parents can be as sympathetic as possible with their frustrated child, without being overly wordy about it. Saying something simple is helpful, such as, "I know just how you feel, Johnny. It really bugs me to lose something."

Mom and Dad can join the search for the lost item. They can even express their child's outrage for him or her: "It's got to be around here somewhere. We're going to find that stupid thing if it takes all night!"

The effect on the child of the parents' sputtering will be instant calming. If you're going to do the fuming and fussing for your child, he or she doesn't have to work up such a sweat on their own. It can even get kind of funny, and laughter is one of the best ways to clear the atmosphere of frustration. Once the loser begins to relax in their attitude toward the lost thing, their mind might clear enough to remember where it is. If that doesn't happen, you can join the child in praying that God will show both of you where the misplaced item is hiding.

Trying to deal with frustration by a frontal assault on the child's carelessness is like trying to dip ice cream while it's frozen hard as a brick. We'll just break the tool, without getting the job accomplished.

131

That's Life

Some youngsters are extremely sensitive in their emotional makeup. A wise parent will not try to stamp out sensitivity, but will encourage it, directing it into the right channels. When a youngster is embroiled in conflict because of his or her sensitivity, the parent can explain, "That's how it is. Any time you get really involved with life, someone may be unhappy. But how awful it would be not to feel for the hurts of other people. We'd be like zombies."

You can let your sensitive youngster know that there will always be kids who will hate their guts because he or she champions the underdog instead of joining in the attack. No one who stirs up trouble will love the peacemaker. You can explain to your child that there is a price to be paid for any kind of involvement—on the right side or the wrong one.

You can tell your child "I'm proud of you for standing up for what's right." And they'll have a healthy attitude about their own right standing, too.

And then there's the teenager—a creature like no other. Teenagers are not children nor are they adults. They are in the midst of rapid change, and it's not all uphill! They vacillate from one moment to the next. They can respond to us like an adult, and we react in kindness. In the twinkling of an eye, they revert back to childhood. About the time we've adjusted to that level, they've switched back! We're wrong again!

Their emotions go from one extreme to another quickly—from happy and carefree to sullen and overloaded. One minute they're popular; the next, nobody likes them.

These are mood swings. Parents cannot always alter them nor should they try.

Naturally frustrating to the parent, social worker, or teacher, mood swings can be even more frustrating to the teenager. But, again, it's all part of living—of growing up. If we have learned to love our children, we'll survive their roller coaster ups and downs. We'll realize that they'll emerge as mature, stable adults in the fullness of time.

Dianne:

Solomon, the wisest of all men, prayed that God would grant him an understanding mind and a hearing heart in order to judge God's people, discerning between good and bad. The Lord was pleased and said:

> *. . . Because you have asked this, and have not asked for long lives, or for riches, or for the life of your enemies, but have asked for yourself understanding to recognize what is just and right,*
>
> *Behold, I have done as you asked. I have given you a wise, discerning mind so that no one before you was your equal, nor shall any arise after you equal to you.*
> *(1 Kings 3:11-12, AMP)*

The New Testament fulfillment of Solomon's prayer is Jesus Christ—"Christ . . . the wisdom of God" (1 Corinthians 1:24)—and we can ask Jesus for wisdom. God says "If any of you lacks wisdom, he should ask God, who gives generously to all without finding fault, and it will be given to him" (James 1:5). As biblical parents, we need wisdom to understand our children, not just to read their behavior, but to know from God what is behind it—what's the "X"?

7

Your Child and Discipline

Iverna:
Some of the biggest problems in family relationships occur in the area of discipline. In its broadest sense, discipline is preventive. If preventive discipline is handled properly, there will be less need for the kind that is more often termed punishment. Webster's Collegiate Dictionary defines "discipline" as "training that corrects, molds, or perfects the mental faculties or moral character; punishment; control gained by forcing obedience or order."

The paramount goal in disciplining youngsters is to mold in them the character or behavior that will be of greatest benefit to them during their growing years and on through adulthood. The motive in disciplining children properly is that they might come to mature, responsible, and enjoyable adulthood, fulfilling the potential God has placed within them. If the job is done properly, children will emerge as effectively self-disciplined adults.

Good discipline begins when a child is very young. Through their actions, parents train their children to be obedient the first time they tell them to do something—or they train them to stall until they yell at them the umpteenth time with loud, fierce threats, and rising blood pressure. Choices are made here, wittingly or unwittingly, by whether or not parents follow through with enforcing their requirements as soon as they are given.

Good discipline is a relief to a youngster—relief from the responsibility of managing his or her own life before they are old enough to do it with wisdom. Deciding what is right and what is wrong is an unbearable burden in the life of a child. This burden falls inevitably on children who have to grow up without a home. Tragically, the same weight is often felt in allegedly Christian homes where the children are provided for in material ways but otherwise live as if they have no parents.

If You Want Something Done Right . . .

It's always easier for parents to do a thing themselves rather than to teach their children to do it properly. But that's not the point. The point is that parents need to discipline their youngsters.

In the midst of their fast-paced lives, there's not a whole lot of disciplining being done in some families. Everyone seems to be constantly rushing. If the only way to spend time at home with their youngster is to drop something else they're doing, parents better drop it, no matter how worthy the cause. There's got to be some regular disciplining done in the home or the children will suffer.

Do your youngsters know that they're supposed to be responsible for cleaning their room, but their attitude is, "Aw, don't worry. Mom will do it?" Do they know that they should hang up their clothes when they take them off in order to cut down on the washing and ironing that must be done? Or do they throw everything on the floor or in the laundry basket because they know Mom or Dad will take care of it for them?

What parents need to understand is that the purpose of teaching children to pick up their clothes, their toys, clean their rooms, etc., is not so their rooms looks nice (most children could not care less about the condition of their rooms); the purpose of it is to teach them early discipline in their lives. Having a proper place for toys, a proper time for recreation, a proper time for brushing teeth, a proper time for going to bed, isn't to satisfy the parents' needs but to teach their children the lessons of discipline. The wise parent will begin this process while their children are very young and give much reinforcement of praise at any attempt of the children to discipline themselves.

For example, many are the times I had to close my eyes and walk out of a room that had the bed "made" in the eyes of my child, thereby preventing myself from giving in to the desperate temptation to remake the bed so it would be acceptable in my eyes. I knew my child had to realize, "I did it and I did it well; this is the way my bed looks when I make it."

Being a good parent doesn't mean being a doormat for your children. That position does not equip them for living in the world outside the home. Children have to be disciplined to do things for themselves, because the world isn't going to wait on them.

Parents need to let their youngsters know what they expect from them. If they expect them to help around the house, the children should know it. If they expect them to mind, the children should know it. However, the goals must be realistic and reachable, so approval can come enabling the children to grow in love and maturity.

Mommy's Little Man

In the absence of a father in the home, little boys often pick up the awareness— whether or not it has been stated to them—that they are the man of the family—and endeavor to fulfill that position. The unfairness of this is obvious. His natural maturing process is laid aside in order to meet needs in his mother or even younger siblings.

The wise mother will discern her son's inclination and talk to him about how proud she is that he is willing to assume a man's responsibility. Mom should stress that her son possesses his own individual personality. She is responsible, for him and his welfare, as well as for the other children. And she, being a capable adult, needs to make sure that his adolescence is not destroyed because of the absence of a father.

The unwise, or needy, or unwell mother may transfer all of her own needs to this child, latching on to him in ways which are unhealthy for both of them. This can even have a long-term effect on her son, preventing him from forming a proper relationships with girls and, ultimately, with women. In its extreme, over-reliance on the mother's part can make her son feel pressured into never marrying, because of the misinterpretation of maternal love.

It's sad to see adults who were never allowed to be children because they always had to wait on someone or be responsible for them. The resulting frustration comes out in a lot of ways: rebellion, misbehavior, running away, marrying too early, becoming promiscuous, never marrying. Somewhere in their life, a child who was made to grow up too fast is going to have to fight feelings of resentment toward the parents who let it happen and forced them into an adult role too soon.

There are, of course, parents who go to the opposite extreme, never letting their children grow up, keeping them always as infants. This is unnatural. Children want to grow up. From the age of two, a baby doesn't want to be a baby anymore. He wants to be a big boy;she wants to be a big girl.

Early in their children's lives, parents have to begin to allow their offspring to express some independence lest they begin to suppress it so effectively that they begin to take on a perpetual baby role. Perpetual babies grow up physically but remain so emotionally insecure that they're afraid to tackle anything for fear they'll do it wrong. They're likely to be people who think the world owes them a living because their parents always gave them what they needed without disciplining them to effect growth in responsibility.

Knowledge Is Not Inherited

Sometimes parents fall into the trap of thinking that their children are automatically going to grow up knowing everything that they know, everything their parents had to learn the hard way. But that's not the way it happens. They have to be taught. They have to be disciplined.

Consistency is the Key

Much of the disciplining of children is in connection with the basic needs in their lives. For instance, in some homes it doesn't matter how hungry a youngster gets, he or she isn't permitted to eat anything until mealtime. In others, the child can eat all day long.

Which is right?

Either way will do, as long as parents are consistent instead of confusing.

When her son comes in and whines, "But Mom, I'm starved to death," she might let him eat right then or might tell him, "I'm sorry, but supper won't be ready for an hour yet."

In the first case, her son is learning that he can have what he wants when he wants it. In the second case, he's learning control, not indulgence, learning that he can't succumb to the desire to eat just because he is hungry.

Most normal children fuss about doing chores at one time or another. But chores should be done, not merely to have the work accomplished but for what the discipline of regular chores does toward bringing a child to responsible maturity.

When my son was home, he had to keep his room clean. But he kept it clean according to his standards, not mine. He was required to make his bed every day, and to pick up anything lying on the floor. I knew that his dresser drawers were filled with papers that ought to be thrown out, and that his puzzles were never put back together. But if they were out of sight, I didn't complain. He knew where to find what he needed. To me, the room was not clean. To him, it was. Every once in a while, I'd go in with him and we'd have a real throwing-out day. Tons of junk was removed. But in the meantime, we had a workable compromise.

Trading One Job for Another

Responsibilities for chores around the house need to decrease as the child's responsibilities outside the home increase. But the decision needs to come from the parents. Mom and Dad can explain to the whole family, "Now that Tommy is working, he has to get up early, and he's so tired when he gets home that we're not going to expect him to mow the lawn this summer."

Let the job pass to a younger member of the family whose schedule isn't so crowded.

When the younger children gripe about this—and they will—they need to be reminded that their turn is coming—when they'll be freed from some household chore for the same reason. That makes it a little easier for them to take—and helps them look forward to the time when they can go out to get a job instead of having to hang around the house to baby-sit and wash dishes. In the meantime, underneath the complaining, they're secretly proud of being promoted to a new level of responsibility themselves.

Free at Last

Freedom is an essential part of the teaching of responsibility and self-discipline. There must always be flexibility in freedom to adapt to new situations, to new stages of the growth in the maturity of your child. Often, I have found myself giving my youngsters more freedom in a certain area than they were capable of managing responsibly. For example, I'd say, "Dan, I want this, that and the other thing done sometime tomorrow."

He'd give me a sweet, "Okay, Mom," but if I didn't mention the things again the next morning, when evening came I'd find they hadn't been taken care of. Then I'd realize that the freedom I'd given him was still beyond the level of his self-discipline. I'd have to step in and start over, saying, "Dan, I want you to do thus and such a thing right now." He did it, and we both learned something.

Don't be afraid to broaden your child's freedom and then to narrow it back down again if you see that you've erred. Next time, your child might surprise you by showing that he or she can be trusted with a greater latitude of responsibility. It's a matter of constant adjustment and continual testing. Parents must make their standards more exacting when they see their youngster getting slack with his or her own standards.

I'm a great believer in letting teenagers have as much freedom as possible. They cannot be held in close restraint without rebelling against it, inwardly or outwardly.

140

If parents are determined to hold the reins tightly, to be all powerful, always to have the last word, to be considered infallible just because they are Mother or Father, they will never enjoy a right relationship with their teenagers.

On the other hand, teenagers will move smoothly into self-disciplined adulthood if the parents have helped them learn by experience that a proper fulfilling of responsibilities is a necessary prerequisite to freedom.

Whoa there!

When riding horseback, if the horse turns away from the road, the rider must pull the reins in for a while. However, the rider doesn't keep the horse tightly reined for the rest of its life. To bring the horse to maturity, the rider trusts it a little again, releasing the hold a little. If the horse starts to run away another time, the rider must rein it in once more. The whole object is to get the horse self-disciplined so that it will walk at just the right pace and in just the right direction to take the rider safely home, even if he or she should fall asleep and let the reins fall. Likewise, some parents let the reins go slack in their hands while others hold them too tight all the time, never releasing or tightening their hold on their youngsters to suit the circumstances. The child concludes either, "I can't do anything," or, "My folks don't care what I do." There is a happy medium of sensible government with our children.

If you have a little one, and begin to trust him or her with something, you need to remember to praise your child for his or her achievement. Don't saddle your youngster with too much responsibility all at once, but let him or her work up to it gradually to guarantee success. This builds up your confidence in your child as well as the child's self-confidence. If your child fails, don't condemn him or her, but see if you can find and remedy the cause of the failure. There may be a legitimate reason for it rather than your child being at fault.

Comparing Apples to Apples

Not all children mature physically at the same chronological age. One five-year-old may be taught to ride a two-wheel bike in just a matter of minutes, while another tries over and over, falling every time it becomes necessary to balance. The parents' handling of this makes a very big difference in his or her attitude when attempting anything difficult throughout life. If the parents compare their child to another, or even allow their child to compare himself or herself with Johnny, who learned quickly, there will be self-deprecation instilled in the child's mind that will need to be fought for a long time, if not forever.

One way to handle a situation such as this would be, "It might be easier for Johnny to learn than you today, but there will be other things that will be easier for you to learn than they were for Johnny. So let's just keep trying. I will be here with you until it becomes easy for you to do this. And I'll tell you the truth, I'm really proud of you, because you're staying with it until you get it."

Delayed Reaction

What if you tell your child to do something, and he or she nicely agrees to do it and heads in that general direction but never quite arrives at the destination? Parents usually get quite frustrated about such things. The parents don't want to be legalistic about it, but when a child is supposed to clean his or her room every Saturday and neglects it three weeks in a row, there must be dire measures taken.

In order to keep from getting into situations that make your blood boil, a good rule to follow here is, first, to make firm rules only about those things that are really important to you and second, let teens plan their own schedules as much as possible.

For instance, instead of saying, "I want you to clean your room on Saturday afternoon between two and four o'clock," you can say, "I want your room cleaned before you go anywhere or do anything else next weekend." Then the youngster can make his or her own schedule and reap the benefits of having chores done on time—or the penalties of not completing them according to schedule.

The object, again, is not so much to get the jobs accomplished as to use them to help the child achieve the self-discipline of responsible adulthood.

There should be a consequence if your time limit is not met. Children need to know that it is always necessary for someone to "pay the piper." Mom and Dad will help them by being relatively inflexible about this. Think of it as training them so that they won't be fired from their first job for procrastination. Young people have to learn somewhere to "get on with it," and home is the best place.

During the early teens, children need to be reminded consistently before they reap the consequences of their failure to accomplish something. They may call it nagging, but parents should do it anyway so that they won't approach the deadline facing a penalty they forgot they would encounter. Around the age of fifteen or so, it's time to stop reminding them and let them take the consequences of their failure to complete an assignment. Somewhere they have to learn to be responsible for their own follow-through—without a parent's reminder. This helps them learn there is a direct relationship between fulfilling responsibilities and enjoying privileges.

Thanks, I Needed That

Some of the problems parents have in disciplining their children arise because the youngsters do not see the blessedness of discipline while it is going on. If we're honest, most of us don't see the blessedness when we ourselves are disciplined either! And yet parents discipline their children and expect them to bounce right back with a big hug and "I love you, Mommy and Daddy. Thank you for making me clean my room. Thank you for not letting me go to the movie until after I've mowed the lawn."

When parents see a little pouting, or hear their child's bedroom door slam, or see or hear any other outward form of rebellion—instead of such a loving response from their children—they may store it up in their minds and find themselves reluctant to discipline their children the next time it's needed.

Guard against your reaction to their reaction. That a child rebels against discipline doesn't mean he or she doesn't need it. The child probably needs more of it—to instill habits of self-discipline in him or her.

Some parents go to the other extreme, staying on the defensive, declaring, "I don't care whether you like it or not, this is the way it's going to be." Such a dogmatic attitude can close the doors of communication. The situation may get steadily worse until a major eruption occurs and the child runs away from home or does something else to demonstrate rejection of his or her family.

Every home has a right to set standards. For example, "In this house you must wear a shirt at the dinner table," might be said to the son who sees no reason for it since the neighbors don't enforce that rule. But parents have a right to enforce this. Perhaps it is something else in another home. It doesn't matter. This needn't cause a breach between father and son, mother and daughter, etc. and should be talked about on the basis of, "It's offensive to me; it's not something that is right or wrong to you but it's something in this home that is right or wrong and, for our sake, this is what we'd like you to do when you're in this house."

Ignoring the Problem

There are parents who ignore a lot of undesirable behavior in their youngsters, because they simply don't know what to do about it.

After expressing to a father my honest love and concern for his child, he asked if I would follow through with enforcing the necessary discipline on his offspring. This is an extreme example of a parent expecting the school or some other agency to bring up his kids for him—discipline and all.

Parents must overcome the natural instinct that says, "I want to do everything for this child." They need to get to the point where they can say, "Lord, I know this is not my child. This child belongs to You. Help him or her to get from me everything he or she needs to become a healthy, happy, well-adjusted, independent individual. And then enable me to let him or her live his or her own life."

Far more difficult than the proper nurturing of a child is their timely weaning. Remember how that went? You set the date, maybe even marked it on the calendar: "This is the day when the bottle goes!"

But Junior had other ideas. He said, "That's what Mom and Dad think. I love my bottle, and I'm going to hold onto it for a while yet."

And Junior got his way. At two o'clock in the morning, after fighting it out all day long, Mom and Dad gave up, filled the bottle, and crawled back into bed, full of the exhaustion of defeat.

Maybe your motive—to have Junior weaned because the neighbor's kid was weaned already—didn't fit his need. When that is true, your efforts at discipline are sure to fail.

Teenagers are not going to have things taken from them without reacting also. If the parent's reaction or fear of confrontation causes them to just give in because it's not worth the fight, then they are failing at their job of parenting. According to Scripture, parents will give an answer for that. "Train up a child in the way he should go" (Proverbs 22:6)—that's the parent's part. God's part is to hold them responsible and accountable to the faith that has been instilled in them.

It's Not An Option

The need for self-discipline is never outgrown. If a person doesn't discipline himself, he wouldn't be able to hold a job, or clean house, rake the leaves, get up early, read the Bible, or do a lot of other things that are vital to a person's well-being.

If parents can help their youngsters to see that discipline is a necessary part of life and that achieving self-discipline is more satisfactory than being disciplined by others, they will have given them a strong motivation for maturity. If children see their parents disciplining themselves, they will have fewer resentments in areas where they have to be disciplined.

When a youngster says, "I don't want to go to school today. I'm sick of school," Mom and Dad can say, "I know just how you feel. I don't want to go to work either. But we've both got to do it. Have another glass of milk, and let's go." It's good for children to see that their parents are self-disciplined and that they can be, too.

One reason why parents often have more trouble with disciplining a child than with disciplining themselves is that they're so accustomed to disciplining themselves that they do it automatically. On the other hand, when parents have to discipline their youngsters, they are always aware—sometimes painfully so—of what they're doing. Parents need to be reminded that the Scripture says, ". . . the Lord disciplines those he loves, . . ." (Hebrews 12:6). What is true between God and man is true also between earthly parents and their offspring.

When parents find it difficult to discipline, they need to remind themselves of the real purpose, or the long range reason for it. It's not because they're getting even, or punishing their child, it's because they love their child so much that they will chasten them if they need it. This may sometimes cause tension, separation, lack of peace, and other negative responses, but those feelings are temporary in comparison to the wonderful, peaceable, fruit of righteousness that will follow the proper correction.

Oftentimes parents get discouraged, not realizing that real growth is taking place in their teenagers, because they are so close to them. If they could back up and get a little perspective, they would see better what is happening.

If parents want their children to grow up, they will have to discipline themselves to progressively take their hands off them. Let them make some mistakes, do some wrong things on their own. Children learn by doing. Don't we all?

Might Doesn't Make Right

But what happens when the line is crossed, the chore not done, the room not cleaned up on time?

"But how can you punish a kid today?" a man asked me recently, shrugging his shoulders in defeat. "My teenager is bigger than I am."

"Sir," I answered, "I don't accept that excuse, and neither does God. But your teenager does because you've sold him on it. What you need to do is to start over, remembering that, before God, you're still in control."

My mother, who was only five-feet-two-and-a-half, used to stand and look up at my six-foot-three brothers and say, "If I have to stand on one chair and use another one on you, you're going to do what I say." She had a bluff and a half, and it worked. They believed her.

Have you ever said, "I wish my teenager wouldn't do such and such a thing, but what can you do?" Have you been tempted to throw up your hands and quit?

There are lots of things a discouraged parent might try. For a specific complaint, try a specific remedy, and if that one doesn't work, try another. If that doesn't work, come up with something else. Parents have got to become comfortable with the realization that they are indeed placed in charge of the lives of their children as long as they are dependent upon their parents for their physical needs.

Recently, my daughter, Debbie, was counseling a young mother who, in exasperation, said, "I just can't handle my three-year-old. I've done everything I know to do and, if I cross her in anything, she just throws a tantrum."

Debbie's response was, "You had better get control of her and you and had better do it today, or you will be saying this same thing for the rest of your life."

If parents don't understand that they have the place of power and control over their children while they're young, and with that a great responsibility as is taught in Deuteronomy 7 and throughout the Word, they will lose them at a later date. This loss will not only be their relationship to their children, they will also lose the healthy life that God planned for them.

The purpose of discipline is to turn us away from self. All humans are basically selfish by nature and would love to live on the premise, "I want what I want when I want it." But from infancy to the day children leave their parent's home, the responsibility is on the parent to set guidelines and govern the child, beyond his or her selfish desires, to acceptable behavior and proper thinking. That's what parenting really is.

Sometimes teenagers come to me and complain, "My parents are still trying to run my life, and I'm eighteen years old."

"Wait a minute," I tell them at the very beginning. "Do you pay room and board?"

"Well, no," they answer more times than not.

"Are you working? Could you support yourself, pay your own way?"

"Gosh, no. I'm still going to college."

"Then you'd better do what your parents tell you to do. As long as you're dependent on them for your support, you're subject to them in many ways. When you want to move out on your own, fine. In the meantime, follow their rules in their house."

They usually get the point.

A mother came to me one day in complete despair about her son. She said he acted as if he had a devil in him. There was no father in the home. The boy had thrown things at his mother, broken the car windows, and done other destructive things deliberately.

"I just can't handle him," she cried.

When I offered to counsel with him, she told me that he had refused to come for counseling, insisting there was nothing wrong with him.

"Well," I said, "then about all you can do is pick up your telephone and call the juvenile authorities."

She backed away from me in horror.

"Why, if I did that, he'd never speak to me again!" she said.

"Well, then, go home and let him keep beating you up," I told her, and she did.

That tyrant of a kid was only ten years old. He was out of control. We can't afford to let that happen to our children.

One summer afternoon, I looked out the window and saw Dan's dog on the neighbors' lawn. They had pretty shrubbery, always kept

148

their lawn neatly trimmed, and I knew they wouldn't want our dog playing on their grass.

"Dan," I called, "your dog is in the neighbors' yard. Go bring him home."

I heard Dan whistling and calling the dog, but after a little while he came in the kitchen where I was working, a woebegone look on his face.

"Did you get the dog?" I asked him.

"No, Mom," he said, kind of hanging his head.

"Well, why not?" I wanted to know. "If he wouldn't come when you called him, why didn't you walk over and pick him up and carry him home?"

"Well, Mom," he explained, "I'm not allowed to go in their yard."

"Not allowed to go in their yard? Why not? Their kids are always tromping through ours." An unrighteous indignation was welling up in me.

"Well . . ." He kind of shrugged his shoulders as if he didn't know the reason either. "I've just been forbidden to go on their lawn, that's all."

I tromped across the lawn to ring the neighbors' doorbell. The very idea that my boy couldn't set foot on their precious lawn!

I soon learned Dan had thrown rocks at their little girl. "Pretty good justification for telling him to keep out of their yard," I thought. I could understand, of course, why Dan hadn't bothered to tell me about that. I marched back home and dealt with him about the situation.

In a case like that, punishment was plainly called for, and I administered what I thought was proper.

A Little Leeway Goes a Long Way

But we should never give our children the idea that they can't get by with anything. That's a devastating feeling. I have to be able to get by with a few things in order to live. My kids do, too.

If I was constantly in cahoots with the parents of every youngster on the block and my kids knew that absolutely everything they did was going to get ratted back to me, they'd find new friends in another part of town.

Parents need to let some things go by if they're not important and they can afford to overlook them. Parents can just breathe in and breathe out, be glad they know, but not advertise everything. It's not necessary to deal with every minor infraction that they happen to learn about.

Taking a firm and consistent stand to punish real misbehavior that cannot be tolerated—throwing rocks at little girls—and overlooking the kind of rule violation that doesn't actually matter are two guidelines for happy and successful parenting.

This isn't just for the welfare of the child. It has real survival value for parents, too. If you can't turn your eyes away from some things that are admittedly less than perfect, your life will be used up in over-managing your kids.

There are many problem areas between parents and children that ought to be overlooked occasionally.

The Clean Plate Club

Suppose your children don't want to eat all of the meat on their plate and so they sneak a hunk of it to the dog under the table. That's probably not the time for an angry tirade about how hard you have to work to earn the money to put meat on the table. Neither is it the time to make their lack of appetite take the blame for the starving millions in India who would be glad for the tiniest morsel of food.

It's probably the time for you to look out the window and pretend you don't notice what's going on. Be thankful that your children love the dog instead of being angry that they don't like meatloaf with onions in it. Failure to eat all the food on their plate is not a life or death matter for the child. In fact, if they can learn not to be a clean-plate eater, he or she may avoid obesity in later life.

I don't believe in forcing children to eat. Youngsters will eat properly and sufficiently for their needs if the right things are offered to them at appropriate times. Making children eat when they aren't hungry creates many a mealtime scene that should never have to take place. Some children don't need as much sleep as others—some don't need as much food as others. You can't legislate appetite.

You can, however, do something about making sure that your kids don't fall into the habit of eating exclusively snack-type foods that are just not nutritious enough. Such snacks can take away their appetites for the nourishing foods their bodies need to stay healthy. There is even medical evidence that certain digestive disorders can result from a diet that concentrates on very refined foods.

As the children grow older, and are around the house less, you can't keep a constant eye on their eating habits. But you can make sure that home eating habits revolve around balanced meals and healthful snacks like fresh fruits, nuts, veggies, cheese, etc.. Snack foods and candies can have their place as a part of family celebrations like birthdays or as an occasional accompaniment to TV watching— best of all, after a healthful, nutritious meal. It won't work to put snack foods on the "verboten" list—that will just make them all the more attractive once the children get free of the rule. It's best to find a balance and stick to it.

Mealtime should be a happy time. If children accidentally spill their soup, or their milk, you can lighten the incident by a quick clean-up, maybe even helping them laugh with you as you share an incident of your own clumsiness.

If they don't seem to have a hunger for more than one main meal a day, don't punish them by taking away the things they want to eat at other times. Yes, they must have the proper nourishment throughout the day, but if they take it all in one meal it isn't going to hurt them to skip another meal or have peanut butter and crackers at another time. I sometimes jokingly say, "Pizza is health food," but very honestly there's much healthy benefit even in a piece of pizza. Try to keep in mind that cake and cookies contain not only sugar but usually milk, wheat flour, and eggs. Excluding sugar, these are all healthful foods and contribute to a well-balanced diet.

Parents can increase the nutrition level of cakes and cookies, in a lovingly insidious way, by taking advantage of the many delicious recipes available that utilize whole grains, honey, fruit, tofu, yogurt, etc. In other words, keep the balance to life and as much as you are able, make it fun to eat in your house.

If all punishment for not eating was repealed, think of the hassles in family life that would be avoided!

Discipline in Money Management

It's very difficult to teach teenagers the value of money if there hasn't been some of that teaching instilled in them at a younger age. Each family has to discover at what specific age it needs to begin training the children about the value of money. Some children could learn it as early as age seven or eight, while others would have no occasion to learn this until they had their first paper route at age eleven or twelve. It's a necessary lesson for youngsters to realize that money doesn't just flow from Mom or Dad's purse or pocket. They must understand that God gives us responsibility for handling money, just as He gave Old Testament people responsibility for handling flocks, herds, gardens, etc. Children must also learn to recognize that everything we receive comes from His hand. This is a likely place to teach tithing and offerings, rather than to just hand them a dollar as they go to Sunday School. Perhaps parents could give their children an allowance that covers enough to pay a tithe and an offering.

If you give them a three-dollar allowance, explain that thirty cents of it already belongs to God. Suggest that they might like to give a little more beyond that, helping them along in this to see the benefits. Anytime an aunt, an uncle, or anybody gives them something, or they have an opportunity to walk a dog or mow a lawn for money, let them see that as the blessing of God. God always blesses those who give.

Parents must also teach their children how to properly spend money. It's not fun to get an allowance if you're taught that you have to save it all. Teach proportionate savings to them—saving for a specific event or towards Christmas. Make certain there is sufficient left for them to do something they enjoy doing or purchase something that they normally wouldn't have if they had spent all their allowance on something else. This is the beginning of discipline, and it starts just like it does with adults—with dimes and dollars before it ventures into hundreds and thousands.

Methods of Discipline

Where both mother and father are working together for the common purpose of bringing their children up to maturity, they can administer correction for misbehavior in ways exactly opposite and not harm their children by it.

For example, there can be a father who never punishes except with a spanking. Perhaps the mother never spanks, but always uses verbal correction, a withdrawal of privileges, or maybe just raises an eyebrow or uses some other expression of displeasure. Still, if the mother and father show respect for one another, upholding one another in whatever they do, and if they're bound together in love with the welfare of their youngsters at heart, it will be all right. The youngsters can understand that Dad gives the lickings, that Mom hands out the looks of displeasure, but the whole picture is one that gives the youngsters confidence and security in facing the world. They know somehow that they're being brought up right.

A father may say, "I'm not around enough. I let my wife handle the kids."

Or a mother may say, "I'm not strong enough. I let Dad do it all."

It doesn't matter who dishes out the punishment, just as long as it gets dished out.

Sometimes a father will come in and make a big declaration, really laying down the law, and then take off leaving the mother to see that an overly-harsh edict is carried out. That's less than ideal. Whenever possible, the parent imposing the discipline should be the one to see that it's enforced.

Are you a parent who finds it difficult to inflict physical correction on your youngster? If it's hard for you, maybe you have a tendency to go overboard. Maybe you're the kind of Mom or Dad who has to leave a welt, who has to use a board, who thinks that if

153

you really beat a child good one time all your problems with him or her will be over and you'll never have to punish your child for anything again.

If that's how you're thinking, think again.

There isn't anything that alleviates guilt more quickly than a good old-fashioned spanking. But a brutal beating is never necessary. The amount of pain inflicted, or copious tears, are not the measure of whether or not you've gotten your message across. If you've broken the rebellion, you've won, whether it took one spank or fifteen.

In spanking, your goal should be to establish a conditioned reflex in the child that says, "What I did was wrong. If I do it again, this will happen again. I don't want this consequence, so I won't engage in that action."

Don't spank your youngsters while you're still infuriated at what they've done. Give yourself a little time to cool down first.

After your emotions are under control, you are ready to spank in order to correct the child, not to dispel your anger. Then you won't feel guilty for correcting your child.

Spouses would be well-advised to pray when an irate mother or father decides to take a too-firm hand in punishing a child. If either parent goes at it with a grim approach, "One good licking will straighten out all his behavior problems for all time," the spouse can get out of sight and on her knees.

Sometimes the youngster you've just spanked comes up to you and wants a hug immediately afterward. Will your words of love and physical expression of affection make your child think his or her wrong behavior was right after all? No. Actually, refusal to hug a child after you have administered a spanking will give him or her the erroneous impression that you love them only when he or she is pleasing you. Your child needs to know that your love is a constant thing, just like the love of God, a love that keeps on loving no matter what the child has done.

After administering a spanking is an ideal time for positive reinforcement, for cementing love, drawing the child close. Explain that the punishment was meted out because you love him or her and want them to do right, so he or she will grow up to be a happy person.

After they get a little older, children are less immediately forgiving of their parents for punishing them. They might find it difficult to receive your love, much less express any of their own. But an expression of love from you won't minimize the effectiveness of the correction. It will actually help the child of whatever age to be more obedient, because he or she will want to please you. You can make it clear that you've punished him or her because you don't want them consigned to a life of frustration and unfulfillment.

The Punishment Should Fit the Crime

Punishment for rebellion—for breaking known rules—should always be in direct relation to the offense. If, for example, your youngster is supposed to be in at ten o'clock and his or her friends persuade them to stay out until eleven, it would be well for you to let your son or daughter make up the time by putting a nine o'clock limit on the next outing. If that works, fine. If not, sterner measures are in order—maybe a denial of the going-out privilege the next time. A consistent reward for keeping a rule, and a consistent withdrawal of privilege for violating it, will achieve the result for which you are aiming.

You can use a lesser punishment for a first offense than for subsequent instances of the same kind of misbehavior. For example, if your son has never stolen anything before, and one day a playmate talks him into taking money out of your purse to buy ice cream cones, you don't have to take drastic measures. For a first offense, you can explain why taking the money without consulting you was wrong, tell your son he is never to take money from your purse again without permission, and let him go. If the same "crime" occurs again, it's time for some form of correction.

The punishment should be just—not unduly restrictive or severe. It should be only as harsh as it needs to be to correct the behavior pattern.

155

Parents would never go in for the "you're grounded for a month" kind of punishment if they put themselves in their child's shoes. He or she will have to live with the restriction for thirty days. That can seem like eternity and give the child a hopeless, what's-the-use attitude.

If your youngster has misused the car privilege, you can take the car keys away, but if he or she has misused the telephone privilege, you don't take the car keys away. Imposing the same kind of punishment for a variety of different offenses lets the child grow up thinking that every breach of conduct is a mortal sin, that every time he or she is wrong, it's a national emergency. It's important to keep punishment within a sensible perspective. An accidental mishap should not carry the same penalty as an act of deliberate, malicious destruction.

Take Shelter!

What if your child throws a tantrum? First, never reward the shrieking child by giving in to him or her. If you reward tantrum behavior, your child will have tantrums with increasing frequency.

Second, don't hang around to watch the tantrum. Walk away from it. Deprived of an audience, tantrums go away more quickly than they would with any other response. Should the tantrum take place in public and it's impossible to walk away, pick up the child and take them to a place where you can be alone. Lovingly, but firmly, hold the child, regardless of the kicking, screaming action. When you're alone, set them down and look directly in their face and say, "I love you so much." See if that doesn't bring some quietness to the action.

At a later time, when they're in total peace with you, you can say, "I want to talk with you about what happened today. Do you remember it? Do you remember why you got started in that?" Then you can rectify some things—or at least discover what brought on the tantrum.

Perhaps the child will honestly say, "I don't know why I do it." You may be dealing with a situation similar to epilepsy or some other condition that needs to be checked physically by a doctor. If it's just a matter of anger, then you can instruct your child against giving way to anger like that. Talk about how you sometimes become angry too, but can't act it out in those unacceptable ways.

To Tell the Truth

To me, lying is one of the worst forms of misbehavior. If I can count on my youngsters to tell me the truth, I go easier on their punishment. I encourage my youngsters to admit their wrongdoing. That doesn't mean that I fail to punish them—but I always reward the honesty somehow.

"Dan, I want you to know that I really appreciate your telling me the truth about what happened. You know that you were in the wrong, but now help me decide what we should do about it to keep this kind of thing from happening again."

In every case that has come to my attention, the child has suggested a far harsher punishment than the parent would have thought of imposing.

Children are hard on themselves. They're likely to say, "Well, all my privileges should be taken away for a week, and I should have to do all the chores around the house, and I shouldn't get an allowance for the whole month."

What such suggestions say to us is, "Mom, Dad, I have a tremendous load of guilt about what I did wrong, and harsh discipline will relieve me of some of it."

Parents need to accept this from them, saying, "I understand what you're saying and I appreciate it. I think, however, that . . ." and then explain what they, as the parents, feel would be a fair response to their action.

"I think it would be sufficient for you to . . ." Be sure to reinforce your appreciation of their feeling the need for severity in their punishment.

You Must Be Mad!

What are you supposed to do with your feelings when your youngster has gone absolutely contrary to all that you've required of him—when he or she has ridden roughshod over all your careful training? It's natural to get mad.

Some parents have gotten the impression that they should never get mad, never show resentment, never exhibit hostility toward their youngsters no matter what they do. That's unreal. More times than not, such parents end up leaving the children free to suit themselves. They can break their parents' standards, tear down their home, beat on their siblings, and yet Mom and Dad never respond with a normal, instinctive reaction of anger.

Is that an ideal we should strive toward? Never.

When I'm mad, my kids know I'm mad. They know why I'm mad, too, because I tell them.

Sometimes I would say to them, "Don't talk to me right now because I'm mad."

They got out of my way, believe me! They didn't feel rejected when I told them that. They recognized that I'm reacting to a situation, not to them.

Some parents attempt to handle their anger by simply not speaking to the child. They pout in their corner, without any explanation, and the child naturally picks up a rejection message. When you're mad, say so. Children can cope with that. They can't cope with what happens inside them when they think, "Mom or Dad doesn't love me anymore."

"Well, you didn't say good-bye to Mommy, so Mommy isn't going to say good-bye to you." Or, "You don't think I'm so wonderful, so I don't think you're so wonderful." This kind of rejection is the most damaging thing that can happen to youngsters. It makes them reject themselves.

In dealing with children, you're dealing with indescribably tender emotional babies. You can't afford to play "this for that" with them, because everything that goes to make up their emotions and their egos is lying wide open, just as if they were split down the middle and turned wrong side out. They're completely exposed, totally vulnerable. It doesn't take more than a stern look from Mom or Dad to crush them.

At the same time, they may act as if they couldn't care less. They may even say, "Yecch. Here we go again," but on the inside, they're saying something else, something that sounds like, "Mommy, Daddy, I hurt."

Don't Rain On My Parade

When one of your youngsters has caused anger in you, you shouldn't try to assuage your feelings by banging out a couple of Broadway tunes on the piano. Don't pretend that nothing is wrong. There's a cloud hanging over your relationship. Don't ignore it. It must be dealt with.

If, when the storm is calmed, you've decided not to punish this time, you should tell the child the score so he or she will know where they stand and not be afraid you're going to lower the boom any second.

"Honey, what you did was wrong. But it's over and done with, and I'm not holding it against you."

The child is suddenly set free to heave a sigh of relief along with you and to do better next time, without a threat hanging over his or her head. Then you can pray with your child:

> Lord, we come to You with thankfulness that You died for us on the Cross; that You have borne all our sins. Thank You, Lord, that no matter what sins we've committed, You still love us, and when we come to You, You wash all our sins away. You make us clean and You don't hold anything against us. Thank You that You won't even remember our sins any more. They'll all be gone.

When you've closed the prayer, you can say to your youngster, "It's so good to be free, isn't it? Now, let's both walk in freedom." After punishment or a decision not to punish, it's a time for starting over with a clean slate.

Paying the Piper

Sometimes parents try to pay the price for their youngsters, to take all the frustration, all the pain, all the responsibility for their childrens' actions upon themselves. But it doesn't work. It can't be done.

Children brought up in such an atmosphere have a hard time maturing, because they have the attitude, "All parents are wrong. All adults owe me a living. Other people are responsible for my misdeeds—it's all their fault."

Unless children are taught to accept the responsibility for their own failures, they will continue to believe that society in general— whether it be the nation, the community, the school, or parents—is responsible for their problems. There is no healing or health in that.

Parents best help their youngsters learn from their mistakes when they punish them for misbehavior. That's what punishment is all about. Once you understand that, you'll stick with it until you have accomplished your purpose as parents who love your children and want the best in life for them.

Dianne:

"Richard," Mom calls out as he enters the house from school, "How was your day?"

Richard ignores her and goes to his room. "Richard," Mom calls out, "Where are you?" The lack of response from him causes Mom to search the house for him. Coming to his room and finding the door is shut, she knocks. "May I come in?"

Richard quietly says, "Yes."

Mom opens the door, looking inside she says, "Is everything okay?"

"No," he replies.

"Do you want to talk about it?"

"Well, I lost my jacket, Mom."

"Your new jacket that I spent a hundred dollars on?"

"I knew you'd say that, Mom. I knew you'd start yelling at me. I don't want to talk about it."

160

"Well, young man, I want to talk about it. Do you understand that I didn't spend that kind of money on a jacket you'd lose the first week of school? You're right to be in your room and you stay in here until I talk to your dad when he gets home."

Mom leaves the room and shuts the door.

Does this sound familiar? Of course it does. In a bonded parent's home, the child will be socialized regarding clothing and the discipline of taking care of things. But in a biblical parent's home, God has given us different standards for training.

In Ephesians 6:4, reading from *The Amplified Bible*, we're told to ". . . rear them [tenderly] in the training and discipline and the counsel and admonition of the Lord." Our goal is not just to deal with behavior to modify it, but to train the heart so there's a heart change. Our concern is not simply to have a peaceful relationship in the home by whatever means, but also to have a home that functions in respect and in regard for the Lord. This necessitates the changing of the inner being. The aim is to nurture our children until their character is changed.

The word nurture has in it the idea of disciplinary correction and may be translated in some places as chastisement. The biblical parent must discipline with whatever is needed for the truth to be laid to heart. They may need to use physical acts such as spanking, or docking money, time outs, and restrictions. Parents admonish (to train by word and counsel) their children by rebuking them or warning and counseling them against fault or oversight.

The key to biblical parenting are the three words, "of the Lord." The parents must be under the anointing of God when they train their children, when they speak the counsel of God, and when they use physical acts to correct their children's behavior. It's not a matter of what the parents think is right, or what the book they've read says is right. The Lord must teach and train parents how to nurture their children.

There are different kinds of parenting styles that are automatically taken in to family and parenting situations.

Some of these styles come from watching how your own parents parented and modeled specific behaviors. Another way is by obtaining knowledge from books, workshops, TV, and other parents—learning proven techniques. Parenting styles are also picked up by trial and error. But none of these are under the direction and anointing of the Holy Spirit.

God wants parents to learn how to nurture their children, train them according to His precepts, and guide them by His Word in conformity to His mind and will. To do this, parents need to discover the parenting style in which they are automatically walking. What did you learn by watching your mom and dad, by reading books and manuals on parenting, and by trial and error? You need to discover your natural parenting style, so you can allow the Holy Spirit to change it into His style.

By looking at parenting styles, you may be able to discover your own, where you need to change, and the value of training your children according to the directions of God, not according to your socialization.

Style 1: The Authoritarian Parent

". . . fathers, provoke not your children to wrath" (Ephesians 6:4, KJV). This is the authoritarian parent. They can be further identified by some of the following:

The parent is overly strict. The authoritarian parent will establish rules and boundaries and enforce them in a very exact, legalistic manner with very little room for mercy.

The parent confronts in anger. Correcting the child will usually be done in anger and hostility, name-calling and non-verbal communication such as shaking the finger, raising the hand, stamping the feet. Correction will not be done in a gentle, calm, reasonable tone of voice.

The parent attacks the child, not the problem, in order to motivate behavior. Dad comes home and notices Ted's room is not cleaned up and says, "You slob, you never clean up your room. It's always messy. Now clean it up or you won't get any supper."

Mother says to Kevin, "Please take out the trash." A few minutes later, she notices it's not taken out, so she attacks Kevin by saying, "You lazy person, you never do what I say."

The parent is always right. The motivation of the parent is that this parent knows what is best for the child and this produces the attitude of always being right, and an "I told you so" relationship between child and parent. Johnny calls home from the gas station to tell Mom and Dad he's going to be late because he's run out of gas. Dad yells, "I told you so. I've told you to fill up your tank before you go out of town." The impression is, "I'm always right and you're always wrong."

The parent looks for and creates conflicts. This parent may see siblings having a conflict between themselves and will enter into the fight, trying to resolve it because he or she is right; this creats more conflict, because the parent has become involved in a   negative way.

The parent becomes so involved with the child's life that he or she begins to control it. Control may be accomplished through the child's fear—fear of the anger, fear of being put down again, or fear of being told they're dumb and stupid. Out of fear, the child complies.

The parent manipulates. A common manipulation is using guilt. "When will you ever learn?" "I've told you a dozen times not to . . ." "Look what you've done to your mother."

The parent uses the Word of God as law and not grace. "Hello," Dad says as he answers the phone, "You've caught Philip shoplifting at your store? Yes, I'll come and pick him up. Thank you." In the car on the way home, Dad begins to quote the Word of God. "Don't you know what the Bible says against stealing?" and Dad begins to lecture Philip using the Word of God.

The parent disciplines the child but shows little love. This parent corrects behavior, sets up guidelines, rules, and regulations, but has a hard time getting involved emotionally in the life of the child. The parent wants the rules and regulations obeyed at the expense of grace and mercy, so the child only feels the love in the rules and regulations, not from the parent.

The parent establishes a win/lose relationship. Because he or she is right, uses the Word of God, and is forceful in mannerism, the parent usually wins, but does not realize that he or she has lost the relationship with the child. The child has been provoked to anger through the pain and the rejection of the relationship.

The parent is physically, verbally, or emotionally abusive. Attacking the person, not the problem, causes a tendency to be abusive in words said, in the physical discipline imposed, and by the lack of love, grace, and mercy that is in the discipline. The authoritarian parent is quick to impose physical discipline, and when angry, can become abusive.

The parent establishes obedience as the goal. The parent wants obedience to himself or herself, and their personal interpretation of biblical standards. This obedience is based on a dogmatic relationship, not a relationship of love.

Style 2: The Permissive Parent

"Our fathers disciplined us for a little while . . ." (Hebrews 12:10).

Lack of consistency or follow-through in disciplining is characteristic of the permissive parenting style, along with the following:

The parent is too lenient. Usually, the permissive parent is too lenient because he or she is an easy going, laid-back person who wants to go with the flow of things. Rules and regulations seem to stifle spontaneity.

The parent is afraid to take a stand. This parent's ruling emotion seems to be fear rather than anger. Dominated by fear, he or she fails to establish definite parameters and guidelines in the home—out of fear that the child will dislike or reject the parent.

The parent avoids conflicts. He or she can be in the midst of conflict, yet not see it or hear it. They will walk away from it, choosing to ignore what's happening around him or her. A permissive parent can see his or her son smoking dope in his room and walk past the room as if nothing was happening.

The parent becomes overwhelmed by problems. This parent is usually an avoider of situations. If two problems come up at the same time, he or she has a tendency to shut down. The more children a permissive parent has, the more he or she becomes overwhelmed and doesn't handle anything.

The parent has very little control. This parent tries to gain control by talking. The idea is that if he or she can talk the child out of the bad behavior, then the bad behavior will stop.

The parent has very little control and few regulations, but much love for the child. The permissive parent wants to give grace and mercy all the time, not enforcing the regulations and boundaries of the home.

The parent doesn't have rules. This parent doesn't have rules, because rules require enforcement. This parent doesn't want to spend the time, energy, and effort to remember the rules, to enforce the rules, and to give consequences because of broken rules.

The parent establishes a win/lose relationship. Permissiveness causes the loss of the child's respect and the child wins in a conflict, because the parent backs down and the child gets his or her own way. Ultimately the child loses, however, because he or she lacks the discipline needed to grow up in a healthy manner.

The parent is non-punitive, non-directive, non-demanding. If the child were to ask for direction, the parent would say, "I don't care, Honey. Do what you want to do." The parent becomes the child and the child becomes the parent.

The parent does not control. The permissive parent does not stand in the role as the authority of the home and has a tendency to see authority as abusive.

Style 3: The Neglectful Parent

"... a child left undisciplined ..." (Proverbs 29:15, *AMP*). The neglectful parent has not only left the child undisciplined, but has left the child:

The parent isn't there, in time, self, money, or discipline.

The parent establishes no boundaries or no rules. There is no training, no support system, no nurturing. The child is left to parent himself or herself.

The parent considers the child a burden. This parent sees the child only as someone who is in the way and wants the child to take care of himself or herself. The parent loses and the child loses.

The parent loses by not having a relationship with the child and not taking the role as parent. The child loses because he or she doesn't have a support system and a love relationship, but is left to parent and nurture himself or herself.

The parent wants no control and gives no love. The neglectful parent gives none of himself or herself to the relationship.

Style 4: The Nurturing Parent

As parents, we are to nurture our children (Ephesians 6:4). Specifically this would cover the following:

The parent is not strict or lenient, but consistent. Being directed by the Holy Spirit when to give grace and when to enforce the rules, this parent becomes consistent in the training and nurturing of the child.

The parent can confront in anger or in peace. This parent doesn't discipline according to the emotional climate, but trains the child according to the situation. He or she can get angry but not sin. He or she can walk in peace, and yet not use that peace to avoid conflicts.

The parent attacks the problem and not the child. When Ted doesn't clean up his room, he shouldn't be called a slob, but dealt with about why the room was not cleaned up. When Kevin forgets to take the trash out for Mom, she doesn't attack him for being lazy, but says, "The trash hasn't been taken out yet. When were you planning to do it?" In this way, the nurturing parent attacks the problem and not the person.

Daniel and I are at the dinner table eating and he spills his milk. If I was an authoritarian parent, I would say, "You careless child, can't you hold a glass in your hand? What a klutz you are."

As a permissive parent, I'd just minimize the problem, hush it up, and start cleaning up the mess, wanting peace at any price.

If I were a neglectful parent, I wouldn't even be there to see the milk spilled.

But as a nurturing parent, I say, "The milk is spilled. Let's clean it up." The family would get involved in dealing with the problem, and not attacking the person.

166

The parent is not looking to be right, but looking for the relationship to be right. This parent's focus isn't on the right or wrong of an issue, but on keeping the relationship healed and restored at any cost. When Michael called from the gas station saying he would be late, the nurturing father would have said, "I'm glad you called. Thanks for telling us what was going on. How can we help?" In this fashion, not only is the nurturing parent establishing the relationship, but attempting to build it as well. Also, he recognized Michael is at the gas station getting gas and is, therefore, solving his own problem and doesn't need to be put down or told right or wrong. He is learning by natural consequences.

The parent deals with reality and the real problems, not looking for problems or avoiding them. This parent is motivated to use life situations for training and nurturing the child under the direction of the Holy Spirit.

The parent becomes involved in the child's life to discover the disposition of the child and not to control the child.

The parent tries to discover what God has created in this child—not trying to live out his or her own fantasies through the child. If, for example, while growing up I had a dream to be a beauty queen that was never realized, as a nurturing parent I will recognize that dream as mine, and not try to reproduce it in my daughter, but release her to be what God has called her to be.

The parent trains the child and doesn't manipulate or avoid them. If the parent allows God to deal with his or her own manipulations and avoidance of life's problems, this training will enable the parent to reproduce these skills in his or her children. As God admonishes the parent, the parent will be able to admonish the children.

The parent loves the Word of God. The Bible is used as a manual and not as a mallet. The Holy Spirit brings revelation and wisdom through the Word of God, which can then be imparted to the child in training and discipline. The child will also see the parent modeling and walking out the reality of these truths.

The parent loves the child through discipline and through relationship. Discipline brings love, and a relationship with a living God brings love. This parent knows the balance between discipline and emotional support.

The parent has a win/win relationship. This parent trains; the child learns—so both grow and mature and both win. When the Holy Spirit is in charge of a relationship, He brings justice that produces a win/win relationship.

The parent is physically, verbally, and emotionally supportive. The goal is that in every encounter with the child, the child will feel valued and valuable as a person. Therefore, the parent's words, physical actions, and emotional responses will say to the child, "I want to restore a relationship with you."

The parent establishes a heart change and relationship through Christ, not just obedience. Obedience will come as the heart is changed.

The parent uses the power of the Holy Spirit to train and correct—not his or her own power or avoidance of power. Because this parent knows he or she is accountable daily to God for this enabling, direction, cleansing, and forgiveness, this parent will daily seek God for his or her own heart to be cleansed, for repentance, and for forgiveness to be released in the home. Confident that it's through the power of God in the home that hearts can be changed, wisdom can be given, and restored relationships can be ongoing, this parent yields control for power to the Holy Spirit, so that He will have His will and way.

The following inventory may be helpful in discovering your parenting style.

Discipline Style Inventory

YES   NO

____   ____   1. When I discipline, I deal with the issue right away.

____   ____   2. When I discipline, I'm usually angry or speak in a loud voice.

____   ____   3. When I discipline, I sometimes call my child names like "lazy," "forgetful," or "sloppy,"

YES	NO	
____	____	4. When I discipline, I do it when I know I am right.
____	____	5. When I discipline, I usually know what is the best solution.
____	____	6. When I discipline, the results some times are conflicts where there is mutual raising of voices; someone walks out; someone becomes silent and sulks; or someone becomes physical.
____	____	7. I think it is the parent's responsibility to stay in control.
____	____	8. As a Christian parent, the Word of God has been given to give absolutes that need to be constantly enforced or the child will become irresponsible.
____	____	9. I love my child and have rules of the home that teach obedience is more important than the child's value
____	____	10. I am not afraid of my child's reactions to my discipline
____	____	11. I will usually physically discipline my child before we will "talk" about the problem.
____	____	12. I see my authority as a parent necessary to establish my disciplinary rules.

YES   **NO**

____   ____   13. I find myself too busy to deal with the
discipline issues at home.

____   ____   14. In our home, we do not have set rules
boundaries, or regulations.

____   ____   15. I find that I'm too pre-occupied with
work, etc., to discipline the children.

____   ____   16. I find that I do not want to make my
children unhappy with my discipline.

____   ____   17. I try to avoid conflict because it
It usually causes hard feelings anyway.

____   ____   18. In our home, I find that "talking to
the child works instead of punishment.

____   ____   19. I believe that loving my child means
to be there for them and to allow the
child to be their own disciplinarian.

____   ____   20. I believe peace at any price is an
example of a Christian home.

____   ____   21. Sometimes I am too overwhelmed
with other problems to effectively
discipline my children.

____   ____   22. I believe that many problems just need
to be ignored and they will work them-
selves out.

____   ____   23. I would rather be my child's friend
than a parent who disciplines.

____   ____   24. There are times that people have said
I am too lenient.

Please mark how many yes answers you have. How many yes answers were in the first 12 questions? How many yes answers were in the last 12 questions? The number that has the highest number of yes answers is your parenting style. Questions 1 - 12 reflect the authoritarian style. Questions 13 -24 reflect the permissive style.

We may also look at our children's reactions to our discipline and insights from the Word to help us discover our parenting style.

Fear. 1 John 4:18 says, "There is no fear in love." When you're nurturing your children and desire *agape*—unconditional love—to flow, your children will not be afraid of the punishment. That's the goal. If you see your child is fearful of you, you may be an authoritarian parent trying to control, or a permissive parent who is not establishing firm boundaries around your child.

Wrath. "Fathers, provoke not your children to wrath" (Ephesians 6:4, KJV). Signs of wrath from your children (verbal or physicall aggression) can indicate you are not nurturing under godly direction. Wrath is anger that has become sin, expressed in aggressive behavior. The authoritarian parent attacks the child. The permissive parent gives no guidelines, so the child is free to express whatever he or she wants without consequences.

Disheartened. Colossians 3:21 says not to provoke your children, not stirring them up to the point of discouragement, disheartenment, or feelings of inferiority. Low self-esteem in your children can be established by an authoritative or permissive parent. If you see this, you can ask the Lord, "Is it my disciplinary style or is it something happening at school?" Then you can do an effective intervention.

Rejection. Proverbs 15:5 says that a fool rejects a father's chastening and instruction. When discipline does not drive out natural foolishness in the child's heart, he or she will reject instruction. The goal is the correction and training of the child, not just that the child will not reject the instruction. If you become either permissive or authoritarian, you can produce rejection in your child. This doesn't mean that a child won't reject a nurturing parent who has just established new boundaries, but you look for rejection as a sign to ask yourself, "Did I not nurture?"

Grievous. Discipline may seem grievous at the time, but, if a child is trained by it, it will produce the fruit of righteousness (Hebrews 12:11). A child reacting negatively to discipline does not necessarily mean you've been authoritarian or permissive. If your goal is to train the child, regardless of his or her response, you'll pray for the heart change to come.

Respect. You are to have the authority in your household that enables you to control and command the respect of your children (1 Timothy 3:4-5, *The Amplified Bible*). Godly authority is based on humility and *agape*—unconditional love—as well as God's righteousness, values, grace, and mercy.

Love. Proverbs tells us that in reproving a wise man, he'll love us, and if we love our son, we'll discipline him (Proverbs 9:8; 13:24). Nurturing and admonition in the Lord will bring forth *agape* love as a fruit and benefit.

Not fainting. Hebrews 12:5 says not to lose heart, or give up, or faint when you're corrected by the Lord. As parents, you are asking the Lord to strengthen you to be consistent and strong in your discipline and asking that your children will learn to embrace it and not faint.

Thinking lightly. Hebrews 12:5 says not to despise or think lightly of discipline. Your children will ultimately respect the training because they will see the health they receive from it.

Enduring. Hebrews 12:7 says you're to bear or endure the chastening of the Lord. Authoritarian parents want their children to endure their angry, manipulative correction. Permissive parents establish no rules to endure, while the nurturing parent prays for the Holy Spirit to enable and empower all in the family to embrace God's chastening.

Focusing on relationship. Hebrews 12:6-8 reveals that God disciplines because He's producing sons. What's your goal for discipline? Do you want obedient children who do what you say, or is your goal to produce a relationship with the eternal Father and do everything to please Him? The nurturing parent receives his or her role model from God.

Repentance. God uses both goodness (Romans 2:4) and godly sorrow to bring us to repentance (2 Corinthians 7:9-10). A nurturing parent knows that admonition and chastening of the Lord are to produce repentance, salvation, and healing.

Cheerfully submitting. When you cheerfully submit (Hebrews 12:9, *The Amplified Bible*) to the training and discipline of the Lord, you'll be able to teach it to your children.

Obedience. "As an ear or nose ring of gold, or an ornament of fine gold, is a wise reprover to an ear that listens and obeys" (Proverbs 25:12, *The Amplified Bible*). As you are learning to nurture your children, God's love through you will produce obedience. Jesus said that if you loved Him, you'd obey Him (John 14:15). Obedience comes from a love relationship. As you begin to *agape* your children—love them with God's unconditional love—obedience will be a natural by-product of that relationship.

Where do you go from here? Have you discovered your style? Do you know in what areas you need to repent? It is through daily repentance and forgiveness that you make a way for God to help you nurture your children. When you see in your children inappropriate reactions to your discipline, that's when the Holy Spirit wants to train you in His counsel. As you repent and ask your children's forgiveness, you are modeling for them how God wants to continue to nurture and train all of His children.

8

Your Child and Siblings

Iverna:

Almost every parent who has more than one child has been aware at some time or another of feelings of jealousy between the children. It's called sibling rivalry, and it can make life miserable for everybody.

Every child needs to feel secure in the love of their parents. No child can bear to feel left out or even put in second place. It doesn't do any good for anyone to sputter to a child, "Look, I'm not being partial to your brother. It's all your imagination. I love you just as much as I love him." The children will not hear such protests. Instead, they will continue to react to what they believe to be the truth. Parents must deal with their child's perception of the truth, not with what they, as the parents, know is the truth.

After Dan was born, I came out of the hospital with him and saw Debbie waiting in the back seat of the car.

"Here's your baby," I said to her as I put him in her lap. At the moment, the relationship that existed between them was a beautiful thing. But when Debbie was around eleven or twelve, something made her think I was showing partiality to Dan.

"I know you love me, but I think you love Dan more," she sniffed.

I sat down beside her on the couch and said, "Debbie, before you were born, when Daddy and I knew that we were going to have a baby, I never referred to it as 'the baby.' In all the letters that I wrote to your father when he was overseas, I always said, 'Debbie this' and 'Debbie that.' I was so sure we were going to have a girl ... "

"Why?" she interrupted me, her eyes wide with surprise.

"Well," I said, "I wanted a girl, and I had prayed to God for a girl with black hair and brown eyes—just like you. When Grandma came to stay with me before you were born, she did everything she could to talk me into thinking I might have a boy, but I wouldn't listen to her. Why, if God had sent a boy just then, I'd probably have sent him right back where he came from."

Debbie had to giggle at that, and I could see I was getting through. I went on to tell her about some of the little clothes I had bought for her and how proud I was to be her mother.

Now, Debbie didn't suddenly give me a lot of verbal feedback. She didn't throw her arms around me and cry, "Oh, Mama, now I really know you love me as much as you love Dan!" but her face gradually relaxed, and she looked happy. She knew then that I had looked forward to her before she was born.

No matter how hard parents try, they can never completely and permanently do away with feelings of jealousy between their children. It's impossible. Children will try to use their parent's partiality, real or imagined, against them as a manipulative tool. If they get what they want from this manipulation, they'll employ it time and time again. Every time Mom or Dad has to say no to one of them, they'll say, "Yes. It's because you like so and so better than you like me."

A child will try to make Mom or Dad back down. But if they do, they have had it. Parents need to be on guard against falling into this trap. At the same time, they have to be aware of their children's need for reassurance.

Sometimes a parent simply has to say, "I ask you to trust me in these decisions," while strongly reaffirming their love for their children.

In certain cases, parents may actually be partial to one child over another. If that happens, they need to be careful not to go to the opposite extreme in order to compensate.

This is especially a danger in homes in which retarded children are growing up. In such cases, parents tend to overcompensate. At its worst, this kind of over-reaction can literally destroy the potential of the "normal" children in the home, since it deprives them of the nurturing parenting they need. In the natural, the parents may prefer them, but because they devote so much of their attention to the one retarded child, the others feel rejected.

Another feeling of rejection that comes later seems to be a natural part of growing up. At about age eleven, a lot of kids decide that they were probably adopted into their family. They think they don't look like the rest of the children, and they know for a certainty that they're not treated as well as the others. This is a typical manifestation of the age of insecurity. An extra measure of love from Mom and Dad will usually effect a cure.

Taking thoughtful inventory of their actions, parents may realize that at a certain stage they are being overly indulgent toward the child who's mentally slower than others, who finds it harder to get along in school, who has a physical disability, or who doesn't have many friends. An honest appraisal forces these parents to agree that their partiality hasn't really helped the youngster as much as it has fed their own need to be needed. In fact, the result has probably been further rejection of the child by his or her brothers and sisters, making the problems worse instead of better for the children and the parents.

If there is a youngster within the family who from birth has been an I-can-do-it-myself creature, Mom and Dad may have a tendency to turn too much attention to the less-outgoing child in order to assuage their own feelings of rejection by the independent one. It's important for parents to be aware of and to guard against this in themselves if they want their children to love one another.

This kind of attention encourages dependence by the less outgoing one and independence by the more outgoing one and can set a pattern for their life if it's not guarded against. Parents need to encourage dependency in areas to the very capable, so he or she can recognize the necessity of having other people participate in their lives, and independence in the over-dependent one so that he or she can learn to function in society as an individual.

Parents may be more comfortable around one of their youngsters than another because one is more sensitive to their needs. Perhaps one child just seems to know when Mom or Dad is feeling out of sorts and leaves them alone. Not only that, but they run interference for Mom or Dad with the other children, telling them "Leave Mom alone today. Can't you see she's tired?" or "Dad wants to take a nap. Don't make any noise."

When Mom or Dad is sick, that child is the one who cleans up the dirty dishes and then comes in and waits on their "patient," all unasked for. Sometimes a parent's subconscious says, "That child likes me better; that child loves me more than the other children do." Without being aware of it, Mom or Dad may begin to show partiality toward the helpful and considerate child.

It's easy to play favorites and to find excuses for it, but it's dangerous business for the peace and harmony of the home.

Dianne:
One of the causes of conflict in the home is favoritism. Genesis 25:27-28 tells the story of Esau and Jacob. When the boys grew up, Esau was a cunning and skilled hunter, a man of the outdoors. Jacob was a plain and quiet man dwelling in tents. Isaac, the boys' father, loved and was partial to Esau because he ate of Esau's game, but Rebekah, the boys' mother, loved Jacob. The rivalry that was set up between these two boys came because each parent favored one child over another. When this happens, the child that is not favored feels the "X"—feels less than the other, feels neither special nor valuable. This "X" sets them up to fight or flee.

The favoritism came because of the qualifications and qualities of the children. Esau was a hunter and was the macho, masculine boy, and Isaac didn't like Jacob sticking around the house and cooking. To Isaac, such work was wimpish. I'm sure there were times in the tent when Isaac made a fuss over Esau—how good he was at hunting and how delicious the game was that he brought home. Isaac's silence in regards to Jacob's accomplishments would loudly express his feelings of favoritism.

Fathers can show favoritism by focusing on one son and his abilities over another son. If one son has a tendency to be more intellectual and likes to study and read, while the other is more athletically-inclined, the father might focus his attention on the athletic son. In so doing, he puts down the son who would rather read than go out for sports. Or, a father might show favoritism between two sons that are athletic by giving more attention to the son who is more proficient in athletics than the other. This produces competition between the sons, resulting in conflicts.

With Isaac showing favoritism to Esau, Jacob's desire for attention went unfulfilled. He may have thought to himself, "Well, Dad might listen to me if I learned about hunting. Maybe he'd talk with me." Because Isaac favored Esau, Jacob received an "X." He felt rejected and that situation caused strife between Jacob and Esau.

Proverbs 12:10 says that hatred stirs up strife. In the conflict between Jacob and Esau, hatred flared between the two brothers. One day, Jacob took advantage of Esau's hunger, causing him to give up his birthright to satisfy his hunger. Esau hated Jacob from that day on.

Jacob needed affection from his dad, and when he didn't receive it, strife and conflict occurred with his brother. The issue between Jacob and Esau wasn't the stolen birthright. The issues were the "X"s—the unmet needs. To resolve the conflict between Jacob and Esau, we'd have to resolve the favoritism and the resulting devaluing that occurred because of the parents' actions and attitudes.

Iverna:

How can parents divide their attention among their youngsters in a way that will be most beneficial? They can begin by giving their attention to the child who is most needy at the moment. Sometimes they can involve two or more children at the same time in what they're doing. When it's necessary to make an arbitrary choice, wherever possible parents can decide in favor of the teenager. Mom and Dad may have years left to deal with the younger child, but what they don't give the teenager now, he or she might not be around to get later.

Suppose Mom starts making a cake with one youngster and the other comes in demanding attention. If she says, "Okay, Susie will mix it, but you can pour it into the pans," Susie may very well leave the scene. Her attitude may be, "Forget it. If this isn't going to be special—just you and me, Mom—who cares about making a dumb cake?"

Making the cake was not what was special to Susie in the first place. The cake-making was just an excuse for being with Mom for an exclusive dose of her attention for a little while. Admittedly, the youngster she turns away may be out of sorts for a while, but she can make it up to him or her later. Including them when the other is not welcoming mass participation hurts them both, and Mom is worse off than when she started.

She can say to the one who wants to intrude, "No, you can't help just now. Susie and I are doing this. Next time, maybe you and I will make a cake." She might suggest something the other child can do instead, and be firm about it.

The resolution of this conflict is actually helpful to the child who first needed the attention. Mom's attitude says to her, "See, I am meeting your needs exclusively right now." When she is satisfied that she is the center of Mom's attention, then she might become more willing to include everybody in the picture. The parent in this scenario must be careful not to let a child feel that everything is mass treatment and that there's never anything special just for him or her.

When one youngster has provoked another to wrath, don't just try to stop the fight. Try to find out what really happened. Then, try to interpret their reactions to them. When you explain to each of them why the other felt as he or she did, why he or she reacted in such a manner, and point out that the offended child would have reacted in the same way if the roles had been reversed, you're helping them to understand themselves and the other person. This paves the way for a behavior adjustment the next time a similar situation arises.

Dianne:
Step-children

With the rise of divorce and remarriage, we now have complex situations in many homes and another reason for conflict between siblings. Many children have two moms and two dads, eight grandparents, two homes, maybe two states that they commute between, and visitation conflicts. Children in these situations are grieving the loss of a parent, grieving the loss of a home, loss of time, loss of position. These children feel no family loyalty and wonder which home they belong in. Where do they belong? Where is their place? They feel rejected or abandoned by one parent and now have to share the other parent with "outsiders." They feel rejected by these strange step-children.

These children feel insecure because they have to deal with the differences in the value systems in each home—one home is disciplined, one isn't; one gives allowances, another doesn't; and so on. Often these children are angry because they feel out of control. They had no choice in the divorce. Many feel guilty because they think it might be their fault. They think, "Maybe if I had behaved, this wouldn't have happened." These children fear that they've lost one parent and that maybe they'll lose another parent to this step-parent. Sometimes these children wistfully think that one day the parents will get back together and they will live happily ever after.

The problems between step-children are obvious. Because of their "X"s, they come looking for conflicts. Conflicts can occur when:

(1) A child is the baby in the family and the new family has a younger child—now they're no longer the baby;

(2) A child may be the oldest of the family and this new family has older children;

(3) There wa an only child and now they're around more children with parental attention becoming divided.

Added to the children's conflicts is the parents' favoritism. One of the biggest problems in parenting step-children is the natural tendency to favor the biological child over the step-child. Biological parents want to protect their own children and uncover step-children—to side in arguments and conflicts with their child against the step-child. Rivalry comes by virtue of the basic dynamics of bringing two families together to live under the same roof. Add to this the other reasons for conflicts: sensual desires, comparison, natural competition, the lack of or differences in a justice system, and you have a potentially explosive situation.

Wayne and I have step-children. Michelle and David are my children from my first marriage. Casey is Wayne's child from his first marriage, and Daniel is our child. We have had to learn to communicate, allowing the Holy Spirit to convict us when we take sides, when we want to get even, when we show favor. Then we allow the Holy Spirit to continue to search our motives and reasoning. If I find myself wanting to take sides with my children against Wayne, I say, "Wayne, pray for me. Help me. I want to get back at Casey. He's just picked on Daniel and instead of ministering to Casey I want to get back at him." Wayne and I continue to talk with each other, being honest about our feelings, not just to expose them, but to allow God to deal with them. Over the years, we've watched God heal us and continue to help us establish a justice system.

When David felt I loved Casey more than I did him, I prayed, "God, give me wisdom to minister to my son so he feels just as loved as Casey. I don't want to go overboard to prove my love for Casey and reject my own son. Give me wisdom. Show me how to meet David's need. Show me how to meet Casey's need. Show me how to parent and raise these children under Your standard according to their bent (disposition)."

Wayne and I recognized the dynamics that were involved in bringing two families together and watched for those signs. We knew there would be natural competition in children—plus, with step-children, there was even more competition for our attention. We were aware that there would be favoritism in the family, more so because of our situation. We were constantly before the Lord. One reason the statistics are higher for second marriages ending in divorce is because of the ready-made families with their ready-made conflicts.

The War Cry

"Let go of my sweater," screamed fourteen-year-old Jennie. "Just because you're my sister doesn't mean you can take my things."

"But you said I could wear it," yelled Beth, Jennie's twelve-year-old sister, as she continued to hold the sweater as tightly as she could while Jennie yanked and yanked.

"I told you last week you could wear it, but I want to wear it today to the party I'm going to," Jennie said as she continued to pull the sweater.

"Well, I'm going to the party, too, and I want to wear the sweater," Beth snaps back.

"Well, you can't," and with a big tug, Jennie yanked the sweater from Beth's hands, but ripped a sleeve of the sweater in the process. "Now, see what you've done! Mom, Beth ripped my sweater and she has to buy me a new one!" Jennie cries in anger as Mom enters the room in the midst of the conflict.

This a common occurrence in our homes. But why do children fight and war?

Sensual Desires

This question is asked in the Book of James. What leads to strife, discord, and feuds? How do conflicts, quarrels, and fighting originate in our midst? They arise from our sensual desires that are ever warring in our bodily members. We are jealous and covet what others have and our desires go unfulfilled. We become murderers, because to hate is to murder as far as our hearts are concerned. We burn with envy and anger and aren't able to obtain the gratification, the contentment, and the happiness for which we seek. So we fight and war (James 4:1-3).

One reason conflicts occur between siblings is because of their own natural desires. The definition of the word desire means to want something so badly we fix our attention on it. This can be for the positive or it can be for the negative. The Word of God says to covet or desire the good things (1 Corinthians 12:31). The Word says to desire the kingdom of God, to seek God's highest, and to seek God's kingdom (Matthew 6:33).

Human beings desire the four A's: affection, attention, approval, and affiliation. When these desires are not met, they can turn negative—becoming lusts—lusts for power, prestige, pleasures, and positions. Pride takes hold.

What did the two teenagers desire? The sweater wasn't the issue—the sweater would give them what they desired, what we call the "X." They wanted to wear the sweater to the party to get attention, to get approval, maybe ultimately to get affection. So the conflict came between the two girls when they had a basic desire that needed to be met in a certain way and they focused on the same object—the sweater.

Pride

Proverbs 13:10 says that pride leads to contention. How can pride bring about conflict in the home? Johnny feels he's superior to his sister, Suzie, so he has a tendency to call her names and lord over her. He feels he has a right to correct her behavior. When Suzie feels belittled because of Johnny, what is her natural desire? What is the "A" that needs to be met in Suzie's life? Does she need attention? Does she need approval? Certainly she's not feeling affiliated to Johnny. From this "X," Suzie will move into conflict with Johnny's pride.

Remember Jennie? Her sweater is fixed, she's wearing it, she looks great. She's getting her desires met. She's getting approval and the attention she wants. Looking great, she begins to drift into prideful thinking, "No one looks as great as I do in this sweater." One day, Beth, her sister, asks to borrow the sweater. Jennie thinks, "Oh, no big deal. Sure, you can borrow my sweater." But Jennie knows that Beth is not going to look as good as she does in it and when she sees Beth come out of her room wearing the sweater, Jennie is going to make sure Beth knows this. So she says, "Well, it doesn't look too good on you. I think it looks better on me." We now have the beginning of a conflict.

What's the real issue? First of all, Beth feels talked down to, feels less than Jennie. Anytime one person feels less than another person—not valued—that's an "X" and they're going to respond accordingly (fight or flee). Beth might respond, "Well, I don't think you look so good in it, either." That would be a fight response to the situation. Or perhaps Beth chooses a flee response—passive-aggressive—and wears the sweater to the party, spilling something on it, knowing that would get back at her sister. What is the real issue? What is Jennie's "X"? In her pride and self-righteousness, she's feeling unloved and insecure. Jennie has had to use her sweater to make herself feel loved and valuable, because she doesn't know she's valuable without the sweater. To bring a conclusion to the situation with Beth and Jennie, we'd say, "Jennie, what do you need to ask forgiveness for from your sister?

"I talked down to my sister."

"That's correct."

"Beth, for what do you need to repent of to your sister?"

"Well, I got even with her. I yelled back."

"That's right. You can be angry, have an "X," but not sin."

Then through prayer, Mom or Dad can ask the Holy Spirit to begin to minister to Beth, so she'll know she's valued and loved just because she's Beth and for Jennie to know she's valued and loved just because she's Jennie. They can ask the Holy Spirit to meet their needs, the natural desires they have, so that they can minister to one another *agape* love—not pride and self-righteousness.

Iverna:

In cases where sibling quarrels are just a bid for attention, ignoring the situation can be the best solution to it.

185

A woman told me about her daughters who began bickering the moment they got home from school each day. She had tried to settle their arguments so many times that she was tired of dealing with it. One day, she just went into another room when the girls began to quarrel and acted as if she didn't hear what was going on. Finally, their curiosity got the best of them, and they peeked through the doorway to see if their mother was still among the living. Seeing her calmly sitting in a chair reading a book, they were astonished.

"Mama!" one of them cried, "you don't care if Sally kills me!"

Sally cried, "Mama, you don't care if Laura kills me!"

Mama turned the page of the magazine on her lap and looked up to answer.

"That's right, Laura! That's right. Sally; I don't care." Mama went back to her reading, the girls looked at one another in open-mouthed amazement and were soon giggling together happily.

Dianne:
Comparison/Competition

> *However when they measure themselves with*
> *themselves and compare themselves with one another,*
> *they are without understanding and behave unwisely.*
> *(2 Corinthians 10:12, AMP)*

Another reason for conflict in the home is competition—the comparison of one child to another.

It's a sin to compare ourselves to one another. It's also unwise, as evidenced by the account of Saul and David when people around them brought a comparison (1 Samuel 18:5-11). When Saul felt he was valued less in the comparison, jealousy rose up in him. The way he heard it, the numbers made a difference to the people. They didn't just sing about the enemy being defeated, they sang, "Wow, David has slain ten thousand and Saul only a measly thousand."

Often parents do the same thing. Some were taught to motivate their children through comparison. When my kids were growing up, my daughter's temperament included being very neat and orderly. She cleaned her room without being asked, the clothes in her closet and in her dresser drawers were color-coordinated, her socks were neatly folded together, and her shoes placed on the shoe rack. My son, David, by temperament, was quite different. He thought that if the clothes were in the room, they were put away. If underwear was on the floor, in his mind, it was put away because it was in his room. I thought I could motivate David to clean his room by saying, "Why can't you clean your room like your sister?" But this caused rivalry, not motivation. What he heard in the comparison was, "David, you're bad because you aren't like your sister. There's something wrong with you."

I had to apologize to my children for using a comparison of their natural abilities as a motivation. That's a sin—it's unwise. Then I said, "You know, Michelle, this is a natural ability you have. Can you help David by teaching him?" Now that's a different approach. It's not saying, "David, you're bad," but it's saying, "It's just not naturally in your temperament to do it, but you need to learn how."

Parents may have a tendency to compare their children in their looks, trying to motivate them with statements such as, "Why can't you lose weight like your brother?" That comparison creates an "X" and the hurting child is going to fight or flee. For example, in the same family there is one daughter who is very pretty and one daughter who is unattractive, with a tendency to overeat and gain weight. The parents try to help by continually harping on the issue saying, "Don't eat; stop eating; you're going back for seconds; don't do that; your sister doesn't do that." What the child hears is "I'm bad." From that "X" they'll fight or flee. They'll fight by getting even, become anorexic or bulimic—passive/aggressive—or continue to overeat.

God brought healing to my daughter's weight problem by healing her "X"s, not dealing with her weight. God taught her how

187

to discover the places she needed approval, which in today's culture comes if you're beautiful and have the desirable physical measurements. No wonder our daughters have low self-esteem if they don't fit the model and the pattern. God, help us to let our daughters know they're valued not because of what they do or how they look but because they are human beings created in God's image.

It's natural for children to compare themselves with one another, but it's sin. When one person compares himself or herself favorably to someone else, it causes pride. If one person compares himself or herself unfavorably to someone else, they develop low self-esteem. The only comparison should be in relation to Christ and the standard He set for us while on the earth.

What a fascinating journey for parents and their children—to discover the standard God has for them. How does God want them to look? What does God want them to do? Not the parents' standards, not what the parents want them to do, but God's standards and God's design for their children's lives.

There was a day that I would have felt guilty that my daughter, at twenty-three, was not married, because the standard said, "Oh, she's going to be an old maid." I would have personalized that comment by comparing her to the daughters of other women my age and felt that I had somehow failed. However, I want Michelle to live the standard God has given her.

Several years ago, the Lord showed Wayne and me that we had raised Michelle according to a double standard. We had raised our boys knowing that they would eventually support a family. Unconsciously, we raised Michelle with the concept that she'd be married and have someone taking care of her. We apologized to her, because we hadn't raise her according to God's standards but according to our own mentality.

Michelle is still not married. She's working full-time as an executive secretary, supporting herself. It was necessary for us to backtrack, teaching her skills we had not thought she would need because she was a girl. Not only has she forgiven us, but we've begun to pray for God to restore to her what she should have had by the standard God had on her life, not the standard we imposed on her.

What's the antidote to comparison and competition? Each child finding the place that God has appointed for them—their calling, their ministry—without comparison to another child's call and ministry. What gifting do they have? If God has given them one gift and someone else five, God has given them that one gift for a reason, and He loves them and wants to achieve the highest potential with that one gift. The person with five talents and the person with one talent are each expected to do the same thing—use their gifts (Matthew 25:15-28).

God forgive us for valuing the one who has five talents over the person with one. We need to allow God's unconditional love to be ministered to each of our children as we discover their inherent (in Christ) tendencies—the standard God has for their life—the anointing and ministry He's ordained for them.

And Justice for All

Another reason for sibling rivalry is the lack of a workable justice system within the home. When the lawbreaker does not get caught or is caught and set free without consequence, it sets up a rivalry.

Three-year-old Timmy got into his sixteen-year-old brother's stuff and broke something. Ralph, the sixteen-year-old, goes to Mom and Dad and explains the situation. Mom and Dad say, "Oh well, he's just a little kid," and do nothing about Timmy's transgression. Ralph feels resentful because his things were violated. Apparently, there is no justice system in the home. He gets even with his younger brother, Timmy, when Mom and Dad aren't watching.

If the younger child's "space" is violated or he or she is picked on, and Mom and Dad don't stop it, the younger child will get even by breaking toys, interfering when the older child's friends come over, or by just being a pest. Mom and Dad need to look beyond the child's behavior to what's really going on.

Ralph has his things and whether they are special to his younger brother or to his parents is not the issue—they are special to him. Timmy needed to be corrected and needed to make restitution for what happened. Then the parents must set guidelines concerning Ralph's room and possessions. Consequences should be established at the same time.

When God sets up a justice system in a home, obedience to the rules is required of everyone. Younger doesn't mean guiltless. Older doesn't mean stronger, or more powerful and therefore exempt from certain rules. When the home's justice system is under the admonition of the Lord, the rules apply to everyone. In families where the mom or dad feels the rules don't apply to them, the children will feel resentment and begin to violate the system in order to get even and, in their eyes, balance the unbalanced scales. The days are over when Mom or Dad can say, "Do what I say and not what I do." God holds the parents responsible for the example set—the modeling—for their children.

Mom and Dad should be honest with their children about the areas where God is working in their life that aren't changed yet. They should show them that they are working toward that change. Parents should not excuse their behavior; they want God to change it. When Jesus Christ is Lord in the home, He requires that every knee bows to Him. Every person repents if they've lied. Every person repents if they've stolen. Every person repents if they've violated someone else's integrity. *Agape* love values each person the same way. Just because they're Mom and Dad does not give them a right to violate God's laws.

Many years ago, Wayne had the rule, "What is yours is mine and what's mine is mine." Our home was established by that rule. If the children wanted to use his tools, they had to ask. But Wayne could use anything that was theirs because in his rationalization, he had spent the money to buy it—it was in his house, so it was his. When Wayne bought David a motorcycle, in Wayne's thinking, it was his motorcycle, because it was in his house and he had spent his money to buy it.

One day, David came running in the house screaming because he was so mad and so upset. He was yelling, "Dad requires me to ask to use his tools, but he didn't ask to use my motorcycle." Wayne was outside riding David's motorcycle without asking permission. Of course, Wayne didn't feel he needed to ask permission, but David was right; he should have. God's wisdom in handling this was to say, "David, you're right. I'd be mad like you are. I'd feel violated, used, abused, not cared about, not understood when things were taken without being asked for. I'd feel all of that. But right now, that's the standard your dad has. So you have a choice. You can choose to forgive your dad for the sin he walks in or you can harden your heart and get even because you're angry. But I don't want you to be angry and sin because the anger isn't the issue, It's the "X." David, Wayne wants God to change him but that's not something God has changed yet, so let's pray for God to encounter him in this issue, because God is just and He will correct this."

We prayed, asking God to forgive Wayne like Paul was forgiven by Stephen when Stephen was being stoned to death by Paul. Stephen had prayed, "Lord, lay not this sin to their charge" (Acts 7:60, KJV), and as Jesus had prayed on the Cross (Luke 23:34), "Father, forgive them; for they know not what they do." We stood in the garage praying for God to forgive Wayne—he didn't know what he was doing. We prayed, "God, encounter him." This incident taught my son that God is a living God, as he watched Him change his dad.

God is going to establish His justice system according to His Spirit, not according to what His children feel is right and wrong. His Spirit will make an eternal change in hearts.

Talebearing

> *Where no wood is, there the fire goeth out: so where*
> *there is no talebearer, the strife ceaseth.*
> *(Proverbs 26:20, KJV)*

Another reason for conflict between siblings is talebearing. A talebearer is someone who gossips and slanders.

191

In this scenario, let's suppose that Beth and Jennie resolved their conflict over the sweater. Jennie now goes to her brother, Bob, and starts talking about Beth, "Do you know what Beth did to my sweater?" Jennie is now a talebearer and is causing strife to come between Bob and Beth.

Mom needs to recognize that there are still some issues with Jennie. Is she still angry? Does she feel that the system set-up was unfair and unjust? Is she still hurting emotionally? Does she still feel it's not fair and still want to get even? Or does she like to gossip? Does she like to talk about others because it makes her feel better? Is she so insecure that she feels better about herself by putting Beth down? It could be all of these or none of these reasons, but Mom needs to help Jennie.

Some boundaries need to be established in the home concerning reporting an incident to another sibling instead of dealing with it in a straightforward manner—and only with the other person involved in the situation. The Bible is very clear—go to the brother (or sister) you have offended or who has offended you.

Proverbs 25:9-10 says, "Debate your case with your neighbor, and do not disclose the secret to another; lest he who hears it expose your shame, and your reputation be ruined" (NKJV). Ultimately, a talebearer will gain a reputation as a gossip. If a child will gossip at home, he or she will gossip with friends and ultimately will lose trust with them. Parents need to help the talebearing child to deal with the root of the problem, not just deal with gossiping. Why do they need to talk? Do they feel devalued?

"He that uttereth a slander, is a fool" (Proverbs 10:18, KJV). When Jennie reported the story to Bob, she became a fool in God's eyes. Proverbs 17:9 says, ". . . he who repeats a matter separates friends" (NKJV). When Jennie repeated the matter to Bob, Bob developed a picture of Beth that unconsciously created a separation between he and Beth. Bob began thinking, "Beth was not right in doing what she did," and by thinking this, he began to take sides against Beth.

To bring healing, Jennie needs to apologize to Bob and Beth for repeating the matter, and Beth and Bob need to forgive her. It's important for one or both parent to pray with Jennie specifically for the "X" area that caused her to repeat the tale. Beth will need to deal with her hurt and feelings of inadequacy. By agreeing and siding with the report, Bob laid hold of a concept about Beth that he must now change through prayer.

We can't change our own hearts, but Jesus Christ can. He came to save us from our deceitful, wicked hearts. Don't expect your children to stop gossiping, rather ask them to allow the Holy Spirit to change their hearts. When the heart change occurs, your children will stop gossiping.

Iverna:

Sibling rivalry doesn't disappear when one of the combatants leaves home. Older children are not immune to the feelings that cause conflict either.

Just because a youngster becomes old enough to go away to college doesn't mean he or she no longer needs Mom or Dad for anything except money. A mother of a large family told me about her twenty-year-old son who came in wanting her attention one day when she had her hands full taking care of a little one. He could see that she was busy, but he just stood in the doorway, his presence demanding her attention anyway.

Frustrated at being torn in two directions at once, the mother complained, "Son, can't you see that I have all I can do to take care of this situation just now?"

Well, he saw, of course, but he stood his ground for a moment before turning to go out.

"All right, Mom," he said. "But it seems like you're always too busy for me. I need a mother, too, you know."

The mother got the message loud and clear, and she was careful to be all ears the next time he favored her with his presence.

Never let your children feel rejected, even when they are old enough to be more or less on their own, when they get married, or when they go away to college. You can't afford to divorce yourself from the child who may be coming home only for occasional weekends. Do all you can to keep the family unity, to encourage the youngsters to feel a part of one another.

Try to arrange to be at home when the child who lives away drops in. Make yourself available to meet his or her needs. Don't turn their old room into a guest room their first week away from home. Don't move his or her things to a storage closet or smaller bedroom. Let them keep on sharing the number-one spot with brothers and sisters. Let him or her know that they are still an important member of the family setup. That knowledge is vital to the child who lives away from home.

Another important thing to realize in preserving the closeness of the family relationship with grown-up children is that parents don't have to become a slave to their visiting-for-the-weekend college student. Sure, they'll bring in a loaded laundry bag of dirty clothes, but if you've brought them up right, they'll remember how to use the washer and dryer for themselves. It will be good for them to resume their usual chores when home for a few days. What better time for a mother and daughter to visit than when they are washing and drying the dishes together? Or for a father and son to have real fellowship than when they're raking the leaves in the front yard on Saturday afternoon. Mother and son can refresh their relationship while she shows him how to replace a missing button on his shirt. Dad can reassure himself in regard to his daughter's safety and strengthen the bond between them as he helps her change the oil in her car.

It's not necessary to blow the budget on a standing rib roast for your visiting older children either. They'll feel more like they're still really a part of the family if you serve them canned soup or a peanut butter sandwich once in a while, just like in the old days. It's the quality of love you give them, not the cut of meat, that makes them secure in their place in the family.

One mother found herself with two daughters away in college at the same time. Both were in nearby schools, so they were able to come home almost every weekend. There was no need for a lot of letters back and forth, because the family would be together for the weekend almost before a letter could be delivered. In emergencies, it was even possible for the mother to get through to the girls via the dormitory telephone.

One of the girls took the matter of an empty mailbox in her stride, realizing her parents were busy with many other things. But the other girl was upset about her empty mailbox and insisted that her mom write to her often.

At first, the mom felt quite indignant that her daughter was so demanding of her. Then she recognized a real need in that child to have the assurance of family love in her new away-from-home life. Disciplining herself to write her daughter a note of some kind every single day for a week, the mother found her own attitude toward the child's attitude softening. What she began as a grit-my-teeth-and-get-it-over-with chore became a time of real blessing to her.

It seems to be a law of life that whenever we do something to meet the need of another person, love for others grows in us. Expression of love is needed, and everybody is benefited from poured-out love. And as we submit ourselves in love to one another, our own needs are met.

Dianne:
How to Minister to Conflicts

By dealing with their "X"s, siblings can learn how to love, support, and nurture one another through the power of the Holy Spirit.

Greg, a sixteen-year-old, has just hit Joey, a ten-year-old, in the nose. Joey then runs in the house crying, "Greg just hit me in the nose." What is the best way to resolve this conflict?

Remain objective. Parents must remain detached from a situation such as this, doing whatever is necessary to recognize their own issues. Do they have a favorite whose side they're going to take? In this conflict, they may be thinking, "Oh, my goodness, the bully has picked on the baby," automatically taking the side of the youngest because they see the bloody nose. But they don't yet know the conflict or the situation.

Another issue the parent must deal with might be in comparing their children. If they've compared their assertive sixteen-year-old, Greg, to a passive sixteen-year-old, they'll think, "Here he is again being aggressive," and are against him already. Or, if they've compared him to another one of their children who never hit, they think, "Why can't he be like so-and-so?" These feelings will keep them from staying objective in solving this particular conflict.

Maybe Mom and Dad have a tendency to believe the first person who gets to them. Proverbs 18:17 says, "The first one to plead his cause seems right, until his neighbor comes and examines [or scrutinizes] him" (NKJV). The natural heart's tendency is to believe the first person who talks to them until the second comes and questions it. Questions such as, "What about this and what about that?" bring the story into perspective. It's not that they are lying—they're only telling their side of the story, not the whole story. To remain objective, parents must hear both sides.

Remember the goal. The role in conflict resolution is to teach and model biblical problem-solving—it's not just to have the children stop fighting, or to have one win and one lose. Parents must allow the Holy Spirit to teach them His way of resolving conflicts.

Biblical Problem Solving

Luke 17:3-4 says to pay attention and always be on your guard. If your brother sins against you, you should tell him so, reproving him. If he repents, forgive him. Even if he sins against you seven times in a day and turns to you seven times and says, "I repent," you must forgive him. This means giving up resentment and considering the offense annulled.

Matthew 5:23-24 says that when you've sinned against a brother, you must leave your gift at the altar and make it right with him. Then you can offer your gift.

Principle 1: "Take heed to yourselves . . ." (Luke 17:3, KJV). Look at yourself first. In Luke 6:39-42, the passage concludes with, ". . . first take the log out of your own eye, and then you will see clearly to take out the speck that is in your brother's eye" (NASB).

Teach your children to take heed to themselves by looking for the log that is in their eye. When Joey comes wanting to solve the problem of being hit by Greg, according to principle number one, they are both to look at their own part of the conflict. What's the log? Is it jealousy? Natural desires going unfulfilled? Was there a comparison or competition? Did they not feel loved or special? What's the issue?

God requires His children to first take responsibility for their own behavior, not report and place blame on the other person. If Greg had said, "If Joey hadn't kicked me, I wouldn't have hit him in the nose," he would have been placing blame on somebody else.

Because it is difficult for an individual to recognize what motivated an action—what was in their heart—it is wise to have your children ask the Holy Spirit to show them their own heart. He is the Spirit of truth (John 16:6) and the One who can search the heart.

When I first began teaching David this principle, I sent him to his room to pray and ask the Holy Spirit to show him why he had hit his sister. He came back saying, "I didn't hear anything."

"Then go back and pray again."

As he went back to his room, I prayed, "Lord, I'm asking You to forgive David for his sin that has hardened his heart so he can't hear You. I ask You to speak to him." Then I asked the Lord to show me David's issues so I could train him.

Sure enough, a few minutes later, David came out of his room saying, "Well, I don't know if it's God or not; I don't know if it's my own thoughts or not." He told me what he was thinking and I was able to say, "Yes, that was God, to one point," and "No, that was just your own desire," to another point.

This is an excellent way to teach your children how to hear God. It's exciting because when God speaks there is no argument, and the child has a revelation from the Holy Spirit. With the revelation comes the grace and whatever is needed for the healing.

Once both children have come to the place where they know what their issue was and for what they need to repent, then they should tell Mom or Dad what it is. If Mom or Dad agrees, they say, "Okay, how are you going to say it to your brother/sister?" Then they can show them how to approach their sibling and role model it for the child. If Mom or Dad doesn't agree with what they've said, they should send the child back for more prayer till they agree with it, knowing it's what God is saying. When both children are ready to repent, then they are ready to deal with each other.

Once the children have gotten the log out of their own eye, they can see clearly the speck in their brother or sister's eye. The Holy Spirit has already begun to work change in their hearts, preparing them for repentance and forgiveness. When the Holy Spirit does His work, the children don't want to get even and prove their point. This makes them ready for principle number two.

Principle 2: Reprove your brother or sister. Set a time for the two participants in the conflict to come together and talk. This can happen in minutes—it doesn't have to take days or hours. It can become so automatic the children can do it right on the spot. By simply stopping and saying, "Wait a minute. I need to ask God to show me what this is," they can then reprove each other right away. But Mom and Dad must teach them how to resolve conflicts. So establish a time for the siblings to come together.

In reproving their brother or sister, their attitude must be according to the Word of God. Galatians 6:1 says to be controlled by the Holy Spirit, which starts happening as the children are asking the Holy Spirit to show them their issue—the motivation for their conduct. They're beginning to allow the Spirit to be in charge of it. 2 Timothy 2:25 says to correct your opponent with a spirit of meekness, hoping God will grant them repentance. When the child goes to their brother or sister to reprove him or her, or deal with the issues that are there, do they want their sibling to repent or do they want to get even? If they want to get even, or to get their sibling in trouble, they're not in the spirit of meekness and not looking for repentance to come.

God corrects His children because He loves them (Revelation 3:19). So look to see—are the children being motivated by *agape* love, unconditional love, or self-love that wants to get even? If it's self-motivated, then the children need to pray and ask Father for His love.

"Open rebuke is better than love that is hidden" (Proverbs 27:5, AMP). Children should be taught to deal with each other up front—to love one another enough to speak face-to-face and not to talk behind each other's back.

Now that the children have searched their hearts, praying for the Holy Spirit's guidance in their attitudes and reasons for the reproving of their brother or sister, it's time to repent. As each child begins to apologize to the other, the love of God begins to flow—healing begins to flow. Then they reprove each other by stating what they think they saw in the situation, the reason for "I hit you in the nose," and the reason for "I provoked the hitting in the nose." Once both sides of the story are told, the total picture will be seen, the "X"'s will be revealed, and everyone will see what the motives were behind the behavior.

The story with Greg and Joey as told by Greg: "You broke my favorite record. I had asked you, Joey, not to come into my room, but you did, even after I told you three times not to. I felt the only way you'd listen to me, and get out of my room was if I hit you in the nose." The whole story comes out as to why the teenager hit the child, even though the hitting was not appropriate.

Principle 3: If brother or sister repents, forgive. Now that each child has told their side of the story, repenting for what he or she sees as their responsibility, they need to forgive each other. This forgiveness involves the mind, the will, and the emotions. Emotional forgiveness has to do with being able to love your enemy, bless your enemy, and do good to your enemy (Luke 6:27-28). That's emotional forgiveness. The participants in the conflict need to pray for the Holy Spirit to totally heal the hurt, the brokenness, and the wounds. When this occurs, the children will be able to wholeheartedly bless their enemy (their brother or sister) and do good for their enemy (their brother or sister).

The parents' responsibility is to lead the children in prayer for this kind of healing, cleansing, and restoration. The Holy Spirit is the One to heal the brokenness, the "X"'s (where they felt violated, unloved, misunderstood). After the parents pray, they should have each child pray for his or her sibling. Teach them—model for them—how to bring the Holy Spirit in to enable them to do good; to be honest enough to say, "Father, I still hurt and I still want to punch my brother in the nose. Give me the grace to bless my brother. Show me how I can bless my brother."

After prayer, the parents should ask each child to think of a way they can bless their brother or sister. In the preceding scenario, Joey could say, "I want to do good for you and buy you a new record." Greg might say, "I want to do good for you. I know you like to play basketball so I'll take you to do that." Let the children come up with their own blessing for their sibling. The goal here is a restoration of the relationship—teaching them to come to the place where they're no longer enemies but blessing each other and doing good to the "enemy" they had.

Principle 4: Restitution. If there is a situation where the healing does not come right away and the combatants still want to get even, then the parents and children should pray until the healing is a fact. Deal honestly with the pain until it's healed. How long will it take? Until it's healed. There's no set time—pray until they can do good for their enemy. Pray daily, moment by moment, week by week, month by month, until they can come back and bless their enemy.

The goal is not behavior modification—the goal is a change of heart. It's not enough for them just to kiss and make up and yet still hate each other. The children must be honest and say, "I still hate. I'm still hurting. I still feel angry." If this is so, then Mom or Dad can say, "Okay, let's take that before the Lord telling Him, 'Lord, heal us. We're angry. Give us Your love. Give us Your grace. Give us Your mercy. Give us Your longsuffering. Whatever we need, we're trusting the Holy Spirit to reproduce that in our lives.'" Having done this, then parents and children can go on about their day or business. If a day later, the child is saying, "I still hate him. I'm still mad. I'm still hurting," then pray again, "Jesus we're asking You to continue to heal. Pour in the oil and the wine, cover us with Your blood, until the cleansing and healing comes." Healing does come. God does a total work, a complete work, but until it's healed, don't confess what isn't true. The truth is Christ heals and He will heal it.

If You Do the Crime, You Gotta Do the Time

Despite the repentance and restitution of the participant's in the conflict, the parents are required to establish consequences. If the hitting was inappropriate, discipline with consequences needs to come. If the record was broken by younger brother, restitution needs to be established. If a younger sibling has messed up their room, it needs to be cleaned up. If money was stolen, it needs to be given back. Then whatever the justice system established in the home dictates for inappropriate behavior, it must be followed through. This brings total healing. Wrong behavior is corrected. Hurts are healed. The "X"s—the needs of those in conflict—are met and ministered to by God.

One family had a boy who continually stole, and as an adult, kept right on doing so because he had reaped no consequences growing up. There wasn't true biblical restitution and resolving of the conflict by dealing with the "X"s of why he stole. Often, he stole from his younger brother because the younger brother was getting attention he wanted. Stealing wasn't the issue. They didn't discover the "X," so there was no healing for the boy. If healing had come, restitution of what was stolen would be part of his healing.

<u>Principle 5</u>: Establish a justice system. Every home must have a justice system. It needs to be established, enforced, renewed, or updated when needed. There are certain rules to be established that everyone in the home must know. For instance:

Children are not allowed to have fun in destructive ways.

Each child's things, or space, or room, are to be respected. When the sign on the door says, "Don't Enter," or the teenager says, "Don't come into my room," no one should enter the room.

Older children are not allowed to tease the younger children.

The younger are not allowed to harass or bug the older ones.

The children don't always have to play with each other.

201

They ought to have their own friends—have their time alone—or they will resent each other.

When Daniel was little, the older kids were available to take care of him. Because we were willing to pay for the baby-sitting, we didn't create resentment and the teenagers sometimes had a choice. They didn't have to baby-sit just because they were in the family. We respected each of them as a person, saying, "You're valuable, your time is valuable and we want to pay you for the time when you take care of Daniel." There were also other times they took care of him without being paid, because they were part of the family.

Principle 6: The justice system is just, not fair. It's harder to establish a justice system when you have two teenagers and have to handle each one differently according to temperament, maturity, and emotional development.

When David was twenty-two and still living at home while he attended college, his room was in an organized mess. He worked full-time along with going to school full-time. Casey, his brother who was seventeen, had a messy room and we were on Casey, training him in how to keep his room clean. He didn't see us get on David's case to clean his room, so a rivalry was setting up between the two of them because Casey did not see the system as just.

We had to explain why the different expectations of David weren't fair, but were *just* according to our justice system. God was doing something different in Casey's life at that time in training him than what He was doing in David's. Casey needed to know he was going to have to deal with this "unfairness" all of his life. He would be in situations where God was focusing on one thing in his life and not the same thing in someone else's life. He would think it unfair, but it would be just.

Years ago, we were having a financial problem and I was praying for God to bless us financially. We went to church and someone stood up and shared the miracle God had done financially in their life. I was hurt, and mad at God because I didn't think it was fair. God said, "I have children who are crippled. Do you want Me to be fair or just?" I realized fairness meant "even Steven" so God was saying, "Some of My children are crippled. Do you want fairness? Then that means you're crippled, too. You're only looking for the blessings, not for what is just."

God knew how to handle me financially and He knew what was *just* for me. Did I like it? No. But I asked God to change my heart so that I could embrace it—see the value in it—not the fairness but the justice in it. God is a just God and He wants us establishing a justice system in our homes.

The justice system has to be established according to the child's age. Casey must clean his room in a way not expected of Daniel, but each one has an expectation that they're to live up to—and if they don't, there are consequences. Those consequences are spelled out very clearly for each one. Casey might not be able to use the car, but for Daniel it could be not being able to play a video game. Each one has their own justice system within the family justice system. It's according to age and personality and development, not according to "even Steven."

Principle 7: Agreement. It's not enough to establish a justice system, but every one has to agree to it. Do they understand the terms? Do they understand the boundaries? Do they understand the rules? This is the time to say, "I don't agree with it," or "I'm mad," or "I'm sad about it." There's not a penalty for a child being upset about the system. The issue is what will bring them to an agreement? Where do they see it as still unjust? If they don't understand and agree to the justice system, they'll undermine it and get back at us.

Make sure when restitution is established that there is agreement to the restitution—and follow-through with it.

If there are different values or standards between the step-children because of the different homes, parents must establish "us" rules. These rules should not be what was in this home or what was in that home, but what are *our* rules and values. What are *we* going to do in this home? In that home he may do that, but here, we're going to do this. As the family begins to walk this out, they may find that what they thought they agreed to is not what they really want, because they sabotage it by getting even. That's when the family needs to continue to work toward a system where the agreement finally comes out in behavior.

Principle 8: Open communication. Psychologist John Powell established a concept of five levels of communication. The first level is cliché, "Hi, how are you?" The second level is talking about others or the gossip level. Number three is sharing what we think about situations. The fourth level is sharing our feelings, and the fifth is total open communication.

Biblical homes need to be at the fifth level of communication. This means there is freedom to share what each family member thinks and feels without being intimidated or feeling stupid. There should be times when they come together and clear the air, saying what they're feeling and thinking, sharing what they feel is unfair. In this open communication, the parents need to continue looking to see if sides are being taken or favoritism is present. They need to talk it through so that conflicts can continue to be resolved. In open communication, it's necessary to learn to speak the truth in God's love, so that *agape*—unconditional love—will surround them and teach them how to minister His truth to one another.

God Will Supply the Grace

Whether this system of conflict resolution is established in your home or not, God does gives you the grace to do it. He doesn't just give His children rules, laws, and regulations but grace and mercy to walk it out in the power of the Holy Spirit. Parents can daily choose to have life in their homes. They can choose to minister God's health and wholeness—to repent, to forgive, to allow the Holy Spirit to bring healing. Parents and children alike may choose not to be a talebearer, not to compare and compete with each other or their children.

The family can choose to allow the Lord to teach them how to love and value each person, so that His Spirit of love and life will be evident instead of the spirit of strife and contention. Dad, Mom, and each child can learn how to build up one another, edifying and thinking the best of each other because of the Good News of the Gospel, so they don't rival one another, but in love, restore one another.

9

Your Child and Sex

Iverna:

The area of physical and sexual relationships seems to be one of the most difficult for parents to handle, yet it is of the utmost importance that it be handled properly.

At first glance, it would seem that this responsibility could be broken down into two main areas: providing sound information and training right attitudes. The two are so closely interrelated, however, that it's difficult, if not impossible, to separate one from the other. This is good. It means that parents have an opportunity to teach their children right attitudes along with every bit of information they impart to them.

The human body is wonderfully made, and answering children's questions about their bodies is one of the greatest privileges of parenthood. With every question their child asks them, parents are handed an opportunity to guide their child's life.

I'm often asked by parents, "When should I begin to tell my child where babies come from?" No one can set down a hard and fast age limit because children are not all cut from the same pattern. Some children develop a curiosity earlier than others. As a general rule, when a child is old enough to ask a question, he or she is old enough to handle the answer to it. Certainly parents should never turn aside their youngster's questions about the origin of life, because if they don't answer those questions, someone else will, someone who may instill wrong attitudes in the process.

In attempting to answer children's questions, parents need to be sure that they have really heard and understood what their children are asking. Only then can they be sure of making an appropriate reply. For instance, a child's "Mama, where did Uncle Harry come from?" is likely to require a simple, "From Atlanta," instead of a lengthy birds and bees explanation.

Beginning at preschool age, youngsters develop some awareness of their sexuality. Certainly a large percentage of boys under nine years of age have had a sexual experience of some kind with themselves. Your child's baby-face appearance is no excuse for not teaching a youngster about his or her sex drives.

"But I'm too reticent and shy to talk about sex with my kids." Instead of being proud of their reticence, parents should strive to put aside their embarrassment and shyness and learn to talk with their youngsters about the things that concern them.

If Mom and Dad absolutely cannot make themselves uninhibited enough to respond to their child's needs in this area, they can give answers indirectly. Public libraries, church libraries, and religious bookstores have many beautiful and sound sex education books written from a wholesome Christian perspective. After examining some books on these subjects, parents can buy or borrow the ones with which they feel most comfortable.

It would be wise to acquire these aids before their child comes to them with the loaded questions. Mom and Dad may be surprised at how easy it is to sit down with their questioning youngster and read through the books together. Hopefully, they'll find their own inhibitions relaxing as they read about how wonderfully God has planned for Christian marriage to provide loving families for new babies born into the world. Parents may gain a new respect for their own bodies and be educated along with their child.

Dianne:

The Word of God has been given to us as our manual for every aspect of life and it includes principles in the area of sex. Because there is little mentioned about reproduction or menstruation, we look at books on the market that give us those specific details regarding our sexuality. We cannot afford ignorance. There are many good books that help explain in detail the biological aspects of our sexuality, and we mustn't let pride, embarrassment, or shame keep us from studying and learning in this area. The more we know, the more comfortable we will be in imparting knowledge to our children. Even though our educational background may have taught us much about sex, we need to update what we learned in school with the latest information on human sexuality. As parents we should keep studying and finding out what's being discovered today. (For a list of suggested books, see Appendix.)

Iverna:

From the ages of two to five, youngsters are quite naturally interested in reproduction, particularly if there's a new baby on the way. There's no need to turn their curiosity aside if there's a pregnancy in their family. Mom and Dad can make it beautiful and precious to them.

My Debbie was five when Dan was born. She enjoyed putting her hand on my abdomen while we counted the unborn baby's kicks together. We talked about whether it would be a boy or girl. She helped me pick out a name for the baby. Sometimes, I must admit, she asked me some rather embarrassing questions. But they shouldn't have been embarrassing to me. A child's curiosity isn't embarrassing. It's natural, normal, and wholesome, and it needs to be satisfied.

If an otherwise normal child has not asked Mom and Dad any questions about his or her sexuality by the age of nine or ten years old, the parents need to initiate some discussions on the subject. Again, well-planned books can be a big help in breaking the ice and in overcoming barriers of false modesty or embarrassment.

Perhaps their youngster has already entered his or her teens and the parents are certain that he or she has received basic sex information from peers or teachers, but they haven't personally discussed anything in this area with him or her. That's not justification for putting it off any longer. Their child needs to feel that he or she can come to Mom and Dad with questions and problems in this area. If the right opportunity doesn't seem to present itself, the parents can create an opportunity on their own. The same libraries and bookstores that have helpful sex education books for smaller children have many soundly-written books for teens, giving Bible-based answers to the questions they might ask.

Mom and Dad don't have to sit down and read these books with their teenager, of course, but they should read them before they hand them to him or her. They can say, "Here's something I found in the bookstore the other day that might be interesting to you." If that direct approach is too tough for them, they can leave a good book or two on their teen's dresser or desk where he or she is sure to see it. They can add new books to the collection from time to time, doing all they can to open a channel of communication.

Boys will need help from their parents to understand what happens to their bodies at puberty, so they won't be afraid or ashamed. They need to know why they feel how they feel, and what they're supposed to do with their feelings. They need to be taught how to handle their sex drives. This very essential instruction must be given at home, regardless of school education on the subject. Home should be the safe place to learn by asking questions and feeling support in working through frustrations.

Hands Off!

Problems concerning masturbation sometimes arise in teenagers who develop social problems due to lack of or improper teaching about it. Some boys grow up thinking they are different from everyone else, condemned by God, and condemned by society because of masturbation or the unavoidable wet dreams.

If youngsters are to grow up with a satisfactory sexual adjustment to life, they must be taught to understand themselves and their sexuality. Little boys and girls should know that they're going to have certain feelings, certain dreams, and certain reactions to actions or remarks from the opposite sex. Early knowledge will help children to develop tools with which to handle feelings without guilt and fear.

When their little girl questions them about her normal biological reaction to something a boy has said to her, Mom and Dad don't have to squelch her with an outraged, "That was a naughty little boy to talk to you that way! I don't want you to speak to him again as long as you live!" That would set up, in the girl's mind, a dangerous rejection of her sexuality. She'd begin to feel that sex is a dirty word, a no-no.

When parents find their youngsters handling their own genitals, they must not rant and rave, saying, "That's terrible!" or "Jesus doesn't like that!" Doing so would plant seeds of guilt, and later on, when their sons or daughters are supposed to have a beautiful honeymoon with the man or woman of their dreams, their subconscious may prevent it. A better way to handle such a situation is simply to say matter-of-factly, "It would be better if you didn't do that." This needs to be taught in the light of the entire teaching on masturbation. "It may feel good, but it isn't necessary for you to do it just because it feels good."

If they are very young, give them something else to occupy their attention. In the case of a teenager, Mom and Dad can talk with them about what's going on in their life and they may find it is simply a reaction to frustration in other areas for which they are trying to compensate. It would be a wonderful thing for the father to talk with his son and share his own frustrations, i.e., pressures from work, expectations from other people that he can't meet, etc., and how that affects male sexual drives. Likewise, it's wonderful if the mother can say to her daughter, "We all have frustrations and want to just escape the world at times, but there are other ways to do it than this." Such understanding, absolutely void of any guilt projection, will be helpful to the youngster. It doesn't have to be an issue, and Mom and Dad don't have to be psychologists to handle it.

The Sins of the Mother

An attractive young married woman came to me for counseling. She claimed to be in love with her husband, but she confessed, "I just can't stand for him to touch me in any intimate way. Our sexual relations are pure agony for me."

As she told me about her life, going way back to her childhood, we found the root of her problem. When she was four years old, her mother had found her with a little boy in a barn. She had her panties pulled down and the little boy was standing there, looking at her. The mother was furious. She spanked the little girl hard then and there, shamed her with loud indignation, marched her into the house without her panties, and made her stand before the whole family and tell them what she had done. Then the mother went to the little boy's house and made the child go through the same nightmarish scene with them.

The child herself didn't realize how scarred she was from the experience until she grew up and got married. She had assumed that it would be natural for her to make a normal sexual adjustment to marriage, but her life was hell. After she realized where her frigidity had begun, she was able to receive forgiveness and let the inhibiting scar tissue be done away with.

There is no need for parents overreact when they catch small youngsters looking at each other's external sex organs. This is a common result of a natural curiosity. It is not necessarily or automatically naughtiness.

When parents discover youngsters looking at one another in this way, they sometimes make loud noises of disgust and move in immediately to separate the youngsters. A harsh scolding follows, often accompanied by a severe spanking, and a guilt-producing, "I don't want you to play with Johnny ever again—he's a nasty boy!"

Maybe the incident wasn't Johnny's fault. Their own precious little darling Lucinda might have suggested the new game.

No matter who was at fault, parents can't afford to set the stage for the child to think that sex is evil.

They can approach the youngsters calmly, and speak to their own child loud enough for the others to hear, but without condemning and angry language. A simple "I don't want you to do that anymore" is adequate. An acceptable activity can be suggested for everybody. After that, of course, Mom and Dad will want to supervise their child's playtime more closely for a while. They can provide the setting for happy, acceptable recreation and do away with the temptation of garages or other concealed play areas by putting locks on doors or otherwise making them effectively out-of-bounds.

It is not necessary for parents to be forever spying on their children, but they shouldn't wear blinders, either. They should trust their children as far as they reasonably can. If they find evidence of forbidden behavior a second time, they should handle it as calmly as they did at first. If the misbehavior persists, they can employ some form of punishment that will dissuade future action along the same lines. It's important to make clear to the child, however, that the spanking or the withdrawal of privileges is not because the thing he or she did was so wrong in itself, but because he or she had been disobedient to their parents rules.

Sex Education Begins at Home

Schools today offer sex education classes but this in no way lessens parental responsibility. As the children bring books and information home from school, a door is opened that can help parents to relax their hang-ups so they can talk about such things. Parents who are already doing their job at home can feel confident that their kids won't be led astray by what the teacher says at school. And parents who haven't done anything at home are sometimes challenged to begin—in order to counteract what they feel is wrong teaching at school.

A nineteen-year-old girl said, "Iverna, so help me God, my parents are Christians, but I have never discussed menstruating or sex with either one of them in my whole life. Two people have taught me everything I know—a girlfriend and a boy who almost got me in trouble."

In this country, with all its looseness and immorality, there are still young people entering marriage with only the sketchiest information about sexual relationships. They are discovering what sex is about only by active participation. A good program of sex education in the schools can help to correct that situation. But the schools cannot take the place of parents in teaching the right attitudes toward sexual relationships. Parents do not always realize this. They may turn away from the God-given responsibility for training their children because the children have more formal education than the parents.

One day, I was speaking with the father of a teenage boy who knew very little about sex and yet whose drives were at their peak. The boy was behaving in some ways that were socially unacceptable, and his mother had asked me to persuade the boy's father to talk to him.

"Me? Talk to my kid about sex?" the father blurted out at me. "Why, my son knows a lot more about sex than I do."

The son, who had gotten his limited information about sex from school and friends, couldn't possibly know more than the father did, unless he'd had more experience. Physical diagrams on the blackboard in a hygiene class, or teaching of the sex act between male and female in sex education class, do not constitute adequate training about sex. What he had learned from his peers probably told him little more than, "Sex is the greatest thing that ever happened to anybody. Man, you ought to try it!" 'Trying it' in the back seat of somebody's car, scared to death he'd get caught, would increase his need to learn what his father could teach him in the area of attitudes.

Homosexuality

Godly parents have the opportunity to impart information based on the Word of God concerning the sexual act that will never be taught in the school. In schools, unfortunately, it is being taught that some men prefer men and some women prefer women, and if that is their preference, they should be allowed to pursue it without prejudice.

Christian parents, while teaching against homosexuality, must make clear to their children that it isn't all evil people who are engaged in this act and that they, with the Lord, must learn to hate the sin, but love the sinner. Parents should not teach them to reject people who are in this lifestyle, nor even to be afraid of them. Christian parents need to help their children establish godly standards of their own so that they are unaffected by homosexual behavior—neither tempted by it or moved to hate the person involved. Their children can then be a light and witness, showing the benefits of the heterosexual relationship, causing the homosexual to be free in conversing with them, enabling the children to win them for Christ.

The Word of God teaches that there is male and female and that is what constitutes a marriage. Parents not only have the right to teach their children that, but they have the responsibility.

Dianne:

Much is being taught about alternative lifestyles, but the Word of God is very clear on homosexuality and lesbianism. There is no debate. It's a sin, explicitly stated in Romans 1:24-32; 1 Corinthians 6:9-10; Leviticus 18:22; 20:13, but it is sin that can be repented of, forgiven, and the person can be cleansed of its stain. So while we continue to study about our human sexuality, whenever that information is contrary to the Word of God, His Word is the final authority. Homosexuals today want their "rights," believing they were created to be same-sex lovers, but since the Word tells us it's not normal, we need to keep opening the Scriptures to our children for God's perspective and viewpoint.

We need to protect our children from same-sex sins. We must wisely discern all who come in contact with our children on a regular basis—every soccer and little league coach, baby-sitter, or Sunday school teacher—in order to guard our children from those who will turn their hearts from the Lord. We must prayerfully observe the boys with whom our sons play and the girls with whom our daughters play. We cannot let our children play at homes where older children are demonstrating homosexual behavior.

We need to be alert that the gay community has a plot and design for our children. In the "Gay Manifesto" (an article printed in the *Gay Community News*, Feb. 15-21, 1987 and printed into the

Congressional Record), it is recorded that gays have vowed to go everywhere the children are—boy scouts, little league, Big Sisters/ Big Brothers, church, even the school (as shcool bus drivers). We don't need to fear, but to be alert and wake up to guard our children from every form of perversion.

Iverna:

Even in the natural intercourse of male and female there is much to be taught by the godly parent that is not even understood by the ungodly. Love between a man and a woman is not simply consummated in the sexual act. This love encompasses their entire lives, and expressed in marriage in intercourse brings a closeness that was not known before. This gives reason for parents to teach their young people not to carelessly engage in sexual intercourse with one another, but to wait for that moment of awareness of love and commitment that goes hand in hand with it. This is not generally accepted teaching in society, so if children are to receive it, it will have to come from us in the home.

The Parents' Responsibility

When parents assume their children know all there is to know about sex, they make a big mistake. Even if they've had sex education classes and talked much with peers, it's the responsibility of the parents to clearly define sexuality and the guidelines they expect to be observed—and the consequences of them.

Where parents have neglected their responsibility to communicate with their children about sexual matters, they find it necessary to communicate over a tragedy later—a pregnant, unmarried daughter or a son who is being sued for paternal involvement.

Communicating with children doesn't mean lecturing them. Communicating means to sit down with the child and find out their opinions, what the input has been to their lives, how they view things, what feelings they are frustrated with, their fears, their sense

214

of inadequacy, etc. It's only then that parents can give them the proper tools of management that they need.

It's not unusual to hear a heartbroken mother say something like, "I just can't understand how she could get pregnant. I know that she knew better." Or hear a father say about his son, "I can't believe he was so stupid as to get a girl pregnant. He should have known better." These are sad, tell-tale signs that communication between parent and child was not there.

As a counselor, it's somewhat common to have a conversation with young boys just coming into a dating age who don't communicate with parents but bare their heart in the counseling session and say, "This probably sounds silly, but I don't even know how to act on a date. I'm afraid if I kiss a girl, I'll go too far," etc. While this may sound like an antiquated statement, be assured that it's still a prominent one today.

Some young men, because of a passionate experience, fear that they may be "oversexed" and finally will come around to stating this fear to a counselor. In most cases, if proper discussions with their fathers had taken place, the young men wouldn't have had to seek an outsider to get some help for their frustrations.

It's also not uncommon for girls to feel they have done something wrong because every guy they go out with tries "to put the make" on them. If she hasn't had proper guidance about dress and actions from her mother, she may certainly be inviting such behavior. If indeed she has had guidance and declares she has done everything she knows to discourage such behavior, then perhaps Mom or Dad needs to help her discover the kinds of young men she's dating.

Sympathetic Sex

This is a generation who have, by and large, disregarded manners in the name of "freedom." Many children are growing up in homes where there is no such thing as parenting—home is simply a place for eating, sleeping, and dressing. Often, these "pseudo-homeless" teenagers are magnets for the Christian boy or girl who see themselves filling a need for love and understanding in this person. In giving guidelines to their children, Christian parents must be careful not to produce prejudice toward these teens. It's not the child's fault that his or her parents have not seen fit to raise them properly, but neither is it your child's responsibility to "take care of" the neglected teen. Prayerful compassion can be shown toward this person without the Christian teenager becoming personally involved in their life. Such involvement often leads to the downfall of the Christian, unless his or her parents are diligent in keeping channels of honest communication open between them and their teen and are able to help them to prayerfully resist any temptations that might arise.

The Teenage Parent

It must be said that, regardless of all the teaching and communication that the parents endeavor to do with their children, there are those children who will violate such teaching and, for a variety of reasons, step out to experience what they have been taught is wrong.

Should parents find themselves with a pregnant teenage daughter who is unmarried or a son who is involved in a paternity suit, it's a demand upon them to overcome their sense of failure as parents and not to take out their frustration in ranting and raging and severe punishments. In rising above their own hurts, Mom and Dad can see the need to help their child through this situation with as much grace and justice as possible.

An adoption agency that I have been so impressed with through the years counsels the unmarried mother who wishes to release her child at the same time that they are counseling the would-be parents. This agency literally brings the two parties together so that they may understand that each is ministering to the other. The unwed mother is bringing to the potential parents what they cannot have on their own, and God is allowing her to make this possible. In turn, her child is going to grow up with love and proper parenting.

In this day and age, many natural mothers are coming back on the scene at a later time causing heart-breaking situations, which has

216

caused some hopeful adoptive parents to fear adopting. It's wrong, however, to throw all of the potential of adoption out simply because there's been a violation and because the godless courts don't know what is right at all.

There are some teenage mothers who desperately want to keep their child, and for them reality orientation needs to begin very early in pregnancy. They need to be guided through the entire nine-month period to realize the responsibilities they're assuming. These unwed mothers need the support of their parents. They need to understand what it is to be a single parent, the financial obligations, the options that are out there for them, etc. There are no absolutes in these situations, but each has to be evaluated individually.

Another reason there are so many unwed mothers today is because of the lack of proper parental teaching of sons. Many parents have put all the emphasis on teaching their daughters to be chaste and clean—teaching them how to behave on a date and how not to—and they've let the boys grow up just any old way. But girls don't impregnate girls.

Many boys have the attitude that they are entitled to take any girl they can get. Perhaps they saw their mothers as servants of all instead of as partners with their fathers—the queens in loving relationships with the kings in their homes. If his father belittled his mother, his father was inadvertently teaching his son, "Women are to be looked down upon." If his mother said to the children, "Don't talk to me that way," and Dad heard but didn't follow up, the boy learned from Dad's silence that women could be treated with contempt. How in the world can such a boy be expected to respect the girls he dates and the woman he marries?

Sexual Equality in the Home

Discrimination in the assignment of household chores is another factor contributing to the lack of respect some boys have for girls. Sometimes girls are taught to cook, to sew, to iron, fold clothes, and wash dishes, but because there isn't much wood-splitting or yard work to be done, the boys aren't asked to help. Doing chores is an important part of growing up to responsible maturity. If housework

217

is the only work they have for their boy to do, then Mom and Dad should put him to work at it. It won't make a sissy out of him. It will help him learn responsibility, make him more independent— able to care for his own clothing and meals as well as he does his car or home repairs, and it will help him learn respect for girls, too. Likewise, daughters should be taught to perform the more traditional male chores. She will learn the same lessons as her brother.

The Dating Dilemma

Sons should be taught that every time they pick up a date at her door, they are responsible under God and to her parents for how they treat her. When they deliver her to her door again, she should feel that she has been treated with respect and that her womanhood has been enhanced rather than degraded. God created men and women to be complements of one another, and their sons' actions should reflect that knowledge.

They must also help their girls to realize that it is their responsibility to maintain poise and character, and not become "a tease" by enticing the boy to show affection beyond obvious limits. They need to help their children understand that dating should be fun, not just a "petting" time to see how far each can go. Find out where they're going to go on dates and why.

Encourage participation in sports programs at school and other active pursuits such as bowling, skating, etc., rather than always going to a drive-in movie or something of that nature. Also, in order to maintain family structure, it's a good thing to involve the daughter's boyfriend, and the son's girlfriend, in family affairs. Have them over for an evening with the family and make it fun, whether it's dinner, or games, or swimming, or watching old movies. Getting to know their child's date can often prevent many problems, giving the parents insight on how to steer their children as they date.

The correct age for each child to begin dating is a personal thing, because parents know their child and their maturity level. When they request permission to date, parents need to take an overall look at their acceptance of responsibility in all areas. Is their school work good? Are their home chores done? Do they carry responsibility?

That might be a wonderful time to explain that if they're going to be responsible enough for dating, it needs to show in other areas.

Don't Let 'Em See You Sweat

Parents should beware of projecting fear about what their kids might do. That translates to, "My parents don't trust me," and that's a frustrating thing for young people. When they leave the house, let them leave with the comfort that Mom and Dad do trust them, but they expect them to be in at the deadline time and to call if they have any needs.

Dianne:

Even though there is a bombardment of sex and sexuality everywhere we turn—on television, billboards, and sex education programs—there are still large groups of children who do not know the truth about their bodies, reproduction, pregnancy, and menstruation. Unfortunately, there are also large groups of children who have had first-hand experience of sex through abuse, incest, and molestation, but their knowledge obtained from these experiences is warped, leaving the children tainted, bruised, and violated.

As biblical parents, it's our responsibility to teach our children that sex is a God-given blessing. God created sex with certain guidelines and parameters and presented it to us as a gift. Where there has been abuse, misuse, or violation in the area of sex, God is ever present to forgive, heal, cleanse, and restore sexuality to its healthy blessing.

Before we can minister to our children in this area, we must allow God to teach us where we lack knowledge, heal us where we've been wounded, and cleanse us where we've been abused.

Healing the Past

Obtaining knowledge in the area of sex is the easiest part of our sexual training. The harder part is to deal with the experiences we've had growing up that affect our sexuality. For instance, if we were

219

raised in an environment where touching meant sexuality, or if it was an environment where there was no touching and no affection, either will influence our thinking and behavior today. If we were raised in a home where sexual talk was perverted and abusive, that will affect us today as much as being raised in a home where sex was not talked about at all, inferring it was dirty and a sinful thing. Being raised in a home where we were not protected, guarded, and cared for, or if incest or sexual abuse took place in the home, will affect us today, just as does experimenting sexually before marriage. Every experience we had growing up influences us in the present.

Jesus Christ will bring healing and cleansing to our sexuality if we allow the Holy Spirit to convict us of sin so that we may repent and ask forgiveness. Some areas of conviction might be involvement with pornography, fornication, the abusing of another child, an encounter with a homosexual or lesbian, or using sex to get attention or to satisfy the need for affection.

God establishes the healing in the areas in which we've been abused while growing up, as well as in the results of the abuse, i.e. low self-esteem, guilt, fears, anger, obsessive behavior, lack of trust, panic attacks, eating disorders, pornography, alcoholism, drug abuse, etc.

Today, with so much talk of abuse and it's remedy, it's easy to establish formulas. We get our check list out and if we have five symptoms of the six on the list, we're sure we've been abused. That may be a lie. I can have low self-esteem, lack of trust, flashbacks, panic attacks, emotional denial, and still not have been sexually abused. Therefore, it must be the Holy Spirit who searches our hearts. He is the One to direct our healing and to show us how to walk out of these experiences to health and wholeness.

If you have been a victim of chronic abuse, either through incest or violence or neglect—any form of emotional or physical child abuse—please seek professional help. There are many Christians who are anointed of God to bring healing to these situations. Check with your pastor and see whom he would recommend.

Our responsibility is to teach our children God-given, God-inspired information regarding their bodies and to protect them from abuse. But, if I have been abused, I will probably abuse my children. If I had experiences of incest in my life, I will think it normal to reproduce it in my children. This is why it's important for God to cleanse us, the parents, of all the situations that have happened in our sexuality and experiences with sex. Then we may have God's standards, God's healing, God's perspective on training our children to walk in this area in holiness and purity.

Sexual Abuse

How do I know if my child has already been abused by a baby-sitter, someone at day care, or a relative? Books on the market today give the signs of child abuse, and we discover that they are very similar to the "X"s we discussed—the behavior that comes from having an "X" such as low self-esteem, aggressive behavior, fight/flee, eating disorders, compulsive spenders, retreating to their room, moodiness. This is why it's important to know our children and what's happening with them. We can't just check over the list and say, "Oh, this is what's happened." We need the Holy Spirit to give us revelation and understanding.

There are some very specific signs we can see in the behavior of a child that might indicate child abuse. These are from the work of David B. Peters (see Appendix).

Infants and Preschoolers

Being uncomfortable around people they previously trusted.

Fear of showers, bathrooms.

Nightmares.

Moodiness or aggressiveness.

Sexualized behavior (excessive masturbation, explicit sex play with other children).

221

Latency Age Children

Being uncomfortable around someone they previously trusted.

Specific knowledge of sexual facts beyond the developmental age.

Sexualized behavior (excessive masturbation and sexually acting out with other children).

Wearing multiple layers of clothing, especially to bed.

Being afraid of being alone.

Fear of restrooms, showers or baths.

Any change in personality or behaviors.

Obsessive behaviors, i.e. over-eating, under-eating.

Adolescence

Sexualized behavior (promiscuity, prostitution, sexual abuse of younger children).

Running away, especially in a child normally not a behavioral problem.

Drug or alcohol abuse.

Suicide gestures.

Self-mutilation.

Extreme hostility toward parent or caretaker.

Self-conscious behavior, especially regarding the body.

Wearing multiple layers of clothing, especially to bed.

Moodiness, nightmares, defiance.

All these behavioral signs might indicate your child has been sexually abused. If you suspect it, please seek your pastor for spiritual consultation and help.

Physical indications of sexual abuse will be pain and itching in the genital areas. The child will have difficulty in walking or sitting. In a girl, you'll see a vaginal discharge. They may contract some kind of a venereal disease or have unusual and offensive odors. If you suspect sexual abuse by physical indications, please see your doctor for confirmation. He will be able to take the appropriate measures.

But what if the abuse is being done by your spouse? Then for Jesus' sake, get help. Your children need help. You need help and your spouse needs help. The problem will not go away; it will get worse. If you suspect your spouse is abusing your child, please see someone for help.

If You Suspect Your Child Has Been Abused

Ask your child. Please remember: the younger the child, the more difficult it is for them to remember details and times.

Believe the child.

Let the child know it's not their fault and that you're glad they've told you.

Pray for the child. Ask Jesus to begin to minister to the hurt and the pain and the rejection.

Seek help. Check your local law enforcement agencies for information.

If there is physical injury, see a doctor and inform him of your suspicions.

Take whatever steps you can to protect your child from further abuse.

In the case of incest, make sure the molester, not the victim, leaves the home. Have your pastor or a counselor help you in dealing with the abuse that's happening in the home.

Over the last twenty years, of those people I have ministered to in the area of sexual abuse, ninety-five percent happened in the church. There have been instances involving a Sunday School teacher, the husband of a Sunday School teacher, an associate pastor's son, a youth leader's son. How can that happen in the church? The Word of God says that the heart is wicked and evil above all things (Jeremiah 17:9). Only as Jesus Christ is allowed into our lives to save and cleanse us are we set free from the sin nature.

One time when my daughter visited a new church, her money was stolen. She was so upset. "Mom, why? I was at church." But just because we were at church didn't mean that the someone there who had stolen the money was under the blood of Jesus Christ. People going to church are in the process of cleansing. If the area of their sexuality is not cleansed, they are open for perversion.

Healing the Abused

Once any abuse is reported, that does not mean the child is healed. There must be the restoration of the child to a healthy perspective regarding their sexuality. Jesus Christ can do it. He wants to heal, restore, and save. Many daughters and sons who have been abused sexually by parents, in-laws, baby-sitters, and by the same sex have been healed by Jesus Christ to the place of total restoration. In some cases, it takes a few years; in others, only a few months, but Jesus Christ, the Healer, has come to heal and to set us free. Abuse is not normal—it's not natural. Incest is not normal—it's not natural. Neither is homosexuality normal or natural. According to the Word of God, the expression of sex and our sexuality is to be given in the confines of marriage. Anything other than that is sin.

It's our responsibility to line up our lives according to the Word of God, to repent for the sin in our lives, to allow the Holy Spirit to cleanse us of all the abuse and perversions, and then to teach and train our children to possess their bodies in honor (1 Thessalonians 4:4).

At Calvary, every power of the enemy, every disease, and every perversion was broken—every taint of sin was cleansed so we can walk healed, restored, and healthy because of Jesus Christ. It's the blood of Jesus Christ and the new covenant that enables us to walk in holiness and righteousness.

I pray God to grant us wisdom, revelation, and understanding in the area of our sexuality, so that we may have the gift of repentance that will enable us to walk cleansed, healed, and restored. May He grant us His wisdom and insight in ministering to our children, so healing will flow to them, that they may be recovered from the abuse and misuse of their bodies, and so their bodies may be sanctified and presented holy and blameless before the Lord.

10

Your Child and AIDS

Dianne:

"Dad, I'm really confused about something," John states.

"What is it, Son?"

"Well, today in school the teacher mentioned that Suzie, a girl in my class, won't be coming to school anymore because she has a disease that we can catch and die from."

"Did your teacher explain what Suzie has?"

"No. Just that she won't be coming back because she has something called . . . well, she spelled it and I think it's hives."

Dad interrupted, "Do you mean HIV?"

"Yeah, that's it! How come the teacher spelled it and why didn't she tell us what it is? What is HIV, Dad?"

This scene is not likely to happen in our homes today.[1] Society, as a whole, is now recognizing that AIDS is a subject to be included in the sex education curriculum. Where the subject was once excluded from public education and even public discussion—as those with the virus isolated from the rest of society—this is no longer the case. As biblical parents, it's our responsibility to be current in our knowledge about AIDS and to lovingly communicate this information to our children.

What is AIDS?

AIDS stands for *Acquired* (obtained) *Immune* (safe, protected) *Deficiency* (lacking) *Syndrome* (group of symptoms). The virus that causes AIDS is known as HIV (human immunodeficiency virus). This means that the virus is found in humans and that it affects the immune system. But HIV is different from other viruses like those that cause colds, influenza, or chicken pox, in that it <u>cannot</u> survive in air, food, or water. HIV can survive only in body fluids. Therefore, a person gets or acquires HIV only by direct exchange of infected fluids like blood, feces, breast milk, saliva, and semen. (Please note that, to date, it has not been determined that other fluids like tears or urine can transmit the virus.)

HIV is also different from other viruses in that once it invades the body's cells it stays there for life. Some people die within a couple of years, while others live for 10 years or longer before they actually display any symptoms of AIDS. This is one of the most dangerous aspects of HIV, because the untested infected person will continue to live normally and, if he or she is sexually involved with another person, may contaminate their partner with the deadly virus.

In a society where multiple sexual partners or casual sex has long been the norm, this act becomes as volatile as a match set to a pile of dry twigs that flares and sends sparks flying into the branches of a forest—a small flame becomes an out-of-control, destructive force consuming everything in its path. The most tragic link in this accursed chain, because of the involvement of the most innocent, is the pregnancy that occurs from this coupling. If a child is born infected with HIV, he is literally handed a death-sentence even as he draws his first breath.

How HIV is Transmitted

HIV is transmitted in three major ways. The scientists at the Federal Centers for Disease Control (CDC) have gathered information about each case of AIDS reported. The CDC reports the following about how people with AIDS are infected:

63% - Sexual transmission.[2]

28% - Needle sharing by intravenous drug users.

3% - Transfusion of contaminated blood or blood use products in the course of medical treatment.

2% - Prenatal transmission (from infected mother to fetus during pregnancy).

4% - Not yet assigned a precise mode of transmission.

Communicating To Our Children

Now that we have some basic knowledge about the AIDS virus and how it's transmitted, how do we communicate this to our children? First of all, we need to look at our motives: Why do we want to inform our children?

Because knowledge is power. The more our children know, the better prepared they are to make godly choices and to protect themselves from life-threatening situations.

Because it will happen in their group of friends, or at their school, or in their church. Preparing our children ahead of time will enable them to minister to the infected person without judging, condemning, rejecting, or ostracizing them.

Because by being informed by a loving, biblical, and concerned parent, the child will feel safe, protected, informed, in control, and focused in God's perspective and not the world's. (We are not teaching safe sex, but rather taking the biblical premise that sex, other than in the context of marriage, is a sin, and furthermore, with the threat of AIDS, which is transmitted sexually, it is a life-threatening sin.)

Iverna:

Too often the fear of confrontation prevents us from fulfilling the path of parenting that involves sexual training. Psalm 106:7-44 lists 14 failures attributed to parents by their offspring:

They understood not God's deliverances .

(vs. 7)

Provoked God by complaints and doubts.

(vs. 7)

Gave only emotional service to God.

(vs. 12-13)

Wouldn't wait for God's counsel (accepted their own).

(vs. 13)

Lusted—never satisfied—wanted what they chose.

(vs. 14-15)

Jealous of those in authority.

(vs. 16)

Wanted a god they could control.

(vs. 19)

Wanted freedom without fight or faith.

(vs. 24)

Ignored God's judgments.

(vs. 23-27)

Caused God's leader to stumble.

(vs. 32-33)

Refused to destroy what God destined for destruction.

(vs. 34-36)

Despised their own children.

(vs. 37-38)

Never learned the privilege or power of prayer.
                                                    (vs. 43-44)
Didn't remain faithful.   *(vs. 43)*

The next generation cried (vs. 6), "We have sinned just as our fathers sinned." It has been said, "What parents do in moderation, children do in excess."

As parents, let us confront ourselves first, and then bring the good news of deliverance, protection, and freedom to our children through acceptance of Jesus Christ who enables us to order our lives by His Word.

Dianne:

How do we share this information? Many of us have a hard enough time talking to our children about the "friend" we don't like, or discussing what is making them angry (depressed, sad, jealous), or why they don't like to go to church, let alone talking to them about the very private, sometimes embarrassing, and for sure, awkward, subject of sex. But once we realize that our motives are righteous and pure, we need to set aside some time to talk about AIDS. I would like to suggest some guidelines:

Be honest. Admit your feelings. If you're fearful, say it. Your child will feel it anyway and might disregard what you say because of what they feel from you. If you feel awkward, let them know. "Tom, I feel really awkward talking to you about AIDS because . . ." Share your heart with your child. This will open the door for your child to share with you. Honesty is free from judgment and pride and the child will not feel "talked down to."

Share the information according to age and temperament. Children from the ages of 2-10 or 11 (before puberty) will not be exposed to sexual activity,

231

but need to be taught the basics about AIDS and about being sexually abused by teens and adults. Once the child is interested in the opposite sex (this is not age-determined, but rather by temperament), begin to give more detailed information (such as how HIV is transmitted). As for biblical parents, we need to share God's heart regarding keeping our vessel pure for Him and for our future mate.

Explain that good people do bad things and we are called to love, pray for, and minister to all sinners. Your child's best friend might contract the virus. What will we encourage our child to do? Do we forbid the relationship, telling our child to reject the friend? Do we talk about how "bad" he or she is? Or do we intercede for the friend to find Christ in this crisis? Our children need to see that our God is not only a just God, but also a God of mercy and grace when a sinner comes in repentance and seeks forgiveness and healing. We can be the family to stand in the gap and pray for the infected person to find Christ's saving and healing power. We should not automatically assume that the infected person contracted AIDS through participation in an ungodly act, however. As we observed earlier, according to the CDC findings, approximately 5% of the AIDS victims contract the disease from a medical procedure or through pre-natal transmission. It must also be pointed out that a husband or wife can contract the disease if their life-partner has been unfaithful or has had multiple sexual partners prior to establishing a relationship with their spouse.

Keep it short and to the point. Talking to our children about AIDS should not be a time for us to lecture, preach, induce a fear of dying, or project our lack of trust. Instead, this should be a time to share our love and our faith in God's keeping power.

Keep it open-minded. Your child might know more than you think, so ask questions (don't interrogate!). "Johnny, has anyone talked to you about AIDS?" Johnny's response will tell you where to start. If he says, "No, what is it?" then you start at the beginning. If he says, "No, but I've read some stuff," then you find out what he's read and what he thinks about it. Questions keep the doors of communication open (remember, your tone of voice will give you away. If you sound angry, fearful, or self-righteous, the discussion will come to a screeching halt and become a monologue because you're doing all the talking!). If Johnny says, "Yes, I know all about it," then a loving way to respond would be, "That's great! I'm glad you're on top of things. Would you mind sharing with me what you've learned? I like to keep current, too. Will you teach me what you've learned?" Even if you know it all, you have just told the child that he has something valuable to share with you and that you need him.

Iverna:

As biblical parents, we have been honored by our Lord with the task of molding and shaping the minds and hearts of the children He has gifted us with into His likeness, mirroring His mind and His heart. Our Father is compassionate, gentle, forgiving, faithful, patient, loving, just, pure, and above all, holy. We must endeavor to be no less. We must instruct our children in His ways—they don't come to this knowledge naturally. Not to do so is the same as thrusting our children into a cold and dark night with neither light by which they may see nor a warm coat to shield them from the biting wind.

As flesh and blood, we are not immune to the elements of nature—as Christians we are not immune to sin and its consequences. We should not assume that our children are naturally insulated from the world's evils or that they are blinkered like a race horse, thereby preventing them from seeing the course run by another and the consequences of so running.

We can see clearly the problem of AIDS in the natural. Now may we learn to prevent spiritual AIDS as well. Too many Christians are slowly losing life, unable to stand for godly principles in trying times because they are spiritually deficient.

May we be alerted to the times and that it might be said of us, as it was said of David in Acts 13:36 (KJV), "he . . . served his own generation by the will of God."

Soon—sooner than we may think or wish—we will all know someone whose life is infected, or affected, by AIDS. Prepare yourself as a Christian. As a biblical parent, prepare your child. Protect your child. Pray for AIDS' victims.

[1]In 1981, there were no known cases of AIDS in the United States among teenagers 13-21 years old. Ten years later, at the end of 1991, there were more than 2,500 reported cases. This number is doubling every year.

[2]59% sexual activity between men; 5-9% sexual activity between men and women (March 1992).

11

Your Child and Friends/ Peers

Iverna:

In the first and second grade, it's very common for little boys and girls to be in love with each other. Whenever I noticed that Dan had a new little girl's name inked on his hand, I'd ask him to tell me about her. His sweethearts were always blonde, always clever, always talented. Because I encouraged him to tell me about his girlfriends in the beginning, he was free to tell me about them later when the romances broke up. We kept the door of communication open between us. At first, his explanation was always an ego-saving declaration that he dumped them, but later he came to the point of being able to say, "Jennifer turned me over for Steve."

"Oh?" I said. "How come?"

"I don't know—I guess maybe she doesn't like tall boys."

Being jilted didn't give him any complexes. It was a normal part of life—and he moved to the next crush soon.

Often, first graders bit by the love bug will exchange telephone numbers with one another. It's interesting to eavesdrop on these conversations. A little girl will dial her boyfriend, and he'll be thrilled to death that she called but so embarrassed he can't say anything better than a grumpy, "Well, what did you call me for?"

Instead of answering his question, she'll say, "Well, I gotta go now," and slam the phone down in his ear. Don't worry about that or even get involved with it. This is standard operating procedure for peer with peer. They understand each other. The kids don't call to say anything in the first place; they're just making contact. Later, their conversations will be more than long enough to make up for these early short ones.

When Debbie was in the sixth grade, her teacher said to me, "Your daughter is doing beautifully academically, but she is behind socially." I knew what she was talking about, so I smiled and nodded my head.

"When Debbie first came to this class," the teacher went on, "every boy had a crush on her, but she doesn't seem to have any interest in boys. I'm a little concerned about this, Mrs. Tompkins, aren't you?"

"Not a bit."

The teacher looked at me as if I had suddenly sprouted two heads or something.

"Aren't you concerned?" she wanted to know. "The average mother is worried sick if her little girl in the sixth grade isn't boy-crazy."

"Well, I guess I'm not average, then," I told her. "I'm not only not concerned—I'm glad Debbie isn't boy-crazy yet. She has plenty of time for that later on."

The teacher just stared at me, then shook her head.

The pressure to date weighs heavily on today's teenagers. Everywhere they turn, someone asks them, "Do you have a date for the party? Who are you going with?"

And yet when I talk to the boys by themselves, I invariably find that they enjoy playing basketball, building models, or playing chess—not going out with girls.

Once when my daughter was complaining about having nothing to do, I suggested, "Why don't you just call up a bunch of kids and have them over for popcorn?"

Her response was mingled incredulity and sarcasm.

"Now wouldn't that just be a ball!" she said, shaking her head and looking at me as if she thought I'd lost my mind.

"I think the kids would enjoy it," I told her. But she wouldn't be persuaded.

Later I checked it out to see if I was really that much behind the times. I asked some kids separately, out of earshot of the others, "Say, if we called you up tonight and invited you over to eat popcorn and watch TV, would you like that?"

"Gee, that'd be great! What time can I come?" they asked. The individual response was unanimously in favor of the idea, but collectively they were afraid someone would make fun of them.

Let Them Be Children

Often pressure from teachers, parents, and peers doesn't let children be children long enough. They have to put away childhood and play at adult roles before they're ready. If we encourage them in that direction, we're guilty of stealing from them some important joys of childhood.

Even thirteen-year-old kids who have just gone into junior high school are considered adult and are called on to make important decisions that will affect their whole lives. In many cases, at the same time that they're being asked to make these major life-decisions, they have just gone from being the oldest students in grade school or junior high school to being the youngest in a high school.

Jumping Off the Bridge (or How Far Do They Follow the Crowd?)

Too often, kids are belittled and made fun of if they aren't in rebellion against the establishment by those who are. They're ridiculed if their clothes aren't sloppy enough, and they're held up to scorn if they do their homework faithfully and consistently get good grades. They may be called a "nerd" or a "geek" or a "dweeb" for just being successful. This causes feelings of insecurity and inadequacy or just makes the recipient of such scorn downright

237

uncomfortable. Their world is actually in conflict with itself—they want to live up to their own personal values, please those in authority, and yet be accepted by those who surround them daily.

Where should the line be drawn in determining how far we let our children follow their peers?

The first secret is in finding a balance between the extremes.

One mother who had an unusually good relationship with her teenagers said to me, "I stay alert to their spiritual growth because, to me, this makes a difference in how far I'm going to allow them to follow the crowd. Little things—like hairstyles—I can go along with."

For her, getting used to long hair on boys was easy. For me, it was tough, because I equated long hair on guys with rebellion.

Another mother told me, "I try to encourage my children to apply Christian principles in matters of dress for themselves. We talk about such things as, 'How "cool" should a Christian be?' rather than laying down the law and saying, 'You will not wear thus and such a thing because I don't like it, and that's that.'"

Her approach was wise. To start with, a child who is wearing what he or she likes, something comfortable, something that doesn't set them apart from the crowd, is going to be a lot happier, better behaved, more secure and stable than one who feels awkward and out of place because of what he or she has on.

Parents who don't observe their own children in a group setting are often not aware of how important style is to a youngster. It's easy for an adult to say, "Your skirt is too short," or "You've got to get your hair cut." But the kids who are set radically apart from their peers will suffer alienation all day at school because their clothing or hair differs so greatly from their peers' clothes and hair. It's important for us to try to understand our children's point of view—and to see things their way if possible.

Security among their peers is important to children of any age. If what they want to wear, or how they want to style their hair, is basically harmless, it's well enough to try to go along with their desires.

There isn't anything I loathe more than high-top tennis shoes. They look abominable on everybody, but that's the only kind of shoe my son would wear to school at one time. He had a narrow foot, so I had to special-order his shoes, and I didn't always get around to it as soon as I should have. I remember one day when he had a couple of big holes in the soles of his tennis shoes, but he had a perfectly lovely pair of brown loafers in the closet.

"Dan, why don't you wear your loafers to school today?" I asked him.

His tone of voice told me I must have crawled out from under a rock somewhere.

"You got to be kidding!" he exploded. "Mom, nobody wears loafers to school. I'd rather go barefooted than wear those stupid loafers."

He was so upset about it that I let him go to school wearing his ragged tennis shoes, their soles flopping almost off. It made me feel as if maybe I ought to apply for public welfare. But if I had insisted that he wear his good shoes instead of his decrepit ones, it wouldn't have been because I was concerned that he might take cold from getting his socks wet. It would have been my pride showing.

We need to check our own motives once in a while and encourage our children to examine theirs, as well as the effect their style of clothing has on other people.

One day Debbie went to the gym wearing a pair of cutoff blue jeans. When she came home, she asked me, "Mom, are these pants too tight on me?"

Because I was so accustomed to seeing all Debbie's friends in skintight pants, I hadn't given any particular thought to hers.

"Oh," I said, "I don't know that they're any tighter than anybody else's. Why do you ask?"

"Well," she said, "I just wondered, because while I was in the gym, five different people came along and swatted me on the seat."

"That tells you what you wanted to know, then, doesn't it, Deb?" We both laughed, she nodded, and I could tell that at fifteen she had learned, on her own, that following the crowd wasn't always worth what it cost.

As our youngsters mature, they will begin to weigh one thing against another, to decide for themselves how far they want to follow the gang. When our child comes home and says everybody is going to a place that is anti-God and anti-us, we can say, "Everybody isn't going, because you're not," but in less vital matters, we don't have to be so dogmatic.

In the past, Christians have sometimes defeated their own purposes by being unreasonably extreme in their views. When I was growing up, I was ridiculed in gym class because my religion did not permit me to learn the two-step. My mother and father made such a scene over the dance classes in public school that kids and teachers alike made fun of me. I had to make written reports to the teacher instead of participating in the fun.

Being punished for something that was not my fault made me really bitter. It did far more damage to me than learning the two-step would have done.

We need to look at the long-range effect of our parental actions. As Christian parents, we have to draw a fine line without letting the kids see the chalk, without setting up stumbling blocks. We can let them be a part of everything that will not harm them spiritually. We can let them feel, "I'm one of the gang. I am accepted."

Then the no-nos, the things we can't allow—alcohol, drugs, etc.—will not make them feel estranged from all their friends. Departure from the crowd on a single issue or two doesn't become a traumatic thing in their peer relationships unless we've insisted on a total separation act all along, always pulling our youngsters to ourselves, inferring, "We're better than other people because we're different."

The truth is that we are different, but our little son or daughter in grade school is not prepared to hear it. He or she wants to be liked—and to be like others.

We need to make certain that the line we draw because we are Christians is clear to the youngsters so that they understand the why of doing, or not doing, the activity in question. We need to help them understand that some lines are drawn for reasons other than our Christianity, also. Our children need to understand the principle differences as well. "We don't wear dirty clothes to school because it's important to me as a parent that you begin clean. This has nothing to do with being a Christian, but it has to do with the way we live in this house."

Many of the things we have to make decisions on should be made jointly with the youngsters. I remember a time when my daughter was invited to a school dance and I allowed her to attend. Upon returning home, she talked about the lights and the music, which resulted in a severe headache; she felt there was a very obvious spirit of darkness that prevailed in the dance and said she didn't think she wanted to attend again. Rather than pounce on that, and hold her to it, so that she would feel guilty if she ever did, I simply said, "Well, that's your decision and I can certainly understand where you are coming from on it." Now, many years later, one of the things that Debbie enjoys the most is her Jazzercise class. Part of her enjoyment comes, I think, because she doesn't have to fight through some extreme stipulation that I made, allowing her instead to discover the guidelines of dancing that worked and were acceptable to her personally.

I just used the dance as an illustration. There are many other such things we need to look at. One thing that is very frustrating to parents and kids today is that so many of the sports games are held on Sundays. There can be an arbitrary stand taken that Sunday is the Lord's day and they cannot play, but that eliminates them from participating in some very clean kinds of things they are capable of doing. It might be wiser to find an alternative.

One alternative that my daughter, who now has a daughter of her own, discovered was to participate in the special classes her church holds on Wednesday nights. They exchanged Sunday and Sunday School for Wednesday night classes, which is followed by family discussion in the Word about what each heard in their class, etc. That really becomes their "Sabbath" to them.

I know this won't be accepted by all and each must be true to his or her own integrity in the matter, but there are alternatives. I really believe we should look for these types of alternatives with our children to help them understand that Christianity is a way of life and not just do's and don'ts.

241

The Different Drummer

Christian kids are different from their non-Christian peers because they have Christ inside them. Older kids can understand that and accept their being different and liking different things from other kids. It becomes a positive factor in their own eyes, not something that drags them down.

Taking Sides

How we react in the face of inevitable peer conflicts teaches our child a lot about proper relationships and what it means to be a light in a dark world.

The indulgent parents who always side with their own youngster when he or she comes in with a problem with a friend is teaching their child that he or she does not have a responsibility to get along with others. If a friend displeases the child for any reason, the youngster knows that he or she can run to Dad or Mom and they will take his or her side in the matter.

The less indulgent parents are likely to go to the other extreme and always blame their own youngster when there is a disagreement on the playground. If we always say, "Son, it's your fault," we are teaching our child that the peer will always win over him, that there is never going to be any justice in his favor, and that he must, therefore, be basically inferior to other people.

Even with preschoolers, it makes a difference how you handle their peer relationships. Dan came in crying one day. "I lost my favorite marble," he wailed, "and those kids are bigger than me."

My instinctive reaction was to go out and verbally beat up the big kids for taking a marble from my little kid, but I asked for a little clarification first. Out the window, I could see some bigger boys kneeling around a circle scratched on the sidewalk.

"What do you mean you lost your favorite marble? Did those big boys take it?"

"Well, not exactly," he sniffed. "There's this game, and . . ."

He explained keepers to me, just as if I hadn't grown up playing keepers with my four brothers.

242

"Dan," I told him, "sometimes when you're playing for keeps, you'll win a lot of marbles from some other poor kid who is going to go away crying. Other times, you'll be the one to lose a lot of marbles. Every time you gamble, something like that could happen. That's just the way it is. If you can't learn to be a good loser, you'd better not play for keeps."

From that day, Dan permitted himself to gamble with some of his marbles, but not with all of them. He gave himself an allotment, disciplined himself to stay within that allotment, and didn't expect any pity from me when he lost.

Dan grew up knowing what to gamble with and what not to gamble with. He became comfortable with the truth, "If you're going to gamble, you can lose." He learned to take the consequences. In my opinion, that was a lot better than setting him apart from his peers by telling him he couldn't play for keeps because gambling is wrong.

The Neighborhood Hang-Out

At times, it may be necessary for us to teach our youngsters' friends something when we want them to behave in ways that are acceptable to us.

One mother told me of a trio of economically disadvantaged children who spent their afternoons playing in her yard. The kids would come in the house for emergency trips to the bathroom, urgent drinks of water, and the like. Each trip was used as an excuse to ask for an apple from the fruit bowl. Seeing that their example couldn't be helpful to her child, who had been taught it was not polite to ask for things, the mother decided to do some instructing herself. One day, instead of handing out apples when they were asked for, she explained to the children that asking was impolite, and that they should wait for someone to offer the fruit to them.

That day, she didn't give the children anything except the lecture. Her own child paid close attention. For a few days, the boys didn't ask for an apple. Then the woman instructed her son to offer one to each of them. He got a reinforced lesson in sharing and in good manners at one stroke.

Guilt by Association

When our youngster associates with children from families whose standards are very different from ours, we have to be watchful to discover whether or not our child is being adversely influenced by them. If we see that he or she is incapable of saying, "No" to another youngster who is forever in trouble for setting fires, stealing, or vandalism, we may have to deny our child the privilege of playing with the troublemaker. When we do this, however, we have to keep in mind that excluding one undesirable from our child's circle of playmates does not eliminate the possibility of all wrong companionship. Isolation from bad influence is not by any means the total answer to developing good character.

It is true that our youngster might have a very good sense of right and wrong on their own and still be led into doing wrong things through the influence of peer pressure. However, that our youngster does a wrong thing to please his or her peers doesn't necessarily mean he or she thinks the wrong thing is right. Inside, they might be feeling self-loathing, nearly dying of guilt, the entire time they are engaged in the wrong action.

Group pressure can make them temporarily violate their own standards—but not forever. A child who has real security will come back to family standards on their own as he or she becomes mature enough to buck the crowd and stand up for their beliefs.

Sometimes when kids are asking to do something they know is against our principles, they're asking because of peer pressure. They really want us to say, "No", so they can have an out. They just don't want to admit that to us. Such an admission would be belittling to them. They're not quite adult enough not to care that they're not following the crowd, and they're not quite adult enough in themselves to choose not to follow. When we sense this, we must be the strong support and make the decision for them.

We'll never find out their "why's" by instant moralizing on the subject. To say, "You know better," is to slam the door on finding out their motivations and helping them grow up into self-discipline. Discuss with them the Christian and home standards and why these were violated.

244

Shock Treatment

One night at dinner, my daughter announced that she was going to read a certain salacious novel. I saw her watching for my reaction, wondering whether I'd blow up or what I'd do. Because we had guests (that fact had also entered into her calculations), I didn't make an issue of it. I just let it go with a nonchalant, "Oh?" and we went on with dinner. Later, I went to her room to talk about her announcement. I hadn't read the book myself, but knew from a review that the book was not recommended reading for teenage girls. Instead of handing her a stamp of disapproval, however, I began to question her.

"This book you're planning to read, Debbie, what's it about?"

"I don't know," she shrugged, "but all the kids are reading it."

Just as I thought. Peer pressure. To have read the dirty novel was the status symbol of the hour.

"Go ahead and read it if you want to," I said, keeping my attitude low-key, "but I understand it's a filthy book, and I don't think you'll enjoy it."

I didn't give her anything to react against, and she never read the book. Our open communication didn't forbid her reading it. She wasn't left feeling that she had to rebel against authority and sneak it in the house. Free to make her own decision, she made a mature one.

If, however, Debbie had gone ahead and read the book, I had opened the door for us to talk about the contents of it. When I found out she was reading it, I would have read it as well, to know how to combat the content of it with her.

What should we do when our children want to go along with the gang and watch TV programs or movies of which we don't approve? With preteens, if we've thought it through, we can be firm in our decision, regardless of what they think. But for teenagers, it is well to examine their reasons for wanting to watch certain off-limits programs or movies.

If our child goes to such a movie, comes home and talks to us about it and then doesn't express a desire to go again, we can let the matter drop. Chances are that some need within them has been satisfied by seeing the movie and no harm has been done. But if the same child wants to go repeatedly to see movies we think will not be good for them, we might ask, "John, what is it you get out of going to movies like that?" By phrasing our question in that way, we encourage him to examine his own motives.

I don't believe in simply telling older kids they can't go. I've seen too many become real addicts to such things the minute they get away from home and out from under parental watchfulness. It's best for them to be exposed while they're still at home where we can guide them.

Sex and Violence in the Living Room

We can't prevent our youngsters from seeing violence. We live in a violent world. Kids must learn to cope with it.

Suppose we keep our teenage boys from seeing violence on the screen—it would take a miracle, but it might be done—and then, in their upper teens, they get sent away to war? They may be exposed to violence first-hand, up close, not make-believe but real. Over-protected kids are not equipped to handle this emotionally, and some come home from war ready for the mental hospitals. They may stay there a long time.

This is not to say that we put an over-emphasis on violence, but rather that we don't put an over-emphasis on the protection from it. Even cartoons are filled with violent behavior. Children who have been over-protected often find great difficulty relating to life in general, and, of course, that is not our purpose in proper parenting.

At one time, Debbie was interested in a certain TV show she had seen at a friend's house, and so we watched it together a few times. The humor on the program was very subtle and tremendously risqué in many areas. I noticed that Deb laughed each time I did. Just checking, I asked her, "Do you know what that meant?"

She hadn't understood any of it.

There was a day when naiveté was considered precious, but that's not true any more. It's actually dangerous sometimes. Our kids may be belittled and taken advantage of if they don't know the score. Whenever possible, I've let my kids be in the know, even to explaining the risqué jokes so they won't be seen as funny—or repeated.

Living in a pretend world is not helpful for your kids or mine. Today, more than ever before, they have to know "where it's at" in order to survive. They'll be living in a world with their peers, whether we like it and approve or not. Instead of burying our heads in the sand and insisting that they do likewise, we need to equip them with all they need to cope successfully with the real world around them.

Dianne:

Our children are going to have friends and our goal is to socialize our children to interact in a healthful manner with friends at each stage of their social development, as well as to spiritualize our children in bringing the reality of God into every social encounter or exchange.

We need to know and implement the normal social development of our children, bringing this development in line with God's Word, understanding how we can train our children to relate to Christ, the body of Christ, and the world as friend.

Social Development

There is a normal social development each child goes through to reach adulthood, and if, they proceed through the stages in a healthy manner, they will reach adulthood without being handicapped in social relationships.

Utilizing this social development information, along with the Holy Spirit's teaching in bringing healthy evolution at each stage, our children can become adults who have Christ as the center of their social development.

247

Stage 1: Age 0-2 Years—Within the Family

When a child is born, his or her immediate relationship is the family. In this context, the child has the first social contact; the first encounter with another person. Besides discovering their own body, toes, fingers, ears, and nose, the child begins to find there are other people, different and separate from them. These are the people they begin to respond to through the senses.

This first social contact within the family is through the child's perceptions. What does the child feel by touch from this family? Is the child learning that there is a touch of tenderness, of bonding, of caring? Or is the child learning only that touch is rough, gruff, rejecting, callused, and anxiety-ridden? The sense of touch will begin to give this child a relationship evaluation. The child also makes contact with the outside world through hearing and starts evaluating himself and others through, not what is said, because he doesn't understand vocabulary, but how it is said. Is the child cooed at? Are lullabies sung? Is the tone soothing and peaceful and calm? Or is the child hearing anxiety, anger, contention, strife—music that is harsh and loud?

In this first stage, it is within the family that the child begins to encounter the four "A" needs. From these encounters, the child begins to develop an evaluation of herself and those around her. How is the needs for attention, approval, and affection being met? Is the world meeting the child's basic needs? If so, the child will begin to find social contact pleasing; if not, social contact will already begin to be negative and anxiety-producing.

Stage 2: Age 2-7 Years—Outside the Family

Developing, moving from crawling to walking, the infant comes into the toddler stage and starts moving outside the family via day care center or church Sunday School, etc. into other relationships, discovering others his or her own size. Through the use of mental structures that are now developing, the child starts to establish imagery and from these pictures establishes the ability to relate to someone else of his or her size.

248

The social development of toddlers, evolving mainly through their play, goes through stages. The first stage is called solitary play. The child plays alone, relating within his or her own world and according to what they want to do, without others for feedback and interaction. Toddlers like to play with rattles and balls. While recognizing others—brothers, sisters, other toddlers that will come to play—the toddler still is very much isolated in his own world.

From solitary play, the child develops into parallel play. From about two-years old to four-years old, children can sit next to each other while playing absolutely alone. They are separate—playing in their own arena.

In parallel play, there's the recognition of others within the sandbox or on the swing, but the child is engrossed with how he's going to get the truck to move in the sandbox, not with how the other child's truck is doing it. So it's side by side, but alone.

Stage 3: Age 4-7 Years—Corporate Play

Four to seven-year olds begin to move into group play. There's a recognition of other children, a give and take in their relationship, but based on the child's perception—what she wants and on her own terms. If the other children don't play by her rules, the four to seven-year old will take her toys and go home.

Eventually children learn to share, but at this stage, they're just learning how to interact with other children.

The goal in corporate play is to help children maintain a relationship where they can learn to play with others—learning to establish some rules together and playing those rules through. Usually at this stage, children can play only for a few hours with their friends and then they need to go home. They have a limited attention span or a limited ability to give-and-take until finally they say, "I want to do what I want to do and I don't want to play with you anymore."

When our child's friend goes home, our child doesn't understand or see any wrongdoing. They simply see the friend as not wanting to do what he or she wants to do. There is no understanding of give-and-take. To help our child, we can suggest that since the friend doesn't want to play basketball anymore, couldn't they play video games? Their response may be, "I don't want to play video games. I want to play basketball."

"Well, your friend wants to play video games."

"I don't care; I want to play basketball."

The truth is, the child wants to play basketball more than they want the friend.

How can we help our child work this through? The Holy Spirit is the only One who can convict of sin—convince us about our motives and attitudes. So we pray for our child and ask the Holy Spirit to show him how his friend felt rejected because he didn't want to play with him. We ask the Holy Spirit to minister to our child because he has felt rejected. Our child felt that his friend didn't want to play with him any longer.

"Do you want to ask your friend back?"

"Yes."

Then we ask, "Do you want to play video games or basketball?"

We may well hear him say, "I want to play video games because that's what my friend wants to play." The Holy Spirit came in and gave the child insight and healing, ministering to his need to be right as well as his need to be needed, so he was released to play again with his friend.

There may be times that our child is still stuck on playing basketball because of his age development, and we might suggest calling his friend to come and play something totally different, getting the focus off basketball and video games. Try changing the subject totally, with something such as, "Why don't you call your friend and see if he'll go bowling with us?" The goal is the continual interaction and social development of the child.

Stage 4: Middle Childhood—Ages 7-12 Years—Peers

Once the child enters first grade, moving into the school years, it can be a fun, exciting time. It can also be one of great pain and confusion. The difference is how we teach our children to deal with their peers.

We need to help our children develop certain skills and attitudes regarding their friends—their peers. Here are some skills we need to understand.

Resolving Conflicts

When pre-adolescent children move into relationships at school and begin to develop friends, conflicts are going to happen. The skill they need to learn is how to effectively resolve conflicts. What will Suzie do when her friend Mary tells her secret, or chooses another friend to play with, or gossips about Suzie? Will Suzie retaliate and reject her friend? Will she gossip in return? Or will Suzie learn how to forgive and receive Christ's healing? This is the time to teach our children how to deal with friends who betray them as Judas betrayed Jesus. Every conflict our children have at this age becomes opportunity for growth. If we do not focus on the pain, rejection, and wounds, but center on what Christ wants to do about the pain, we will be able to minister effectively to our children.

Communication Skills

Kids begin to talk on the phone, starting to relate with one another. It's the beginning of socialization—social events—and these encounters necessitate that our children learn how to communicate effectively. Much pain and misunderstanding happens because what we think we said wasn't said—or what we said wasn't heard correctly. When our children get hurt, or are misunderstood, they will have a tendency to want to fight or flee, but we can help them learn how to communicate effectively regarding the situation. For example, Suzie calls her best friend, Mary. Mary says to her, "I don't want to talk to you anymore on the phone," and hangs up.

Suzie comes crying to her mother, saying, "Mary doesn't want to talk to me any more. She doesn't want to be my friend anymore."

The conclusion Suzie just gave the mother is not true. All Mary said was, "I don't want to talk to you on the phone anymore." She didn't say, "I don't want to be your friend." Our responsibility is to find out what really was said and what happened.

251

"Suzie, what did you hear her say? What did she say to you?"
"She said she didn't want to talk to me on the phone anymore."

"Is there a reason why she said she didn't want to talk to you on the phone anymore?"

"Well, she had to go to a party."

"That just meant she didn't have anymore time to talk on the phone with you. When she gets home from the party, why don't you call her back and find out if that's what she really meant?"

This teaches Suzie how to give feedback to what she thinks she heard. It's teaching, "You heard something and you made a conclusion. Is your conclusion true? If it isn't true, you need feedback. If it is true, you still need feedback about why they said they didn't want to talk to you anymore." We've moved from basic communication in hearing what the other person says to teaching Suzie how to resolve what seems to her to be a conflict.

Losing

During the school years, our children will be involved in games and outside activities where there are rules and competition. In any team sport, there's going to be someone who wins and someone who loses, so our children must learn how to lose in a healthy way. It's fun for everybody to win, but one of the purposes in team sports is to learn how to lose and not take it personally. Our child can lose a game and not be a loser.

Biblical parenting brings Christ into the situation and lets our child know he is loved regardless of his behavior. My son, Daniel, loves soccer. When he first started, he was the goalie and was very good at it. Yet when he was scored on, he felt badly, and so did the team. After those games, we'd say to Daniel, "You're not bad. You played the best you could and that's all any one expects you to do." We began to minister unconditional love to him. Daniel wasn't loved or valued because he won or lost—it was because he was still Daniel. Yes, we wanted him to learn to win, but we are not always winners. There are some things we're going to enter into and try and not do well. We need to know that we are loved and valued in spite of that.

Different People

As our pre-adolescents grow older, they will discover among their friends those not like them, not only boy-girl—they've already discovered that. They will also find that there are girls that behave differently than they do. If they are our sons, they'll find there are other boys that behave differently than they do. They have different temperaments. Some boys in school will prefer reading to playing sports. That's not bad or wrong—it's just a different temperament. Certain girls will enjoy playing kickball and not dolls—they don't want to read, or play the more sedentary games, but would rather be playing football with the boys.

Our children need to learn in their social relationships that people are different and different isn't bad. Our differences make each of us unique. God has created each one of us as different as a snowflake, and we need to give that kind of value to our children. It's not based on color or gender. Each person is valued for who they are, and this is where we can help our children find that there is a Creator and He doesn't make mistakes.

Because they're different, they're going to find in the classroom that some have a natural ability to get A's without having to work hard at it. My son's kindergarten teacher said he was very bright, so I would have to watch when he got into his pre-adolescent years, because boys who were not as bright might ridicule him. If he was insecure, he would back down, thinking it was not okay to get good grades. I appreciated this teacher's input and could apply it to every quality my son has. In every aspect where he is different from someone else, I want him to love his uniqueness, not to excuse it or back down from it because of the ridicule from other boys or girls who are insecure. We need to help our children be with other kids and stay true to their God-given abilities.

Who Am I?

Pre-adolescents are finding their own personalities at this stage, and if it's not done in a healthy fashion, they'll become dysfunctional in relationships. What's a healthy fashion? First and foremost, our children need to discover they are worthy—valuable in Christ. The Bible says when we lose our life, we'll find it (Matthew 17:25). Our children need the Savior to save them, and, as they begin to find their identity in Christ, they will be healthy in Him, safe in Him, so they can move out to discover themselves, amidst their peers, and yet not have to become like them.

During this period, children begin to develop cliques. If our children don't know who they are, they're going to be drawn to certain kinds of groups—finding their identity in the trappings of the clique and not in Christ. If they don't find their identity in Christ, they're going to want to possess a special friend, someone that will be there all the time and will meet all of their needs. Yet the truth is, no one can be that to anybody. Yet out of insecurity, they will seek that one person to fulfill what only Christ can fulfill. If our children don't find a healthy identity in Christ, they will look for it in being popular, in wearing the right clothing, in "going along with the group," or they may turn to substances in which to "drown" themselves, such as food, drugs, alcohol, and sex. Or they will choose friends who are popular, athletic, leaders of a certain group or club, thereby gaining identity from someone else.

Our role is to help our children find out who they are in Christ and then friends will be an asset to them. They will choose friends who will have the same values.

They Establish Rules Regarding Friends

Kids begin to discover what they want in a friend and what they like in a friend. From these likes and dislikes, they start establishing rules that ultimately become very controlling.

For instance, "My friend will always call me; my friend will always go to school activities with me; my friend will give to me as I give to him." These rules become internalized and the child begins to operate and evaluate people from the rules, not from discerning the person.

If our son has the rule that a friend would want to go hang out at the mall and listen to the same kind of music, and he meets a new young person in church who listens to different music and doesn't like going to the mall, he will not want to befriend that person. He'll think there's something wrong with the person. We must help our children discover the uniqueness of each person and the freedom to be the kind of friend God wants to produce in the relationship. Our children need to learn that a friend can care for them even though they don't talk with them on the phone. It's not based on what they do for them—it's who they are.

These principles must be taught as our children go through pre-adolescent time. It's in this stage that we're planting the seeds for adulthood. If it's not dealt with now our children will carry into adulthood the controlling rules of friendship, believing they're godly and good healthy rules when they're not.

Stage 5: Adolescence—The Opposite Sex

Once our child reaches high school, friends are still very important to them, but there is a shift from same-sex friends to friends of the opposite sex. Some pre-adolescents have discovered the opposite sex at eleven and twelve, but the focus in high school becomes very much on the opposite sex. At this time, the adolescent begins to look beyond the home to the outside world and independence, which produces an identity crisis as the adolescent begins to shed the "child identity through puberty" and faces the outside world through graduation.

This transition will be less traumatic if our child has discovered their identity in Christ in pre-adolescence. If all stages of social development have been walked through in Christ, the adolescent will accept the opposite sex with a healthy self-image, good communication skills, and the ability to resolve conflicts. All these skills are needed for establishing their own social unit, which is marriage.

Biblical Premises for Friends

In order to help our child work through the issues and transitions to come into a healthy social life, we need to know what the Bible says about friends. What is God's concept of friends, and how does He want us to relate and respond to them.

> *I appeal to you therefore, brethren, and beg of you in view of [all] the mercies of God, to make a decisive dedication of your bodies . . . as a living sacrifice, holy . . . and well pleasing to God, which is your reasonable (rational intelligent) service and spiritual worship.*
>
> *Do not be conformed to this world . . . to its external, superficial customs, but be transformed . . . by the [entire] renewal of your mind . . . so that you may prove [for yourselves] what is the . . . will of God.*
>
> (Romans 12:1-2, AMP)

We have been conformed—taught to think a certain way—to the world's ideas about friends, and we need God, through His Word and by His Spirit, to transform us. This transformation means an internal change where the Holy Spirit alters our whole pattern of thinking regarding friends and teaches us through God's Word and by experience what it is to be a friend.

Jesus lived a transformed life in relation to friendship. One example is found in the Gospel of John, chapter 11. Mary, Martha, and Lazarus were close friends of Jesus. They had spent time together and entertained Jesus in their home. Yet, when Jesus heard Lazarus was dying, He didn't go to him right away.

What concept of a friend did Jesus violate? The world's concept is that a good friend would go immediately to a sick friend's house. But Jesus' response was to obey His Father first, and Father said to wait three days. Jesus had been transformed from the world's concepts of friends. Mary and Martha obviously had another concept of friendship. When Jesus finally arrived, they were angry and felt that if He had come immediately, Lazarus would not have died. They still had man's concepts of friendship, but Jesus had been transformed and wanted to transform their concepts regarding Him.

Jesus wants to do this with our children as we begin to walk through these stages with them. Through experiences of friends, God can teach us how to be transformed, to have our minds renewed, to see friends according to what God says, and not according to our training and the world's concepts of friends.

Jesus wants to be the child's friend. In John 15:15, Jesus talked to His disciples about being His friend. The important thing is to understand that Jesus, as a friend, is ever present. Natural friends come and go in the stages of development through our children's lives, but Jesus will be their constant friend. When that friendship is established with Jesus, all the friends that will come in and out of their lives will do so in a healthy way and not in a possessive relationship.

When my daughter was in junior high, she had a friend with whom she did many things, both during and after school. One day, we received a call from a boy's parents, telling us that my daughter and her girlfriend were seeing their son late at night. The parents explained that when our daughter spent the night at the girlfriend's house they would sneak out to visit this boy and would be out all night.

We thanked this boy's parents for telling us and asked Michelle, who admitted it had been happening. I called her friend's parents to tell them what was happening, but they didn't care. As far as they were concerned, their daughter could do what she wanted. So we knew Michelle couldn't spend any more time with this girl.

Giving up this friendship was very painful, because she was Michelle's closest friend. For one year, we prayed daily for Jesus to be Michelle's friend and to help her to establish new friends. During that year, Michelle was depressed and suicidal, yet, Jesus continued to comfort, heal, talk with her, and fill the gap that was there. The principle Michelle learned through this painful experience is that friends will fail, but Jesus never will. Jesus is a faithful, ever-present friend. What seemed to be a very painful, negative experience became an opportunity for our daughter to discover Jesus as her friend.

257

Ultimate trust cannot be in a friend (Micah 7:5).

> *But Jesus did not commit Himself to them because he knew all men, . . .*
>
> (John 2:24, NKJV)

Jesus Christ didn't commit Himself to the people around Him because He was first committed to the Father. Did Jesus have friends? Yes. He had the twelve disciples, plus Mary, Martha, and Lazarus. In fact, He was so healthy in His relationship with friends, He could pick a Judas knowing the relationship would be one-sided. If your children were going to pick a group of friends, would you want them to include a Judas, someone who would subsequently stab them in the back? Jesus so trusted His walk with God—His relationship with the Father—that He could choose a Judas and still minister to him.

We have some friends because they need us to befriend them, others because we need them, and still others just because we enjoy being together. I want my children to be transformed in their thinking about friends and ministering to people. I want them to learn that it isn't only those who like them that God wants them to befriend, but also those who need what God has given them.

When our children put their ultimate trust in God, they can allow their friends to be human. People do tell lies, they gossip, they fail to keep secrets. But we can help them grow up in the grace and knowledge of Jesus Christ (2 Peter 3:18) by our lives, love, and sharing.

When my daughter was going through the traumatic time of losing her closest girlfriend, she would return from church depressed because no one would talk with her. She not only felt rejected by her closest girlfriend, but rejected by the kids at church. So we challenged her to go to church and find people who were worse off than she was—kids that were hurting and wounded—feeling rejected just as she was—and be a friend to them. And she did it. As Jesus taught her how to be a friend, she became that to others. She didn't need to seek out the popular kids or the ones that would feed her ego. As God began to heal her and minister to her, she could give that kind of love and friendship to others.

"A friend loves at all times and is born like a brother for adversity" (Proverbs 17:17).

The only way our children, as friends, can love at all times is through Jesus. In the natural, we have conditional love. It's only as our children encounter *agape* love that they will be able to give that love to others that God brings into their lives.

This Scripture also tells us that friends are developed through a crisis that makes them seem closer than a natural brother or sister. We cannot be offended if relationships are established outside the home that seem to be stronger than the ones inside the home. Jesus makes it clear that in the end-times, brother will turn against brother and children against parents (Mark 15:12). But Jesus Christ promises to establish us in His family—God will be our Father, and give us brothers, mothers, and sisters (Matthew 12:50).

A true friend will cover or correct a friend and not gossip about him.

> *He who covers a transgression seeks love, But he who repeats a matter separates friends.*
>
> *(Proverbs 17:9, NKJV)*
>
> *A perverse man sows strife, and a whisperer separates close friends.*
>
> *(Proverbs 16:28, AMP)*
>
>
> *He who belittles and despises his neighbor lacks sense, but a man of understanding keeps silent.*
>
> (Proverbs 11:12, AMP)
>
>
> *He who states his case first seems right, until his rival comes and cross examines him.*
>
> *(Proverbs 18:17, AMP)*

> *Be not a witness against your neighbor without cause, and deceive not with your lips.*
>
> *(Proverbs 24:28, AMP)*

> *Argue your cause with your neighbor himself . . . disclose not another's secret.*
>
> *(Proverbs 25:9, AMP)*

> *A man who bears false witness against his neighbor is like a heavy sledge hammer, and a sword, and a sharp arrow.*
>
> *(Proverbs 25:18, AMP)*

> *Ointment and perfume delight the heart, And the sweetness of a man's friend gives delight by hearty counsel.*
>
> *(Proverbs 27:9, NKJV)*

> *As iron sharpens iron, so a man sharpens the countenance of his friend.*
>
> (Proverbs 27:17, NKJV)

It is natural for every child to gossip, slander, and tell tales. Our responsibility is not to deal with the whispering and gossip, but to find out why. Out of insecurity, pride, self-righteousness, and self-hate, a child will gossip. We need to help our children to allow the Holy Spirit to bring healing to those places of insecurity and repentance to those places of pride. When the Holy Spirit transforms our children, they will be able to speak the truth in love—to cover their friend and not repeat a matter.

When we discover that our children have told a secret or gossiped, it is an opportunity to bring Christ in to change the heart.

Jesus came to transform the heart of every human being so that from it would flow love, joy, peace, longsuffering, gentleness, and goodness (Galatians 5:22). That takes bringing the Cross—the blood of Jesus Christ—to the experiences our children have as they develop socially and encounter friends. It is a great opportunity to teach our children how to give a good report—or cover their friend when their friend lies or repeats a matter.

In the Sermon on the Mount (Matthew 5:43-48), Jesus told us that it is easy to love those who love us. But we will show that we are sons of God when we can love those who hate us. This takes Jesus Christ becoming our friend, healing us, and loving us unconditionally, so that we can give that ministry and love to others.

One of the reasons why gossip is believed is revealed in Proverbs 18:17, "He who states his case first seems right." It's hard for us to believe that the first person who gets to us has only told us part of the story. Our children must learn that when Suzie calls and says, "Hey, do you know so-and-so said this?" that they are only hearing part of the story or that the story has been changed a little; it's necessary to find out from everybody involved what the truth is.

"Seldom set foot in your neighbor's house, lest he become weary of you and hate you" (Proverbs 25:17, NKJV).

Visiting may not necessarily be a positive. We can have a rule from the world's standards that a good friend is always over at someone's house. Yet the Word of God tells us that we need to be careful that we don't become a bothersome person in someone's house. Our children need to learn to be sensitive.

Some people are trained culturally that the door should always be open for anyone to come in at any time. Yet, there are places in this country where the opposite is taught—it is rude not to call before you come over. We must teach our children to be sensitive to people. It can be rude to just show up or it can be rude to come over all the time. Some people are very social and outgoing and want you there all the time, while others say, "I really don't want to see you this weekend. It's not a personal thing—I just don't want to see you."

Our children need to learn it's not personal, that there's nothing wrong with them, that it's a right a person has.

There will be some friends who will turn on them—some that will have to be taken out of their life. But as they look to God for the healing and ministry, He will turn it around to bless them.

> *All my close friends abhor me, and those whom I love*
> *have turned against me.*
>
> > *(Job 19:19, NKJV)*

> *Even my own familiar friend in whom I trusted, Who*
> *ate my bread, Has lifted up his heel against me.*
>
> > *(Psalm 41:9, NKJV)*

> *Faithful are the wounds of a friend, . . .*
>
> > (Proverbs 27:6, KJV)

When Michelle was going through her experience of losing her closest friend, she felt no one loved her or cared for her. These Scriptures ministered to her, assuring her that she was not alone—others had also experienced it. In the life of David, God brought friends. It was only a season that he went through rejection, but God was faithful and blessed David, and He will do the same thing for us. The God we serve and believe in will also minister to us.

It is indicated in some translations of Proverbs 18:24 that many friends may bring destruction.

In our children's social development, pre-adolescent time is when they like to be involved in groups and with lots of people. But we need to help our children understand that all these people are not friends, they're acquaintances. They are people to whom they can relate, and from whom they can learn. God wants them to develop close friendships within the group, and God will teach us and our children to discern those of His choosing to befriend. It isn't always the popular ones or the one we'd naturally choose but it will be those who will bless our children's lives. They will learn that God knows better than they do, and in His wisdom He knows how to bless their lives beyond what they know.

There will be some "friends" who will come into our children's lives with wrong motives.

> *The poor is hated even of his own neighbor, but the rich hath many friends.*
>
> *(Proverbs 14:20, KJV;see also 19:4-7)*

We need to help our children discover those motives. Usually it will be discovered through pain. For example, if our child is liked because he is the all-star player and then gets taken off the team, whoever departs his company was not his friend, and the true motive will be exposed.

We can help our child know that wrongly motivated "friends" leave, not because of our child's failure, but because of the heart of the other person. Then we can help our child see how we value him—and love him with God's unconditional love.

Deuteronomy 13 teaches us that if a friend entices us away from the Lord, we are to forsake that friend. Proverbs 16:29 causes us to see that a covetous man entices his friend, driving him into the way that is not good.

In watching the influence and effect our children's friends have on their lives, if we see them begin to be drawn away from the things of God—things of value—and from the things that they believe in, not being strong enough to stand against their friends, then we must break the friendship off. We cannot allow our kids to associate with friends who will entice them away. Until our children are strong enough to do it themselves, the parent is required by God to teach them how to forsake anyone that would turn them away from the things of God.

King David and Jonathan were very close friends. But Jonathan never left his father's house when Saul became David's enemy, staying with him against David. David went into the caves and Jonathan missed another place of ministry because he would not give up the palace.

David had to go on in God and leave Jonathan, who wanted the place of comfort, therefore not following David into that place of ministry. We need to help our children discover there will be some Christians who will not give up the palace—the way of the world. Just because the friend is a Christian does not mean Christ rules their heart and they're willing to give up the things of the world for Christ.

1 Corinthians 15:33 tells us we must not be deceived and misled—evil companionships corrupt and deprave good manners and characters. This is why we must break the associations that are moving our children from the things of God. Even Christians who haven't allowed Jesus Christ to change their heart will ultimately affect our children and their character.

Because our children are in the formative stages of learning skills and ways of relating, they need to have godly input and godly role models, not the things of the world and of Satan.

During adolescence, we watch who our teenagers date. If our daughter chooses a drug addict, it shows us how she feels about her self-esteem or the lack of it. If our son dates someone who seems to be really loose and not of value morally, we deal with our son, not the person he is dating. Who they choose to associate with is a reflection of our kid's heart. Our goal is to help our children through what we see around them, and what is happening in their lives, so they can continue to grow in the grace and knowledge of Jesus Christ.

> *"The [consistently] righteous man is a guide to his neighbor"*
>
> *(Proverbs 12:26, AMP).*

As our children allow the Holy Spirit to change them and transform them into the likeness of Jesus Christ, their righteousness will be a guide. They will become a true friend. As I've watched my adult children in their relationships, the righteousness God has established in their lives has become a light, a direction, and a way for others to walk. Because they've allowed the Cross and the life of Christ to come into their lives, they can feed others with that life, teaching them what it is to be a true friend and how Jesus Christ wants to be that in their life.

In Deuteronomy 6:4, we're told that first the love of God has to be in our hearts and then we are to teach it, imparting it to our children. When we allow the Word of God to transform us regarding our friends, and Jesus Christ becomes our best friend, then we can impart it to our children.

12

Your Child and School

Iverna:

Counseling a six-year-old one day, I asked him, "How's everything at school?"

"All right," he muttered, without any enthusiasm.

"Just 'all right'?" I asked him. "What's the matter? Are you having problems at school?"

"No, no problems."

"Getting good grades?"

"Yeah."

"Like your teacher?"

"Yeah."

"How about the playground? Are you getting along with the kids at recess?"

"Sure. Everything's fine at recess."

"Well," I said, "I guess I must be crazy, then, because I have a feeling that something's wrong at school."

"You do?" His passivity had sparked to life. "That's funny, cause my mom thinks there's something wrong at school, too."

Probably, in all innocence, the mother might have looked at an assignment in new math and fumed, "That's a stupid way for them to teach you," not realizing that every word she spoke or didn't speak about school would be indelibly registered in the mind of her youngster.

I remember the first time I was confronted with new math. Dan had come home almost in tears because he had so many division problems to do for homework.

"Don't worry about it, Dan," I had told him. "I'll help you, and we'll get them done in a hurry."

He sat down at the table and opened his book to the page of problems. I started writing down numbers on a piece of paper, saying "That is the answer to that, and that is the answer to that, and . . ." I was doing the short-division problems in my head, of course.

Dan took the pencil ever-so-gently out of my hand, shaking his head as if to say, "Isn't it a pity—she looks so intelligent."

What he said was, "Mom, I'm sorry, but that's not the way to work the problems." He started writing numbers down the side of the page and then adding them all up—or something like that. Being totally in the dark, and overwhelmingly frustrated and embarrassed, I let my exasperation out in words.

"Dan, it's utterly ridiculous for you to have to put five numbers down there and then put that thing at the top. You can work the whole thing in your head. All you've got to do is . . ."

Well, he had to do it the school's way, of course, and I noticed that he didn't talk to me about his math homework any more. My exasperated statement had communicated to him, "You have to make a choice between mother's way and the school's way." He had chosen. And I had learned a lesson—not in arithmetic, however. I couldn't afford to put my youngster in the midst of a conflict between me and the school.

The Man in the Middle

I don't want to put up a wall of separation between me and anything in my youngsters' lives. It's my responsibility to guide them, and I can't if I don't know what is going on. I have a responsibility to keep the door open for communication in every area, because they're emotionally involved with me and what I say matters to them. Kids can find themselves in the uncomfortable middle whenever teacher says one thing and Mom or Dad says another. But if their emotional needs are properly and fully met by parents in the home, they don't have to carry over any emotional response to what they're learning at school in philosophy, social studies, literature, etc. Their attitude there can be a detached, "That's what the teacher believes, so that's how I'll answer the question on the test." They can take it or leave it, in perfect freedom, without frustration.

Debbie was exposed to a little bit of teaching about evolution when she was a junior in high school. When she came home from school one day, she tried to shock me with it, but I didn't shock.

"Boy! No kidding?" I exclaimed, when she told me that her teacher said that man was descended from an ape. My response was, "I wonder if there's any truth in that?"

She laughed, and told me that she knew that in the beginning God created the heavens and the earth and those teaching evolution left God out of everything; besides, if there wasn't any God, how could any thing evolve into being, because it never would have *been* in the first place.

It warmed my heart to realize that at a very young age the truth had been implanted in her life that would prevent error from becoming believable.

It is up to us to maintain such a rapport with our youngsters that they will tell us what they learn from others so we can help them cope with any truth or error they encounter.

One parent called his child to the window one day to show him a rainbow.

"Isn't the rainbow beautiful, Honey?" the parent said. "And you remember from our Bible story book that it's a sign of God's promise that He'll never again destroy the world with a flood."

The child nodded in agreement, but added, "At school today they told me that the rainbow is really just the colors made through the raindrops when the sun is shining."

Dad was able to explain that the scientific explanation was correct, but that it was God who made the laws of science work just the way they do. The child was able to accept both knowledgeable aspects about rainbows without any conflict.

Knowing All the Answers

It's obvious that we won't know as much as our youngsters do about some of the things that are taught in the schools today. We don't have to pretend that we know something we don't. That does more harm than good. But there isn't any loss at all in a good parent-child relationship when the parent says to the youngster honestly, "Son, I don't know the answer to that one." My kids have never belittled me or wanted to leave home because I gave them an "I don't know" answer. We can't know everything.

When I was in school, I hated history. I got by—by the skin of my teeth and my mother's prayers. I didn't care what happened in the dim and distant past, I insisted. I wanted to focus all my attention on living for today.

When Debbie brought her history book home from school, she asked me a question, and I had to tell her that I didn't know the answer.

"Then why do I have to learn this stupid stuff?"

The answer to that was easy, I thought.

"Well, Debbie, you have to learn it because that's what they teach you in school, and later, when your own youngster comes home, you're going to have to know."

She interrupted me with the truth.

"How come *I* have to know? You didn't know. You couldn't tell me."

She had me there. And at that point, I was tempted to get on my high horse and yell at her, "Yes, that's right! I don't know it—and that's exactly why you're going to learn it!" But I would have lost valuable ground if I'd done that. I would have set up resentment and rebellion in her.

That day, I was blessed to do the right thing for a change. I said to her, "Debbie, I know exactly how you feel. You'll just have to do the same thing I did. Read your assignments, get your homework in, and pay close attention in class. It won't last forever."

I didn't have to pretend I liked history. I didn't have to pretend I understood it. I didn't have to pretend I thought it was good for Debbie to learn it. But she had to take it because it was part of the school curriculum.

The Teacher

A true teacher cares about children. A teacher spends more time with our children than we do—and needs us to support him or her in every way we can. The teacher is not always right, but then, neither are we.

There may be times when we have to go to see our child's teacher about some problem area. We can't afford to go until we have handled our emotions. A display of anger may cause the teacher to close his or her mind to what we might have to say. If we calmly approach the subject of concern, the teacher will be able to hear our concerns—and we can be made aware of their perspective. It's important for us to understand the teacher's point of view as well as to express our own. Often, we've heard only the perspective of the story that gives all of the benefit of doubt to our youngster. The whole truth might present a very different picture. We might even be persuaded that our child, instead of being a perfectly innocent bystander, was actually a participant in the matter.

If our child has a teacher who punished the whole class for the misbehavior of one or a few members of it, we can use the situation to teach our youngster that his or her presence with someone who is misbehaving makes them a party to it.

I've told my son, "If you're with a group of boys who rob a store, and you don't even know they're going to do it but you're sitting in the car when they're picked up, you'll be taken before the authorities along with the rest of them." This lesson, hopefully, will teach our children to use discretion in friendship involvements.

If, instead of using this kind of situation as a tool to teach our children something they need to know, we take an extreme negative approach, saying, "Punishing everybody is not right. I agree with

271

you, Son, that the teacher has no right to make everybody stay after school just because a few of them did something wrong," we're keeping our youngster from learning a very important lesson. This also gives us an opportunity to show that one's offense does affect all.

Getting Involved

If our youngsters sense in us a lack of concern for their school—if we never attend school functions, or join the PTA, and we're never interested enough to look over the papers they bring home—they may lose interest, too.

Some parents protest, "That's ridiculous! I don't have time to go to a PTA meeting." There's a way to handle that, too. In our town, PTA meetings were always on Tuesday night which was also my church choir night. There was no way I could be in both places at once. So when the kids brought home the little PTA membership form every year, I filled it out, gave them my money for membership, and explained, "Now, you know that mother can't go to the meetings, because it's my choir night, but you tell the people I'll be glad to furnish refreshments for their socials or do anything else I can to help."

By using that approach, I kept them from thinking, "Mom doesn't care. She isn't interested in my school." They knew I was interested.

Boredom

If our child complains of being bored to death at school, we shouldn't ignore it. Boredom at school is an indication of one of two extremes—either our child is so far ahead of the class that there's nothing to challenge him or her or so far behind he or she has no hope of ever catching up. In either case, we can do something about it.

I've never found a school yet that was not willing to cooperate when the administrators knew that a problem existed and knew what the problem was. Sometimes they put the bored youngster in a higher class, one better suited to his or her capabilities. Sometimes they assigned the child a challenging project guaranteed to stimulate the youngster's interest in a subject. Other times they provided the necessary tutorial help to enable the youngster to catch up with his class.

Positive Reinforcement

Praise and reward are tremendous incentives for learning. Teachers are using it more and more, and we parents should, too. When we look through papers brought home from school, even papers with A's on them, do we automatically inflict some form of negative reaction on the youngster?

Do we begin with a smile, saying, "These are really good papers. I'm proud of you!" but then spoil it with an almost threatening, "Do you have any homework for tonight?"

Don't say, "I'm so pleased with these, but you could do even better if you tried." The emotional reward of praise is negated by a sense that what they achieve is never enough."

Let us learn to emphasize everything for which we can commend our children. Let our praise and reward be full of accentuating the positive. There will be plenty of time later for dealing with the negatives, for dishing out warnings. If we use the positive moments for undiluted positives, we'll find ourselves getting more and more of them.

A wrong response to our child coming in on time might be, "Well, I'm glad to see that at least you got in on time for a change." That response doesn't make the child—or the parent—feel good. A better response would be, "Hi, Honey, glad you're home" or "Is everything OK?" or "Did you enjoy yourself?" or, "Did you get done what you'd planned?" etc.

Afraid you'll make them sinfully full of pride? Forget it. The critical world will keep that knocked out of them. We can counteract discouragement by letting our children know that we are proud of them, pleased with what they've accomplished. And we don't have to wait for perfection before we begin to praise them.

Suppose our child brings home a report card with "F's" in five subjects and "C" in one. We can focus on the "C" for once. It won't really kill us. So what if the "C" is in sports, something he or she enjoys, something where there's no homework? We can let them know we share their accomplishments and we can be glad he or she is good in sports. This conversation can then be followed by, "Let's look at the subjects one by one and see if I can help you find out why there's so many failures. I know you're a smart kid, and I think, together, we can solve this problem."

If we can build into our child a sense of success and capability, and train them not to compare themselves with others who may be "A" students, but to compare themselves with the best they are personally capable of doing, they will achieve that self-acceptance that we're looking for.

The Great Debate

People often ask me what I think about public schools in comparison with Christian private schools.

Certainly, twenty years ago, my answer would differ somewhat from my answer now, in that schools today are so lax in Christian-principled education. In the attempt to give equal rights, some very cultish and unacceptable things are being taught in public schools. Some of these we have covered in previous chapters. But even morals and principles of dealing with oneself and others are far beneath the standards of the average Christian family.

It's because of that that I rejoice with parents who have the funds and opportunity to send their children to Christian schools. It is, however, not realistic to think that the majority of people have those opportunities. Therefore, it becomes more important than ever to maintain constant (by that I mean daily) communication with your youngsters who are attending public school. What are they hearing? What is being taught? What is being inferred? What are the kids saying? What are the discussion groups covering? Questions like these can bring some correction to each situation—and alleviate a lot of confusion.

Keeping the Lines Open

We must be careful not to let our emotions spring forth to eliminate the two-way conversation with our youngster who may have formed a very strong bond with the teacher teaching evolution—or with a peer group that thinks it's just fine to sleep with a date, if you're past sixteen and take precaution against sexually transmitted diseases and pregnancy.

We must allow them to realize that some nice people do err. Some nice people sincerely believe a lie. That doesn't make the person no longer nice, but it let's our youngster realize that they must differentiate from the standards of another because of their own standards, while not forcing them to break the ties of friendship or appreciation.

Home Schooling

Today, there is an increase in home schooling, as well as Christian private schools, and in many cases this is extremely successful.

Before venturing into it, the parents need to be aware of all the ramifications involved. There is a double pressure on the parent who becomes both parent and teacher—and not only for the amount of work that he or she has to put into the preparation of the school. They must have the ability to wear several "hats" and to allow the child to relate to them on these different levels. It's sometimes difficult for the parent to realize that the child related to them as a teacher, not as a parent, in their responses. All of these things have to be taken into consideration before home schooling.

The social adjustment also needs to be viewed. Our children learn a great deal from being subjected to the variety of nationalities, backgrounds, morals, principles, teaching, and training of others in public school. They don't have the opportunity to learn these social skills when they're limited to the family arrangement.

Sports is a very important thing to consider. If you're going to home school your youngster, I strongly suggest you find Christian

275

circles for sports activities where they will learn good sportsmanship and competitiveness under control.

The Bible strongly urges us to teach our children in the morning, at noon, and at night. The inference is not to home schooling, though I am not at all against that. Rather, let us have the standards of Christian life so ingrained in us, that it's a natural way of life for our youngster, whether they're in public school surrounded by sinful expressions, or they're in Christian schools surrounded by competitive friends, or they're being home-schooled.

The important point is not where they're getting their schooling, it's where they're getting their training. We are instructed to train our children. This means to bring them to a requisite standard, to live the life before them, to lay out the godly principles in teaching, to require from them expressions of Christian behavior, and all the things we have taught. We need to come back and watch for these things to be expressed in their lives and correct them where it isn't in evidence—always with love and tender care—and continually communicate with the child whether we expect him to understand the truth of it or not.

Dianne:

A discussion on schooling requires that we look at our child's mental abilities, development, and training and consider what God's Word says about man's mental capacity.

Let's first look at God's perspective of the human mind.

In the beginning, in the Garden, Adam and Eve experienced an intimate relationship with God. They had a good time communing with Him spirit to Spirit. Man's spirit was alive—it was in that spirit that God spoke and communed with him. In the middle of the garden, God planted two trees the tree of life: and the tree of the knowledge of good and evil. He placed very few limitations on the couple, allowing them to eat freely of the tree of life, but forbidding them to eat of the tree of the knowledge of good and evil (Genesis 2:16-17).

In this beautiful setting, the enemy came to Eve, tempting her to eat from the tree of the knowledge of good and evil. The serpent told her that if she ate, not only would she think independently from God, she would be able to think like God—to know as God knows. What a temptation—to know as God knows.

So Adam and Eve chose. They chose to know knowledge apart from God. In so choosing, their soul (the mind, will, and emotions), became dominant over their spirit. Man was cut off from his only source of life—God. Their purpose had been to be able to think like God, but in all actuality, they were separated from God, thereby losing His thoughts and His mind.

Excluded from God, Adam and Eve were left to their own natural (carnal) mind to teach them. All who were born after them were in the same predicament—thinking themselves wise and full of knowledge, yet truly lacking in both and without understanding. Centuries later, Jesus Christ arrived, volunteering to take our place as a propitiatory offering so we might be set free from that position by choosing to trust His offering. In Jesus Christ, we once again have access to the tree of life and the choice to feed from it as we do the tree of the knowledge of good and evil.

When we receive salvation, Christ comes into our dead spirit—separated from God's Spirit. He regenerates us, causing us to come alive again (Ephesians 2:1-5). Our spirit is now but a few days old, but our soul is as old as we are, which means it seems to know better and to be wiser. Through salvation, however, Christ becomes the basis of truth, and we begin a new foundation of knowledge, revelation, and transformation.

Romans 12:2 says, "And be not conformed to this world: but be ye transformed by the renewing of your mind, that ye may prove what is that good, and acceptable, and perfect, will of God." But how are we transformed? Titus 3:5 and 2 Corinthians 3:18 tell us the Holy Spirit is the One to transform and renew us. We can't do it. Transformation occurs by allowing the Holy Spirit to change our thinking according to the Word of God and not according to how we've been trained and made to conform to the world.

"Blessed are ye when men shall revile you, and persecute you" (Matthew 5:11, KJV). Is this how the world thinks? Do they call us blessed when we're being persecuted? No! The world doesn't teach us to love our enemies. The world says, "Don't get mad—get even!" Much of our childhood teaching is designed to mold us into a shape that conforms to the world's specifications. God wants to transform us, line-by-line, precept-by-precept, from glory to glory. This is only done by the Holy Spirit breathing the Word into us.

We must cast down every stronghold that would come against the true knowledge of Jesus Christ (2 Corinthians 10:2-4). Strongholds are formed in the mind; these are: a thought or notion, concepts and attitudes toward family, friends, marriage, sex, holidays, fellowship, finances, careers—virtually all areas of our lives. These strongholds must lose their power, their strength, in the presence of Jesus. This casting, or tearing, down of strongholds is not done in an instant of time; it's a process.

On the road to Emmaus (Luke 24:13-35), Jesus opened the understanding of two men as He walked with them. This is what we need today. We don't come by spiritual understanding naturally—it comes by the Spirit. The natural man cannot discern the things of the Spirit (1 Corinthians 2:13-16), they are spiritually discerned by those that are moving in and being filled with the Holy Spirit. It's not enough to have an experience of being baptized in the Holy Spirit and speaking in tongues, we must be continually filled with the Holy Spirit (Ephesians 5:18). It's a daily process, a daily infilling.

God wants to renew us and train us and teach us how to have our minds set on Christ. We are to love God with our whole heart, soul, mind (Matthew 22:37). According to the Greek translation of Matthew 22:37, the mind with which we love the Lord is a renewed mind. The natural mind is carnal, antagonistic and rebellious toward God. The Spirit of God and the flesh are antagonists—they are in warfare, in constant conflict, on opposing sides (Galatians 5:16-18, AMP). This means we're going to battle our double nature. But God has made a way to change us that we may truly know Him with the mind renewed by the Spirit, not with our own natural mind.

278

Jesus Christ promises us that He will write His laws on our mind and heart (Hebrews 8:10; 10:16). It's a renewed mind that He writes on. When His laws are written internally, we will act from them. This is what we desire for our children—the new hope we have through Jesus Christ. We don't have to remain invalids; we don't have to continue in our carnal thinking. The mind can be changed.

We are to refrain from childish thoughts yet retain the innocence of a child when it comes to evil. That is, when it comes to thinking evil, stay child-like, but mentally, be mature (1 Corinthians 14:20). God is requiring us to grow up in our thinking, and we need to know what normal *child-like* thinking is and what *childish* thinking is.

Now, let's look at how the human mind develops in the natural. In order to know when our child is thinking in a mature manner, we need to understand how their mental, cognitive abilities develop. We can trace the development—the maturation of our children's thinking—from infancy to adolescence.

Cognitive Development

Cognition is the mental process or faculty of knowing, including aspects such as awareness, perception, reasoning, and judgment. Our minds have certain genetically determined structures that cause our intellects to develop and grow. Cognitive development means that the mental structures of the mind are in the process of development.

One of the big mistakes we made in the last generation was believing children were little adults, that they thought like adults. It's just not true. Much pain and agony occurs in the home when the parents believe the child should think as they do instead of recognizing the child's age and stage of development.

Cumulative:

Cognitive development is cumulative—it builds on itself. The child goes from learning one principle to learning two principles to learning three principles and so on. He accumulates information and skills. If the child doesn't learn principle number two, he or she is not going to lay hold of number four or five. The development must happen in a cumulative fashion. If the child doesn't learn to go from the concrete to the abstract, he or she will not be able to understand the abstract.

To play soccer my son first needed to learn how to kick the ball straight. The next skill that needed to be developed was learning to kick the ball with the side of his foot. After this, he progressed to learning how to 'head' the ball (hit it with his head). These skills were cumulative.

Experiential:

A child can only understand what he or she experiences on their own either through imitation—or trial and error. If they don't experience something this way, there is no understanding; the child does not "own" it.

For example, let's say we have a triangle form (a triangle with a hole in it) and a triangle block. A child is going to learn one of two ways to get that block to fit into that form. Utilizing trial and error, the child will take the block and keep moving it around until it fits. If we show the child how to do it, picking up the block and putting it in the form, the child will eventually begin to imitate what we did. Once the child learns the behavior, he or she "owns" it. We can't do it for the child. We can demonstrate how to do it, but it's not owned by the child until he or she experiences it. This is an important principle—at an early age children learn by imitation and repetition, by trial and error.

If children are devoid of an environment with many different stimuli and experiences, they will be limited in their cognitive development. That's why so many children's programs were so successful years ago when they went into the ghettos. These children were not mentally retarded, they merely lived in an environment with little stimulation. The programs expanded their world.

Now, as adults, we have the capacity to learn what, as a child, we did not experience.

For instance, you may have been brought up in a home where conflict was avoided. Therefore you never learned conflict resolution skills. We are not born with the ability to resolve conflicts. However, we can learn such skills by experience, observation, or by imitation. Then we "own" the skills—they become automatic.

Continuous - Assimilation/Accomodation:

Cognitive development is a continuous process where the child learns to adapt and adjust to his or her environment. The baby boy sees a rattle over his crib. He learns if he bats it, it jingles. A face appears over his crib. He bats it; it doesn't jingle, but it does make a funny face at him. By trial and error, the child begins to learn the different options available to him and in essence says, "Well, that didn't fit in this little structure—I'm going to try something else."

In the development of cognitive skills, two processes are utilized: assimilation and accommodation. In the process of assimilation, a child has a concept in his mind. A new idea comes from the child's environment. The child places the new idea into the concept already established.

For instance, Johnny has the concept in his mind that everything with four legs and fur is a dog. That's what Johnny knows. Then he sees a cat and calls it a dog because it has four legs and fur. Later, while watching television, the child sees another furry, four-legged animal. He calls this animal (which is really a lion) a dog. This is assimilation. The new and similar idea (the cat and the lion) is put in the already established mental structure (a dog is furry and has four legs).

As children develop mentally by imitation and trial and error, they learn to accommodate—to develop a new mental structure in which to put a new idea. They learn that there are going to be classes within classes. A sub-class to four furry legs is: four furry legs that roar is a lion; four furry legs that meow is a cat.

Because of assimilation, we need to explain the "whys" to our children that will enable them to accommodate to their environment. When a child asks, "Why is that light on and that light not on?" we don't need to begin a dissertation on the laws of electricity. He or she is not going to understand that explanation. Instead, we simply explain that one switch is on and the other one isn't—a simple explanation.

Parents must be sensitive to how their infant perceives his environment in order to help him accommodate. The first time my son, Daniel, went to the dentist, it was an awful experience. He's very sensitive to noise. The dentist blew air on Daniel's tooth so he could see clearly. Because that noise was so loud, Daniel panicked. The dentist thought Daniel was afraid of the air, so he kept squirting it on Daniel's arm to show him it wouldn't hurt him. The dentist didn't know Daniel wasn't afraid of the air, he was afraid of the noise. The more he squirted the air, the more panicked Daniel became. The next time we had to go to the dentist, Daniel panicked. Just the word "dentist" made him panic. I took him to a specialist who understood young children. When Daniel saw a different man, there was no panic. I helped Daniel accommodate into his environment. Now he goes to the original dentist with no problem.

Concrete:

All children must be able to understand the world in concrete terms before they can think in abstract terms. In other words, children need to touch, see, sense, and perceive something before they can *think* about the image without *seeing* it. Once they experience the ball, they'll be able to picture the ball in their mind without having the ball present. They must see the concrete first. This is why many people cannot think intuitively or deductively; they haven't learned to think concretely.

According to psychologist Dr. Jean Piagit, a child's cognitive development occurs in stages. Let's look at these stages.

Developmental Stage #1: Birth to Age 2 (Toddler)

Dr. Piaget calls the first stage of the child's cognitive development the *sensory motor stage*. Everything that the child can sense is real to them. Everything must go through their senses. The child understands the world by perception. The child will only experience what he or she senses or has direct contact with. This is the stage when babies discover their fingers, toes, ears, and nose. Put a toy in front of a baby. Where does it go? Right into the baby's mouth. The baby wants to sense it—not necessarily taste it. The baby has learned, through bottle and breast feeding, that the mouth is a good sensory avenue for discovering things. That's why parents are counseled to watch what infants put in their mouths, because they'll swallow it. Babies have no concept of danger, therefore parents need to make the environment safe for their exploration. As they move around, they will explore their environment by taste, feel, touch—comprehending through their senses.

The growing infant is beginning to develop primitive mental images. His or her experiences become a mental image in their mind. They begin to acquire *object permanence*. At six months old, what the child sees is perceived as permanent.

The infant child sees a toy in front of them. If Mommy puts the toy behind her back, the child will think the toy doesn't exist because it's out of sight. Mommy knows the toy is behind her back and she can pull it out any time she wants to, but the child doesn't know this. The child thinks the toy is gone. If the toy were to reappear, the child perceives it as a new toy, one that's just been created. The child only knows what he or she can see.

Between approximately 18 to 24 months of age, children learn that objects remain permanent even if they can't see them. The ball that rolls under the sofa is still a ball and still exists. The child will search for the lost item because he or she knows the item still exists even though it is out of sight. Toddlers acquire the cognitive skill of object permanence. They understand that whether or not they can see the object, it's permanent. They are able to represent the object in their mind even when the object is out of sight.

The toddler can see Mommy in his or her mind even though she is nowhere in sight. Children who have a hard time developing this concept experience separation anxiety. When separated from Mommy, they believe she's gone forever—she's not coming back. It takes successive instances of seeing Mommy come back before the child begins to realize that Mommy didn't just "non-exist" and then reappear again. Mommy is permanent.

Once toddlers have learned object permanence, they can play peek-a-boo. A hidden toy becomes a game for the child who eagerly goes after the hidden object.

At this age, the toddler learns primarily by imitation. The child repeats what he or she sees. You clap your hands. They'll learn to

283

clap their hands. You wink. They'll try to wink. By trial and error, once the toddler "gets" it, the skill is now in his or her mind. It's there to use.

All the experiences the child has in this stage of mental development prepares or prevents them from entering the next levels of development.

Developmental Stage #2 : Ages 2-7 years

This is the *pre-operational stage* because the child does not know how to logically think of operations (i.e., A plus B equals C). At this stage, the child is beginning to develop the ability for concepts, but the concepts are still illogical.

Let's look at the characteristics of pre-operational thinking:

Egocentric:

An egocentric child focuses on only one viewpoint—their own. They don't know how to look outside themselves to say, "You think differently than I do." They really believe everyone thinks like they do. They approach life from their own standpoint, their own viewpoint.

For example, if we take a child by the hands and say, "Which one is your right hand?" the child will raise his or her right hand, saying "This one." If, while still holding the child's hands, we ask, "Now which one is my right hand?" the child will point to the left hand of the person holding his or her hands. That's where their right hand is. The child doesn't know how to take the "holders" point of view—only their own.

How many times have you seen a pre-school child nod his or her head while listening to someone talking to them on the phone? In the child's mind, the caller can see the child's nod.

Emotional:

A child's perception and reasoning in the pre-operational stage is emotional—if a child feels it, then it must be. This is because the logical part of the brain is developed after the limbic, which is

284

the part of the brain responsible for feelings. A child will feel and then think.

Absolute:
Children think in absolutes. Everything is either good or bad, black or white. If Mommy yells when she is angry, the child will conclude that all mommies do this.

Young children like to know the rules and will get extremely upset when older siblings don't have the same rules. If the 5-year-old has to go to bed at 8:00, so does everyone else. The child can't reason that since there is an age difference, the rules are different. If we understand this about their thinking, then we can help our young children feel loved even when the rules seem "wrong."

Animistic:
Children of this age believe things are animistic—they attribute conscious life to natural objects.

Between the ages of three and four, my son believed his stuffed animals were alive. I used this whenever he didn't want to go to bed at bedtime. I would make a crying sound and say, " Daniel do you hear that?"

"Yes."

"Who's crying in your closet?" (that's where all his stuffed animals were kept).

"I don't know."

"You better find him."

He would go to his closet and pick an animal. Then I'd say, "This animal is really tired and needs to go to sleep right away. Will you watch and make sure he'll go to sleep?" Well, of course he was willing to do so.

"And will you make sure he doesn't cry any more?"

Daniel would go to bed just because he was doing it for his animal. Bedtime wasn't a problem because I learned to come down to my child's age and to his way of thinking.

Centered:
Children at this stage of development have a tendency to focus on one aspect of something to the exclusion of everything else.

Intuitive:

Pre-operational children think intuitively, not logically. Children at this stage will base their actions on an immediate comprehension of a situation rather than by using a logical process (which, as yet, is undeveloped). For example, take three red balls, three yellow balls, three yellow wagons, three red wagons. When asked to group them, children at this stage will put all the yellow objects together with the idea that the yellow wagon is like the yellow ball because they're yellow. Yet they may take the red wagon and put it with the yellow ball and wagon saying, "These go together because the wagon has wheels, too." The rules change to fit the classification. This is intuitive thinking.

One day when Daniel was playing "farm" with various figures of farm animals and farm hands, I asked him to pick out all the men on the farm. He picked the daddy, the grandfather, and the little boy.

"Why did you put the little boy with the father and grandfather?"

"This daddy has a hat and this daddy has a hat and this daddy has a hat."

Daddies wear hats. Classifying intuitively, not by logic, he centered on the one thing, the hat, and that established his classification. He couldn't get past the hat into thinking, "This is a little person wearing little boy clothes." He didn't know how to think that way.

Transductive:

When a child makes inferences from one particular to another particular, it is transductive reasoning.

For example, "A" flies and is a bird; "B" flies and is a plane; therefore "A" equals "B," particular to particular i.e. Johnny is a boy, daddy is a boy, therefore, Johnny should be able to drive the car because they are both boys.

Creative/Imaginative:

The pre-operational child thinks in creative, imaginative ways. Sally draws a picture and shows it to Mommy. She expects Mommy to see exactly what she has drawn—a box with sheep inside. Mommy sees a circle with three circles on it. Sally didn't draw the sheep that were inside because she knew Mommy would see the sheep just like she does. If Mommy were to ask Sally to explain, she'd say that Mommy couldn't see the sheep now because they were sleeping.

The child in her imaginative thinking saw the sleeping sheep and expected Mommy to because she could. We would call that exaggeration, fantasy, making up things. But pre-operational children are almost magical—not satanic—but magical in the sense that they think they have power to do things others can't do. If there are monsters in the closet, Johnny knows that all he has to do is yell, "Boo!" and they'll go away. This is not supposed to be logical—the child is still pre-operational.

Irreversible:
A pre-operational child fails to see that most things work both ways.

"Sandy, do you have a sister?"
"Yes, her name is Julie."
"Does your sister, Julie, have a sister?"
"No."

Developmental Stage #3: Ages 7-11 years

The child of this age moves from the pre-operational to the concrete—establishing mental operations. At this stage, children use their mind instead of perceptions to make conclusions. It's a fun time for parents, because the child is beginning to use logic— discovering things in a logical sequence and developing concrete operations.

If the child is having problems at school, it may be that he or she lacks development in the cognitive stages. School psychologists can do tests to find this out. Remember that cognitive development is cumulative, and the child cannot go into the concrete until he or she has learned to experience through perceptions and hands-on involvement.

Developmental Stage #4: Adolescence

This level of cognitive development is called *formal operations*. Adolescents are able to think inductively and deductively—able to separate their point of view from another's point of view. They're able to use rules of logic to solve problems.

Egocentric:

Egotism is a characteristic of adolescent thinking, but it's different from the egotism of the 2-7 year old. Adolescents can conceptualize thoughts of self and others, but cannot differentiate between objects towards which the thoughts of others are directed and those which are the focus of their own concern. The adolescent will assume others are pre-occupied with his or her thoughts and behaviors—just as much as he or she is. Adolescents are self-conscious because they are convinced that everyone is as engrossed in his or her physical appearance and behavior as he or she is. They *know* that if they walk into a room everyone will notice the pimple they have on their nose because they know it's there. This is egocentric thinking. The adolescent believes that all thoughts are directed toward him or her and the perceived flaw.

It's important for parents to thoughtfully and lovingly consider their adolescent's naturally fragile feelings regarding their appearance and not to criticize or poke fun at some temporary figure or facial flaw. It doesn't matter how innocent the intentions or seemingly harmless the remark, the self-conscious adolescent mind will magnify the remark, and the flaw, to devastating proportions. It is at this age that many children, boys and girls, enter into harmful, even deadly, practices in order to alter, hide, or escape their perceived physical imperfections. Proverbs 18:21 says, "Death and life are in the power of the tongue." An unkind word, over-zealous, or ill-spoken criticism can be the single "straw that breaks the camel's back," causing the adolescent's feeble self-esteem to crumble. Anorexia, bulimia, drug abuse, alcoholism, promiscuity, gang activity, even suicide—these are all devices utilized by adolescents in order to cope with this highly emotional and egocentric stage of life.

If you have any questions regarding the mental development of your child at any stage, it would be wise to see the school psychologist who will be able to help discover where your child is cognitively and how you can help him or her work through each of these stages. In the final chapter, we will look at the characteristics of maturity in Christ—and at how we can help our child to grow in the Lord.

Iverna:

As parents we need to continuously communicate with our children that we are looking after their very best interests. We're not out to make ourselves look good by the way they express us, but to make them look good by the way they express Christ—and the standards of life that bring success. Because our children acquire certain actions and behavior patterns by imitating their parents, it is our responsibility to be "Imitators of God" (Ephesians 5:1).

13

Your Child Matures

Iverna:

In a society that pressures man, woman, and child alike to conform to the status quo, no matter how corrupt, it is important, indeed necessary, that parents instill in their youngsters a personal integrity platform of their own. The day will come when Mom and Dad will not be with them to say "Yes" or "No"—they will have to make decisions for themselves.

If a grade school youngster asks, "Why can't I do such-and-such," and the parent simply replies, "Because I said no," they haven't helped him or her grow to maturity by explaining the process of or reason for making the decision. Instead, they may have provoked their youngster to frustration.

A teenager said to me, "It doesn't make any difference why I want to do something, no matter how I lay it out to my parents, they always say "No". When I ask why, they answer, 'Just because we said so.'" This young man was understandably angry. Their answer also left him incapable of knowing how to make decisions for himself or of understanding his parents' decisions.

Kids want reasons. No teacher teaches by saying "Because I said so." Teachers prove everything to their students and expect them to prove things in return. Students aren't expected to take the teacher's word as fact. Explanation is the order of the day.

291

Parents need to be aware that children have naturally inquisitive minds. They want answers and will get them one way or another. The parents' only assurance of them getting the right answer is to provide it for them.

In addition to explaining the reasons behind their answers to their youngsters, it's good if the parents question the reason for their youngster's actions. But don't ask why when you really mean, "I don't like what you did." For instance, we shouldn't say, "Why did you come in with mud on your shoes?" when what we really mean is "Clean the mud off your shoes." But we could ask, "Why did you feel what you just did was acceptable behavior, when it goes against everything we believe in?" Give them a chance to answer that.

Parents can discuss the reason for misbehavior with children old enough to think things through. They can ask their motives and try to follow their line of reasoning.

"I did it because I wanted to" is a real answer, but not a very helpful one. Don't stop there.

"Son, let's look at what doing what you wanted cost you."

By pursuing that dialogue, we train our youngster to look at the consequences of his wrong actions. He will see what it cost this person and that one, his parents, and himself. Then we can ask, "Now, Son, what would you have done differently if you'd thought of all these things ahead of time?"

By leading the child through this kind of look at his own behavior, we'll have helped him toward more mature action and responsibility in the future.

Picky, Picky

A young man asked me one day about some of the laws in the Old Testament.

"I don't understand why a God of love would lay down some of those laws," he said. "They sound so ridiculous to me. Don't eat this, don't eat that."

He considered most of the Old Testament laws arbitrary and dictatorial, until I showed him that every law God put in the Bible was a protection for His people. Even seemingly silly little laws about food preparation were given to prevent sickness. (For a helpful explanation, see *None of These Diseases*, by Dr. S. I. McMillen, Spire Books, 1967.)

When the boy realized this, he began to understand that there is a reason for everything God wants in our lives. The commandment that children are to honor their father and mother is a good example (Leviticus 19:3; Matthew 15:4; Mark 7:10). This rule isn't in the Bible for the purpose of making parents feel honored. When children learn to honor and obey their parents, they learn to honor and obey others who have rule over them—and their lives are naturally smoother and happier.

Why? Why? Why?

Children are helped toward maturity if they know the reasons for our actions and our rules. Those reasons won't necessarily make them agree with us, but they do allow them to realize our premise.

We can say, "Jim, please bring in some kindling and a load of logs for the fireplace."

"Why do I have to do it?" he gripes. "Why can't Trevor do it?"

Our response can be, "Because I told you to," or we can say, "Trevor did the yard, and I've asked you to bring in the wood."

He does it. Maybe he doesn't look any happier about it, but at least he has a reason to satisfy his mind.

The necessity for expressing a reason makes us examine our own motives continually. That's helpful, too.

A Little Whine With That?

Children need to learn that they can't change their parents' minds by begging and whining to get their own way in something. Parents will help them most by letting their "No" be no—henceforth and forevermore. If children learn that by nagging and teasing long enough they can wear Mom and Dad down and get their own way, they've learned something very dangerous to their development into maturity. They will always do whatever necessary to get their own way.

Children who always get their own way through manipulation are being rewarded for manipulating—and they'll use it increasingly in life.

Flexibility

However, there are also problems when parents are so unbending that they never change their mind.

Good parents are not afraid to change their minds when their's is a valid reason to do so. After we've listened and heard the child's point of view about something, we ought to be able to admit, if it's true, that we've made a mistake. We should explain why we've changed our minds or suspended a rule. The whole business of rules and discipline doesn't go down the drain just because we make an occasional exception.

When parents are only interested in their word being infallible law forever and ever without change, they need to look at their own security, their self-confidence, their sense of worth as individuals. Inflexibility is not a quality of good parenthood. Changing the rules for special circumstances lets our children see that we really care about them, not just about our rules. It may give them more respect for our judgment, too.

Of course, if we are habitually inconsistent and double-minded, this will water down our authority in the mind of the child. But that's not to say the same thing will happen when, for instance, we've told our daughter that she can't go to a certain place and then we get more information that makes us decide to let her go. We can explain why we've changed our mind, and she won't be left hanging in mid-air, thinking we're wishy-washy.

As we mature in our Christianity, one of the first things that happens to us is that we become more open—better able to admit our mistakes, better able to listen to the evidence and opinion of others without reacting defensively. As this happens to us in full view of our youngsters, it happens to them, too.

A man in his twenties came in to see me one day. He had grown up in a Christian home that had taught the Word of God but had stressed legalistic don'ts—don't smoke; don't drink; don't swear; don't do this; and don't do that. He had rebelled against it all one day, turned his back, and walked away.

"Now," he said, "I do all these things, but there's no joy in them for me. I'm going crazy in the midst of them. I can't really get it out of my mind that all these things are wrong." The young man had rebelled against his parents' teaching, but the teachings were still there inside him, an integral part of him. He would never find happiness until he could weigh his previous beliefs in the light of his current convictions centered in the Word of God. Only then would his inner warfare be gone.

It is God who has arranged for parental influence to be so strong that their word becomes fact in the minds of their children. They will never forget what Mom and Dad believed and taught, even if someone "proves" it wrong.

Training

There is a difference between verbal instruction—or teaching—and what we call training. Our English word "train" means "to bring to a requisite standard, as of a conduct or skill, by protracted and careful instruction; specifically, to mold the character of." The Hebrew word *chanak* comes from a primary root word which means "to narrow."

When we train our children up in the way they should go, we have carved our children, we have molded their character by narrowing them, by disciplining them. Such training involves far more than merely telling a child what's right and wrong.

It has been established that we retain ten percent of what we hear, fifty percent of what we hear and see, and eighty percent of what we hear, see, and participate in. This is why teachers use pictures, movies, and other kinds of visual aids in instruction.

If we really want to train our youngsters—to effectively mold their characters—we have to let them see demonstrated in our lives, in what we say and do, that which we want them to learn. They need to be able to imitate us, and, through re-enactment, make our conduct their own. If what they see in our lives is not consistent with what they hear from our lips, we're in trouble.

Suppose I want to train my son to love animals. I am training him when I say, "We don't hurt animals; we love them," and follow that up by treating our household pets with loving kindness. However, if I permit my son to kick his dog, he will not suddenly learn to love animals. Training must follow through in every stage.

We train our children to love—or not to love—their parents in the same way. When Mommy says to her child, "Love Daddy," and shows love towards Daddy herself, she is reinforcing her teaching. But if she says to her child, "You should love your daddy," and then behaves in unloving ways toward Daddy, she shouldn't be surprised if the child says, "Why should I love Daddy? You don't." Actions truly speak louder than words.

Tell-Tale Signs

In trying to understand what's happened in a home, social workers will often observe children when they're playing house. They learn surprising things this way, getting some real insights into the kind of home children come from.

It tells them something when one little boy or girl is always beating on the other children or when one is always promising their little doll or stuffed animal that they'll be right back.

A little six-year-old boy revealed volumes about the kind of love in the home he came from when he was playing by himself one day in his grandmother's house. He had taken a pile of clothes from the laundry basket and was pretending to iron them on the hearth. When his grandmother passed through the room, he looked up at her and explained, "I don't usually do the ironing, but my wife's pregnant." The grandmother chuckled, assured that there was loving help in the boy's home.

If we tell our children they should be good to those who persecute them and they see us always trying to get even with our enemies, they'll be confused about what is really required. "If you talk it, walk it," is a good rule to follow. What they hear us say and what they see us do has to fall in line.

When Debbie was very young, I began to show her pictures of uniformed policemen.

"If you ever get lost," I told her, "find a nice policeman to help you."

The words I spoke to her were just right, conveying exactly what I wanted to teach her and showing a proper respect for authority. But one day she made me realize that by my influence and example, I was teaching something else, loud and clear. She couldn't miss it—and she didn't.

I was driving my car (crowding the speed limit a little), and I'd let up on the accelerator when I saw a policeman or a patrol car.

"Whoops! There's a flatfoot," I'd say, not intending to undermine authority or my deliberate teaching, but doing it just the same. One day when Debbie was about three years old, she was standing in the front seat beside me—we didn't have seat belts in those days—when she happened to spot a policeman on the corner before I did.

"Uh oh, Mommy," she warned me. "Better slow down. There's a 'flatfoot.'"

I began right then to mend my ways. If I wanted my child to grow up as a law-abiding citizen, I'd have to be one myself. Debbie would have to see me adhering to the laws of the land whether there was any "flatfoot" on the corner or not.

Once, when I had been away on a prolonged speaking trip, I came home to learn that Dan had acquired a couple of speeding tickets. I talked to him about them and about the necessity for obeying the law on the highway as well as everywhere else. It didn't matter that he thought the limit was too low. He had to obey it anyway, because it was the law.

I didn't impose any disciplinary measures at that time, but a few days later, when he came in with a third ticket, I knew I had to take action.

"One more ticket, Dan," I told him, "and you'll have to give me the keys to your car."

I went with Dan to court, and when the judge learned what I had said about the speeding offenses, he let Dan off with a small fine. The privilege of having a car to drive had to lead to an attitude of increased responsibility for obeying the motor vehicle laws. Dan learned it.

Dianne:
We have looked at the cognitive development of the child so that we could understand how a child thinks. Now we shall discover the biblical characteristics of God's sons: the immature, the childish, and the mature.

Biblical Development
As soon as we are born into God's kingdom, we are God's sons. However, as the Books of Galatians and Romans explain, we can be God's sons without being ready to claim our inheritance. In other words, we need to grow up or become mature. According to 1 Corinthians 13:11 and 14:20, there are two stages of development: *nepios*—the Greek word for children—and *teleios*—the Greek word for mature.

> *When I was a child, I talked like a child, I thought like a child, I reasoned like a child; now that I have become a man, I am done with childish ways and have put them aside.*
>
> *(1 Corinthians 13:11, AMP)*

> *Brothers, stop thinking like children. In regard to evil be infants, but in your thinking be adults.*
>
> *(1 Corinthians 14:20)*

The Characteristics of Nepios—*Childish Thinking*

Reveals carnal thinking. Carnal means the natural man dominates, not the Holy Spirit.

(1 Corinthians 3:1-3)

Childish thinkers love the law, depend on the law, focus on the law.

(Galatians 4:1-3)

Childish thinking is dominated by the natural senses.

(Hebrews 5:11)

Childish thinkers can only drink the milk of the Word.

(1 Corinthians 3:2)

The childish thinker is tossed to and fro, easily influenced by whatever teaching comes along.

(Ephesians 4:14)

The childish person talks like a child and reasons like a child.

(1 Corinthians 13:11-12)

Previously, we discovered that a child reasons with imagination, is egocentric, thinks intuitively, and uses his or her perceptions to make decisions and draw conclusions.

The childish one has the natural heart dominating the thinking. Out of the heart comes base and wicked thoughts.

(Mark 7:21)

The Characteristics of Teleios—*Complete or Mature Thinking*

The Spirit controls the mature thinker, not the carnal nature.

(1 Corinthians 3:1-3)

The mature thinker is under grace. The mature, perfect person wants the grace of Jesus Christ in their life.

(Galatians 5:4)

The senses are trained by use to distinguish between good and evil. Because of use, the natural senses are under the control of the Holy Spirit and the person can now see, taste, hear, feel, and touch from God's perspective—not the natural. The mature person sees how God sees, not how they were trained to see. For example, we are trained naturally to see that when a person raises their hand in anger, they're going to hit (because we've experienced this), but a mature person will be able to discern the heart of the person and know if they will or not. A mature person knows that even what's been experienced before as true, may not be true today.

(Hebrews 5:14)

The mature person can eat the solid food of the Word; he can understand the solid things of the Word.

(Hebrews 5:14)

The mature mind is set to know Christ .

(Philippians 3:15)

The mature thinker does not offend in words; doesn't say the wrong thing.

(James 3:2)

In the *logical, concrete, operational* stage of development, we need the Holy Spirit to renew our children's minds so they can focus on the things of the Lord.

Romans 12:2 can be effective in our children so we don't have to wait until they are adults to have Jesus Christ change their minds. He wants to renew their minds now; to change their thinking processes as they develop so that they will think according to His mind.

In the final stage called *formal operations*, the teenager thinks *egocentrically* and *subjectively*. This is when teenagers need the Holy Spirit to heal them, causing their thoughts to be His thoughts, helping them mature in the ways of the Lord, and to start being the *teleios* they've been called to be—the sons of the Most High God. As God's sons, they will learn to walk in faith in Christ, to be peacemakers, and to love their enemies. They will learn to walk in *agape*—unconditional love—eating the solid meat of the Word and continuing to grow in the grace and knowledge of Jesus Christ.

Iverna:

I see three general attitudes among parents whose children are still at home and who are presenting some problems in their struggle for maturity. First, some parents give up the training in self-defeat, throwing all discipline out the window. They stop trying because they feel there's no way they can win.

A second group of parents insist that they're not guilty of any shortcomings in their efforts to bring their child up properly. Apparently he is going bad all on his own.

The third and healthiest attitude is found among parents who acknowledge, "Yes, we've made mistakes and we can't undo them. But we'll try to do better now that we know better."

What if we have failed our kids? We've done the best we could—or we haven't done the best we could. But there's no way to back up and start over, no matter how much we might yearn to do just that. What then? Do we have to be haunted by our failure forever?

No. God has promised to redeem everything we give to Him. One of the first steps in Christian maturity and in Christian parenthood is to become aware of what God will do and what He won't do. Basically, He will do what we can't do, but He won't do what we can do for ourselves. What we can do for ourselves, He doesn't need to do for us.

When we're wrong, we can admit it. We can confess our own shortcomings to our children, acknowledge that we're human, and that we do make mistakes. We can explain to them that we're striving toward the perfection of Christ in us but that we haven't reached it yet. And if we let them see that God is training us day-by-day, they'll take it in stride and be stronger for knowing it.

A woman told me about a word that had come to her from the Lord. He promised her and her family salvation because of her faithfulness to Him. He said that if she would take her hands off her family and release them to Him, and keep continually committing them to Him, He would do in supernatural ways the things her own hands could never do.

God proves that to us, over and over again. We have to keep on committing our children to Him and acknowledge that He is the one who is doing the work in their lives. If we are worried and up-tight about the well-being of our children, we are actually tying God's hands. When we commit them to Him, we let Him do what He wants with them, not what we had in mind. Our own desires for them might not be what His desires are. But when our desire for them is that His desire for them should be accomplished, then He can go ahead and do "exceeding abundantly above all that we could ask or think" (Ephesians 3:20, KJV). At that point, living with our kids will hold for us the kind of joy God planned for us from the beginning.

Dianne:

As biblical parents, we can walk beside our child's natural cognitive and emotional development, allowing the Holy Spirit to cause their minds and hearts to be transformed from the childish into the *teleios*, from the *nepios* to the mature. We must ask the Holy Spirit to show us where we need our own senses to be trained, our own minds renewed, and where we need to walk in grace and mercy, not law. The Holy Spirit will reveal to us those areas where we are still walking in the carnal, natural ways and not in the *teleios*.

> *And be not conformed to this world: but be ye transformed by the renewing of your mind, that ye may prove what is that good, and acceptable, and perfect, will of God.*
>
> *(Romans 12:2, KJV)*

O God, grant us wisdom to learn how to mature, ripen, and grow by the Spirit according to the guidelines and directions and parameters of Your Word. May we and our children be perfect, *teleios*, as our Heavenly Father is perfect, *teleios* (Matthew 5:48).

APPENDIX

Some books to Help You with the Sex Education of Your Child:

Andrey, Andrew C., and Steven Schepp. *How Babies Are Made.* New York: Time-Life Books, 1968. (Ages 3-10)

Beck, Lester F. *Human Growth: The Story of How Life Begins and Goes On.* New York: Harcourt, Brace and World, 1949. (Early teens)

Bendick, Jeanne. *What Made You?* New York: McGraw-Hill, 1971.

Buckingham, Jamie. *Coming Alive.* South Plainfield, New Jersey: Bridge-Logos, 1970. (Grades 5 and 6)

Buckingham, Jamie. *Your New Look.* South Plainfield, New Jersey: Bridge-Logos, 1970. (Junior high age)

Crawford, Kenneth. *Growing Up with Sex.* Nashville, Tennessee: Broadman 1973. (Sexuality in Christian Living) (Junior high age)

de Schweinitz, Karl. *Growing Up: How We Become Alive, Are Born, and Grow.* New York: Macmillan, 1965. (Middle grades)

Edens, David. *The Changing Me.* Nashville, Tennessee: Broadmans 1973. (Sexuality in Christian Living) (Ages 9-11)

Evans, Eva Knox. *The Beginning of Life: How Babies Are Born.* London: Crowell-Collier Press, 1969.

Frey, Marguerite Kurth. *I Wonder, I Wonder.* St. Louis, Missouri: Concordia, 1967. (Concordia Sex Education series) (Ages 5-9)

Gruenberg, Sidonie Matsner. *The Wonderful Story of How You Were Born.* Garden City, New York: Doubleday, 1959. (Middle grades and junior high)

Gruenberg, Benjamin C. and Sidonie M. Gruenberg. *The Wonderful Story of You: Your Body - Your Mind - Your Feelings.* Garden City, New York: Garden City Books, 1960. (Middle grades and junior high)

Harty, Robert, and Annelle Harty. *Made to Grow.* Nashville, Tennessee: Broadman, 1973. (Sexuality in Christian Living) (Ages 6-8)

Hofstein, Sadie. *The Human Story: Facts on Birth, Growth, and Reproduction.* New York: Lothrop, Lee and Shepard, 1967. (Ages 10-14)

Howell, John C. *Teaching Your Children About Sex.* Nashville, Tennessee: Broadman, 1967. (Sexuality in Christian Living)

Lerrigo, Marion O. *A Story About You.* New York: Dutton, 1969. (Grades 4-7)

Lester, Andrew D. *Sex Is More Than a Word.* Nashville, Tennessee: Broadman, 1973. (Sexuality in Christian Living) (Senior high)

Levine, Milton I. and Seligmann, Jean H. *The Wonder of Life.* New York: Golden, 1968. (Grades 5-9)

Madaras, Lynda. *What's Happening To My Body*, (A book for Boys) New York: Newmarket, 1984.

Madras, Lynda, with Ann Madaras. *What's Happening To My Body*. (A book for Girls) New York: Newmarket, 1983.

Narramore, Clyde M. *Life and Love*. Grand Rapids, Michigan: Zondervan, 1968. (Pre-adolescent)

Narramore, Clyde M. *How to Tell Your Children About Sex*. Grand Rapids, Michigan: Zondervan, 1958.

Power, Jules. *How Life Begins*. New York: Simon & Schuster, 1968. (Grades 4-9)

Scanzoni, Letha. *Sex Is A Parent Affair*. Glendale, California: Regal, 1973.

Sheffield, Margaret. *Where Do Babies Come From?* New York: Knopf, 1972.

Showers, Paul and Kay Sperry Showers. *Before You Were a Baby*. (Let's Read and Find Out Science Books) New York: Thomas Y. Crowell, 1968.

Silverstein, Dr. Alvin, and Virginia B. Silverstein. *The Reproductive System: How Living Creatures Multiply*. Englewood Cliffs, New Jersey: Prentice-Hall, 1971.

Strain, Frances Bruce. *Being Born*. New York: Appleton-Century-Crofts, 1954.

Taylor, Kenneth N. *Almost Twelve: The Story of Sex for Children*. Wheaton, Illinois: Tyndale House, 1968.

BIBLIOGRAPHY

Caplan, Frank. *The First Twelve Months of Life.* New York: Bantam Books, 1973.

Carey, William and Sean C. McDevitt. *Clinical and Educational Applications of Temperament Research.* Berwyn, Pennsylvania: North American Inc., 1989.

Curran, Dolores. *Working With Parents.* Minnesota: American Guidance Service, 1989.

Dobson, James C. *Parenting Is Not for Cowards.* Dallas: Word, 1987.

Dobson, James C. *Preparing for Adolescence.* Santa Ana, California: Vision House Publishers, 1979.

Dobson, James C. *The Strong-Willed Child.* Wheaton, Illinois: Tyndale House, 1982.

Dodson, Fitzhugh. *How to Parent.* New Jersey: New American Library Times Minor. Signet, 1970.

Douglas, Paul Hardy and Laura Pinsky. *The Essential AIDS Fact Book.* New York: Columbia University Health Service, 1987.

Elkind, David. *Grandparenting.* Glenview, Illinois. Scott, Foresman and Company, 1990.

Faber, Adele and Elaine Mazlish. *How to Talk so Kids Will Listen and Listen so Kids Will Talk.* New York: Avon Books, 1982.

Faber, Adele and Elaine Mazlish. *Siblings Without Rivalry.* New York: Avon Books, 1987.

Frumkin, Lyn and John Leonard. *Questions and Answers on AIDS.* Los Angeles: PMIC Consumer Health Service, 1994.

Galinsky, Ellen. *Between Generations: The Stages of Parenthood.* New York: Berkley Books, 1981.

Garber, Stephen W., Marianne Daniels Garber, and Robyn Freedman Spizman. *Helping the ADD (attention deficit disorder) and Hyperactive Child.* (A useful resource to consult if your child is hyperactive, inattentive, impulsive, or destructive.) New York: Villard, 1990.

Garber, Stephen W., Marianne Daniels Garber, and Robyn Freedman Spizman. *Good Behavior.* New York: Villard Books. (St. Martins Paperback Edition), 1987.

Gesell, Arnold, Frances L. Elg, and Louis Bates Ames. *The Child from Five To Ten.* New York: Harper and Row, 1946.

Gesell, Arnold, Francis L. Elg, and Louis Bates Ames. *The Years From Ten to Sixteen.* New York: Harper and Row, 1987.

Gould, Katherine. *Clinical Psychology.* Brentwood, California. Unpublished worksheets.

Hein, Karen and Teresa Fay Diguonimo. *AIDS: Trading Fear for Facts.* Yonkers: Consumer Regents Books, 1989.

Huggins, Kevin. *Parenting Adolescense.* Colorado Springs: NAV Press, 1990.

Kauffman, James M. *Characteristics of Behavior Disorders in Children and Youth.* Columbus: Merril, 1989.

Kazoin, Alan E. *Child Psychology Therapy.* New York: Pergamor Press, c 1988.

Ketterman, Grace H. *You and Your Child's Problems.* New Jersey: Fleming H. Revell (now Baker Book House, Grand Rapids, Michigan), 1983.

Le Francis, Guy R. *Of Children.* Belmont, California: Wadsworth, 1989.

Papalia, Diane E. and Salby Wendkis Olds. *A Child's World: Infancy through Adolesence.* New York: McGraw-Hill, 1975.

Peters, David B. *A Betrayal of Innocence.* Waco, Texas: Word Books, 1986.

Piaget, J. *Play, Dreams and Imitations in Childhood.* New York: W. W. Norton, 1959.

Piaget, J. and B. Inhelder. *The Psychology of the Child.* New York: Basic Books, 1969.

Powell, John. *Why Am I Afraid To Tell You Who I Am?* Argus Communication.

Robley, Wendell and Grace. *Spank Me If You Love Me.* Green Forrest, Arkansas, New Leaf Press, 1974.

Singer, Dorothy and Tracy Reneson. *A Piaget Primus: How A Child Thinks.* New York: Plume, 1978.

Stantrorl, John W. *Adolesence.* U.S.: William C. Brown, 1981.

Webster, Linda. *Sexual Assault and Child Sexual Abuse.* Oryx-Press, 1989.

Wright, Norman H. *Communication - Key to Your Marriage.* Regal Books, 1971.

Wyckoff, Jerry and Barbara C. Unell. *How To Discipline Your Six to Twelve Year Old—Without Losing Your Mind.* New York: Doubleday, 1991.